Jane Cumberbatch's

PURE
style LIVING

Jane Cumberbatch's

PURE
style LIVING

photography by Pia Tryde

A DORLING KINDERSLEY BOOK

LONDON, NEW YORK, SYDNEY, DELHI, PARIS,
MUNICH, and JOHANNESBURG

In memory of my mother and for Alastair, Tom, Georgie, Gracie

contents

Book Design and Art Editor: Vanessa Courtier
Design Assistant: Gina Hochstein
Text, Photographic Art Direction, and Styling:
Jane Cumberbatch
**Co-ordinator, Research, Design of projects,
and Styling Assistant:** Kate Storer

For Dorling Kindersley:
Project Editor: Neil Lockley
Art Director: Janis Utton
Category Publisher: Judith More
DTP: Sonia Charbonnier
Production Controller: Louise Daly

First published in Great Britain in 2001
by Dorling Kindersley Limited, 80 Strand,
London WC2R ORL

2 4 6 8 10 9 7 5 3 1

Copyright © 2001 Dorling Kindersley Limited, London

Text copyright © 2001 **Jane Cumberbatch**

A CIP catalogue record for this book is
available from the British Library
ISBN 0-7513-338-91

Reproduced by GRB, Italy
Printed and bound in Spain by
Artes Gráficas Toledo
D.L. TO: 600-2001

see our complete catalogue at

www.dk.com

sources

live

directory

Introduction

Pure Style Living is about trying to live more simply and efficiently: a **blueprint for living** in the new millennium. This is a book about homemaking in a **down-to-earth, practical,** and **realistic** way. It's a **fresh approach** to making a home **stylish, sensual, and peaceful** that will work for any domestic set-up whether single, married, shared, or any other kind of permutation of the contemporary household.

Pure Style Living is timely as life is tough these days. Our consumer society has led to high expectations, but do we really need all these consumer props? And although we live in a super-technological age where emails and computers react instantly, working hours are increasing and chipping away at precious free time.

This sentiment is echoed in the poem *Leisure*, by W.H. Davies (1870–1940), that begins:

What is this life if, full of care,

We have no time to stand and stare?

Although it was written years ago in a cosier English age, it is perhaps more startlingly relevant today. When slaving away on the consumer treadmill it's easy to lose sight of the simple things in life, such as appreciating a walk in fresh air or having a picnic feast with friends.

I have written **Pure Style Living** from the viewpoint of a working mother with three children, trying to make life more **balanced** and laid-back in the face of all the pressures that make up contemporary life. For me, **home** is at the **heart** of daily life, the one place where we can communicate our honest feelings and be our real selves, reflected in the colours and furnishings that we choose to decorate with, in how we sleep, bathe, garden, or in what we wish to eat. Whatever else is going on in the outside world, **home is grounding**, a refuge, and our main source of **warmth and security**. It should be **light and airy**, a living breathing environment furnished with **natural textures** and **uncomplicated design** ideas that minimize the daily grind.

Of course, there's no escaping the fact that money has to be earned in order to have the means to buy or rent, kit out and run a home, however large or small. But we're beset with a bewildering choice of ideas and goods in the shops. This book aims to show the reader how important it is to go back to **basics** when picking the best ideas for the home. It illustrates that there are ways to make a **stylish home** in an economical way but **without skimping on essentials** like good food or a decent bed.

Pure Style Living is about using **functional** yet **good-looking design**. There's no point in having tricksy gadgets or fancy furnishings if they're not well made, **easy to use, or maintain**; for example, in the kitchen a dozen inferior knives are worth less than **one really good steel blade**, and in the sitting room a fussily trimmed velveteen upholstered sofa would be more good-looking and practical in an **honest, plain cotton loose cover**.

Pure Style Living is also about **paring down** and **sorting out clutter** to make the home more **organized**. Having less things to look after and worry about cuts down stress levels. Cupboards, open shelves, boxes, and drawers can all make life easier to run. It is also about **being practical**, and **doing things yourself** that are **achievable**, not impossible. **Transform a chair** with a lick of paint. If you can sew, **run up basic cushion covers**. Make your own cards and decorations. Be **resourceful** and equip your home with **affordable** ideas from chain stores, **junk shops**, and markets.

Fresh, sensual living is a part of **pure style**; painting rooms in light tones of **whites and creams** with **crisp injections of colour**, natural textures of **cotton, linen and wool** for loose covers and curtains. It's also about having **gorgeous scented** flowers such as **hyacinths** and narcissi, or delicious soaps and **natural candlelight**.

And **Pure Style Living** also concerns **health**. We are what we eat, and our wellbeing depends on **good food** from local or dependable sources. There is growing dissatisfaction with mass-produced and packaged food that is high in additives and low in nourishment.

The approach is about putting back the **rituals** into preparing and eating food, with **fresh ingredients** and simple techniques. It isn't difficult to prepare a fresh salad of crisp lettuce leaves or grill a piece of meat, and it is so much more satisfying to set a table simply with a cloth and take the time to sit down and eat.

Pure Style Living is also about being **eco-friendly** around the **home** and knowing that because the earth's resources are finite we should put less strain on an already beleaguered environment. As well as avoiding processed and packaged food, we should buy fruit and vegetables that are grown without harmful pesticides and fertilizers, or even **dig a little patch**, make a **compost heap** and **grow our own produce**. In the home we can **recycle** everything from old clothes to newspapers, and let clothes **dry naturally** to save electricity, or use cleaning products with fewer chemicals.

Pure Style Living aims to make life more **sensual**, **practical**, and **balanced**.

Jane Cumberbatch 2001

sources

Nature

Smell

Texture

Eat

Architecture

Function

Order

Homemade

Fabric

Colour

Nature

Man used to live **at one with nature** and the pattern of his existence was defined by the **sun setting and rising** and seasonal change, however technological advances have long overridden our co-dependence with nature. We can carry on working all hours with the existence of electric light, but early man had no choice but to sleep when it got dark. Similarly in traditional societies, the heat of midday dictated repose and rest, but nowadays in hot months air-conditioned offices and factories ensure that the workers carry on working.

Commercialism has also eroded the meaning behind **seasonal rituals** – both religious and secular – that are linked to the **natural cycle of the year**. Christmas – which replaced a pagan festival to celebrate the passing of the shortest winter day – has become a cynical marketing opportunity, with plastic Christmas trees and Christmas songs appearing in shopping malls in September.

Getting back in touch with nature and the passing seasons, and enjoying life in a simpler way can help us steer away from materialistic concerns.

In **spring** the lengthening evenings and **flowering bulbs** that push up through the grass are tonics to the eye after the long dreary winter days. At home it's time to spring clean and push the windows wide open for fresh air. We blow hens' eggs at Easter, and decorate them with paint for the table (see pp. 206–207), and pick little posies of primroses. In **summer** I head for the sea or park and we **picnic outside**, taking every possible opportunity to enjoy the outdoor elements when they are at their most clement. Summer is when **children learn to swim**, and **grow brown and strong** from running wild. It's a time to cook up sausages on a campfire. Picking strawberries and eating creamy fruit fool made from fat gooseberries are summer highlights. **Autumn** is a voluptuous season, with **smoky November evenings**, reddish sunsets low in the sky, and walks through thick mounds of **papery fallen leaves**, inhaling the earthy and **woody smells of mushrooms**. This is the time to make **lanterns out of pumpkins** for Halloween, to **roast chestnuts** on the fire, and make delicious preserves from apples and quinces.

Celebrate the **long dark days of winter** with candlelight, **warming stews**, sticky puddings, indoor games like charades and cards, and set aside time to catch up on reading. Get out into the elements and **experience the chilling and crisp air** of an open moor, or the white frost-covered common in **bright low winter sun**. We go and **collect greenery** to make a Christmas wreath for the door, and pile the table high with **clementines and nuts**. The children grow a **hyacinth bulb** in a glass of water and watch it sprout and produce **spring colour** and scent.

Smell

The most direct and **evocative** of our senses is smell. Damp scented pines, **sea-salty air**, honeysuckle, cut grass, **toast in the morning**; a whiff of any of these might conjure up a scene or conversation that happened years ago. Smells are **nostalgic** because they trigger images and emotions before we have time to edit them. The fresh **scent of a yellow peace rose** encountered at the park will take me **back to childhood** and playing barefoot in my mother's garden, where she had a bed of these blooms that flowered throughout the summer. Smells fall into a few basic categories; minty – peppermint, floral – roses, ethereal – pears, musky – musk, resinous – camphor, foul – rotten eggs and acrid vinegar.

We don't need to use our sense of smell to survive anymore except to sense danger, but there seems to be a need to surround ourselves with artificial outdoor smells, perhaps to remind us of how we lived at one with nature.

Scented artificial camouflages are not desirable, but neither are unwashed bodies, dirty clothes or a room stale with cooking smells. Again it's a question of balance. Of finding simple ways to make ourselves and our homes smell good.

Start by choosing cleaning products that are unperfumed or as little perfumed as possible. And practise simple rituals such as opening the windows to **circulate air** or letting washing dry naturally, or washing down surfaces with hot water to keep them bright. Keep clothes fresh in drawers with sachets of **dried lavender** or blocks of earthy **cedarwood** for deterring moths.

Fresh flowers are an instant way to bring **natural scent** into a room. Scented hyacinths or narcissi are a joy to the senses in the middle of winter, when you can have a reminder in your bedroom or sitting room that spring is on its way. In summer raid the garden for **sprigs of rosemary**, lavender, **rose blooms**, stems of jasmine, or tuberoses; bring them to the table in jugs for intoxicating scent.

Scented pot-pourris made with dried flower petals and scented candles are also ways to refresh your home. The general rule is to buy the best you can afford for the most authentic and appealing smells. Cheap scents smell just that – cheap and nasty.

The **kitchen** is a place where we can also indulge our nasal receptors each time we prepare food to eat. Enticing scents include **chopped garlic**, mint thrown in with a pot of new potatoes, **grated lemon or orange rind**, and ground coffee brewing on the stove.

In the bathroom buy good-quality soaps and colognes for simple beauty routines. Also use **simple lavender or rosewater** which can be bought from chemists and put in a glass cologne bottle to splash on after baths and showers. Invest in some outrageously exotic lotions and potions for the days when extra pampering is necessary, too.

Texture

We are **energized by touch** – without the chance to hug, or be hugged, we humans become withdrawn, cynical, and grumpy. It is imperative that we experience the **tactile elements** around us and re-play them as visceral memories to **remain healthy in body and mind**. There is nothing more sublime than feeling the **breathy gentle nuzzling** of a newborn baby, the hot sand trickling through toes, the **tingling and breath-taking iciness** of the first swim of the year, or the **enveloping** soft warmness of bedding. But legislation and efficiency-obsessed corporations care little for the fact that our lives are becoming more sanitized, preventing connection with our instincts and natural surroundings. How I wish to fling myself among sweet grass and wild flowers after spending a day travelling through static-loaded, plastic-furnished airport lounges, or sitting in the meeting rooms of an air-conditioned, windowless office.

Health and hygiene rules are also dehumanizing. "Don't touch," said the fierce woman (perhaps anticipating a visit from health and safety) standing behind the crates of fruit and vegetables as a small child **ran her fingers** over the furry bloom on some plump peaches tantalizingly displayed at eye-level at our local market the other day. It is also depressing to have more of our food presented in characterless and antiseptic vacuum plastic or moulded polystyrene. (Full marks to the shops who still **hand-wrap** their goods in **smooth waxed or crisp paper**.) At least we have the power to make our homes into living, breathing spaces, a second skin filled with **natural** and **sensual** textures.

In the kitchen, work with tools and surfaces **in wood**, or honest metal textures, ceramic tiling, marble, or **smooth utilitarian stainless steel**. Eat real food – raw salads, proper cheese, good meat, homemade cakes – to teach tastebuds that over-processed, over-salted, or sugared goods are unhealthy and unsatisfying.

Sleep like a baby among **soft wool** blankets and **crisp cotton** sheets that have flapped dry on the line, or luxuriate in **linen** that is the coolest texture on hot summer nights.

Curl up on the sofa in front of a **blazing fire**, and keep toes warm with a **woolly** blanket. Bring in logs from the woodpile and stack in **rough woven baskets**. Underfoot use natural textures – **tough hairy sisal**, rough terracotta or **scrubbed wooden boards**.

Bathe in deep scented water, and **rub down skin** with a natural **loofah**, or pumice, then wrap up and wind down in a soft towel or cotton robe.

Eat

We should buy the best food we can afford: **fruit and vegetables** that are **in season** from **local sources**, not waxed and polished, and not flown out of season at vast expense from far-off locations; **fresh bread made with unrefined flour**; chocolate high in cocoa solids; good coffee, **proper cheese** made on a farm not in a factory; and meat from **small-scale producers**. Food that is grown **organically** is produced with farming methods that avoid the use of synthetic pesticides and most artificial fertilizers, and instead use crop rotations and good husbandry to promote the health of crops and livestock. Genetic engineering is not allowed in organic systems. **Animals reared on farms certified as organic** by the Soil Association in England have **access to natural light and air**, are protected by rigorous **animal welfare** standards, and are not produced in cramped conditions and fed on antibiotics and other drugs.

I know how wonderful **home-produced** meat can be after we kept some of the local **Iberian black-footed pigs** at the farm in Spain, and fed them on a diet of **acorns, chestnuts**, and **apples**, to produce the most succulently sweet air-dried ham – **jamon** – which the Andalucia region of Spain is noted for, and the most mouth-watering tenderloins that were barbecued on the fire.

Architecture

Home is a notion as old as the human species. For the vast majority of people – whether they live in caves, as many still do in Cappadocia, Turkey, in mud, stone, or straw huts, or in flats or houses – home is the fixed point in our lives, both emotionally and physically. Our homes should be **comfortable**, womb-like and **enveloping**, but **simple in proportions and function** to cope with the frantic demands of contemporary life. A large bank account is useful, but doesn't guarantee instant style, as anyone browsing through the pages of magazines featuring celebrities can see. Getting back to basics with ideas that are **simple and functional** is more likely to make your home **stylish and sensual** without spending whole wads of money.

For inspiration take a look at different buildings around you. **Vernacular buildings** have a pleasing **simplicity** and **unselfconsciousness**. They are the result of generation upon generation continually defining and redefining function, working within the means at the disposal of their builders, and transcending poor ingredients. The appeal of a crofter's cottage in Scotland, a modest schoolhouse building, or a hut for storing food and keeping animals in rural Spain, is visual, as well as knowing that its shape has evolved from pure necessity.

Nowadays when the traditional family set-up is being replaced by more fluid family groupings, we need to be increasingly **flexible** in our living arrangements. Borrow from vernacular principles, such as using **natural materials**, simple detailing, and **maximizing storage space** to make the most of **space**, **light**, and **proportion** in a modern home. For example, the poky dimensions of a 19th-century terraced cottage can be improved with careful knocking-out of walls, and simplifying of the interior. Or, in the countryside the sensitive restoration of old farm buildings and barns can create textural interiors.

In recent years, the **conversion** of many sturdily-built and well-proportioned disused inner-city 18th- and 19th-century **industrial warehouses and factories** into **domestic living space** – or **lofts** as they have become known in estate agent's jargon – has allowed many people to enjoy the benefits of living centrally in environments that are more **spacious and airy** than conventional terraced houses or flats. Three years ago we left a home on five floors, and traded gruelling stairwork for horizontal space in a third-floor warehouse space on the edge of the city of London. **Remodelled** to accommodate five of us it has proved to be a workable and comfortable **multi-functional home and office**, with solid walls and good-sized windows that allow large amounts of daylight to flood in.

Function

There is much to be said for the **simple beauty** of the functional, which was until recently a living tradition and present in every pre-industrial society. In early rural England simple **tools** and **craftsman-made** objects for domestic use had an unaffected artlessness. **Plaited reed flooring**, conical **willow beehives**, wooden bowls waterproofed with grease and beeswax for daily use, a one-metre square wooden corn bin – all were designed to be functional and simple in form. More recently, and a huge influence on modern decoration, the **Shakers**, who lived a life free from the encumbrances of possessions, produced architecture and objects of **simplicity** and perfection, and their artefacts are now sought after as aesthetic objects. Many contemporary interpretations of the Shaker look are now featured in the ranges of designers and interior shops.

In our consumer-driven society our homes are awash with objects that are over-decorated and over-designed. While our grandparents would have made things last at least one lifetime, we are happy to discard them at the slightest sign of wear. In pursuit of living a more organized and simple existence I am ruthless at **paring down** and living life with fewer things, yet functional and simple.

So many **ordinary everyday objects**, such as a **pudding basin**, a **wooden spoon**, a **basic stool**, a **plain school bench chair**, or a **folding wooden clothes airer**, are good examples, perfectly balanced between shape and function. **Cotton fabrics** in plain checks and stripes bring simple pattern and detail to table coverings, blinds, cushions, and chair covers. A plain **white cotton sheet** or wool blanket couldn't be more hardwearing, functional and stylish as a bed cover. **Honest and unaffected** design is evident in many objects used for commercial and industrial purposes, where elaborate detailing is less important than the **functionality** of an object – big **cooking pots**, or cutting tables and chairs from 19th-century **woollen mills**, or **stacking chairs**, pigeonhole shelving, and solid desks made **for schoolrooms**. These ideas can also be adapted for use in the home. The catalogues from catering companies, office equipment businesses, and hospital suppliers are full of good **no-nonsense** ideas – wire-mesh cloakroom lockers, trolleys, stacking boxes, pots and pans. If you hunt in traditional hardware shops you will find **basic everyday** tools – brooms, **metal buckets**, coconut doormats and other functional necessities that look good and cost very little.

Order

The straight line has made man's environment orderly and more efficient, whether it is **neat rows of olives studding a hillside**, tiers of metal shelves for goods storage in a factory warehouse, linear patterns in wooden flooring or lengths of striped fabric.

Traditionally, the mediaeval farmer using oxen to plough developed the straight-sided field seen in the system of strip cultivation because traction was more direct in a straight line. Looking out of an aircraft circling low over London, you see **neat patchworks** of allotment gardens sandwiched between terraced houses and flats, where urban dwellers with a need for links with the land grow vegetables and produce their peas, beans, and potatoes in orderly rows on small plots.

Roman roads were laid out in **straight lines** to maximize their efficiency for marching columns of soldiers from destination to destination. Note that in nature, ants and birds have similarly organized **linear ways** of getting from A to B. In urban development the linear **grid system**, used to lay-out New York's Manhattan, illustrates how criss-crossing straight roads between blocks of buildings produces the maximum **use of space** and ease of passage.

linear order is a feature in commercial areas where efficient use of space for access

and storage is reflected in the smooth running and profits of a business. Consider how shops and

restaurants do it – lines of white **plates stacked in piles** on a shelf or a counter restaurant kitchen,

shoe boxes stacked in neat rows from floor to ceiling in the stockroom of a shoe shop, or coffee

packed in plain white paper bags, simply and stylishly displayed on shelves in my local dairy. These

are all ideas to be inspired by when creating order and dealing with clutter in the home.

In a home office, keep a grip on paper and documentation by **filing things** away in **uniformly**

coloured and **labelled folders** and boxes. Build **vertical open shelving** for storage, with infrequently

used books and papers stowed away at the top. Open shelving is also practical in kitchens for storing

everyday dry goods such as pasta, coffee, and sugar in plain glass bottling jars. **Vertical linear tongue-**

and-groove wood panelling on walls and for doors is a simple and modest architectural detail that

has existed for centuries in vernacular building and because of its characteristics it still remains

appropriate in many different types of interior today.

Homemade

In contemporary England we're not quite used to the notion of being **thrifty** and **economical** when so many mass-produced goods are available that are cheap to buy and often disposable. It's worth reminding ourselves, as we throw away yet another razor or pair of socks with holes, of the incredible **resourcefulness** of people during the last World War. With the make-do and mend approach encouraged by the wartime government, everything was transformed into something else. Curtains and wedding dresses were run up from available materials – parachute silk, butter muslin, and black-out materials. Flour sacks and sugar bags became cushions and loose covers. Fabric used to fill broken windows after air raids was found to make useful tea towels. During the summers of 1941 and 1942, 1,500 tons of jam were made from gluts of seasonal fruits by women's institutes.

No doubt my need to be economical has been influenced by **growing up in the 1950s**, with parents who had experienced wartime rationing of food and other household staples, when my sister and I were **encouraged to sew, cook, and make our own presents**. In adult life, though my credit card yields to some retail therapy, an expensive dress or coveted pair of shoes, my conscience generally asks me why should I waste money on shop-bought things such as cushion covers or Christmas cards when I can make them myself? To be resourceful, buy **cheap utilitarian fabrics**, such as **calico and cotton**, and look out bargains in sales, too. **Collect** a bag of **remnants**, bits of **ribbon**, and other trimmings that could be used to freshen up a collar or the hem of a skirt, or to trim a plain napkin.

There are many shops selling renovated and painted furniture, but why not buy your own **chair** or table from a junk shop, then strip it down and **paint it yourself**?

When cooking it's quick to throw together **easy baking ideas** such as **scones**, flapjacks or biscuits, or a **simple cake**. With a basic recipe it is quite simple and quick to boil up a batch of **jam** with summer strawberries, or in winter **marmalade** with some of the season's tangy Seville oranges.

At Christmas time when funds are stretched, make your own decorations, cards and labels with supplies of coloured paper, pens and paint from an art shop or stationers. A batch of **homemade biscuits** packed in a box and tied with bright ribbon couldn't be a more appreciated present.

Fabric

Fabric in natural cotton, linen, wool, and silk used to trim and decorate windows, sofas, beds, cushions, and other home furnishings and accessories is one of the simplest ways to make your home more comfortable, colourful, and textural.

Plain hard-working **basic utilitarian** fabrics, used for sails, tents, awnings, sacks and other commercial purposes can be bought from specialist suppliers and used to make **textural** and **tough** furnishings at home. Art suppliers are a good source of artists' canvas, which can also be transformed into chair covers or curtains, or hessian used as a canvas backing that could equally make a textural curtain or seat cover. Theatrical and film-set suppliers sell very cheap muslin, which can be tied with loops onto a pole or even just stapled up at the window. I know a good source of felt generally used for commercial backdrops that comes in a range of wonderful colours, including pinks, greens, oranges, and lilacs. There are also quite a few companies who specialize in various basic materials, such as sheeting that you can use to make your own duvet covers and pillow cases, or bright orange, yellow, or green canvas to create your own chair slings and cushions.

Ship's chandlers are good sources of rope for making cord to use on heavy-duty laundry bags or beach bags made from tough canvas.

florals   Back in the 1970s, our sixth form floated from class to class in romantic **Laura Ashley**

floral-sprigged, cotton-frilled shirts and patterned milkmaid smocks, bought with Saturday job money

from her small shop in the Fulham Road, London. Ashley's vision of the English country look, inspired

by **floral-printed chintzes**, dried pot pourris and roses climbing around cottage doors, was cleverly

interpreted in both her clothes and furnishing ranges. After her sudden death, the sweetness and

clarity of her designs was never quite recaptured in successive collections. During the get-tough, get-

rich 1980s aspiring bankers and other would-be money-makers paid interior decorators to recreate

the grand English country house, in mansions and semis alike. Swathes of chintzy wallpaper and

extravagant curtains with swags in bold floral patterns appeared in every interior-decorating magazine.

During the 1990s, the country look went out of fashion to be replaced by more pared-down and

modern trends in interiors. **Florals have come back again**, but in a much more restrained manner,

and in some gorgeous **retro-1940s styles**, as **pretty details** for home accessories. When used sparingly,

florals can look **fresh and crisp** in a contemporary interior.

checks and stripes are **simple patterns** that have been used for centuries in commercial and domestic environments. Blue-and-white striped **cotton ticking** is a traditional mattress covering that has become a stylish curtain, cushion, or chair covering in its own right. Cotton tickings are **tough and good value**, and can be found in black, terracotta, brown, and yellows, as well as blue.

Striped linen, used for roller towels in hospitals and institutions, can be bought by the roll from the suppliers and cut to make table runners, or sewn together to make chair covers. Classic striped linen tea towels can also be given the same treatment.

Checks are basic and **uncomplicated** and have a **sense of order and neatness** – that's why they are used for school uniforms and as table linens in restaurants and cafés. I adopt the restaurant principle at home and use either bright **blue-and-white check cotton** cloths, or wipe-down checked plastic that is highly practical. I also use checked cotton fabrics as cushions or blinds against a backdrop of plain walls and furnishings. A local Spanish supermarket is my coveted source of mesh shopping bags – ordinary, dirt-cheap, and stylish carriers for my *pan grandes* and vegetables.

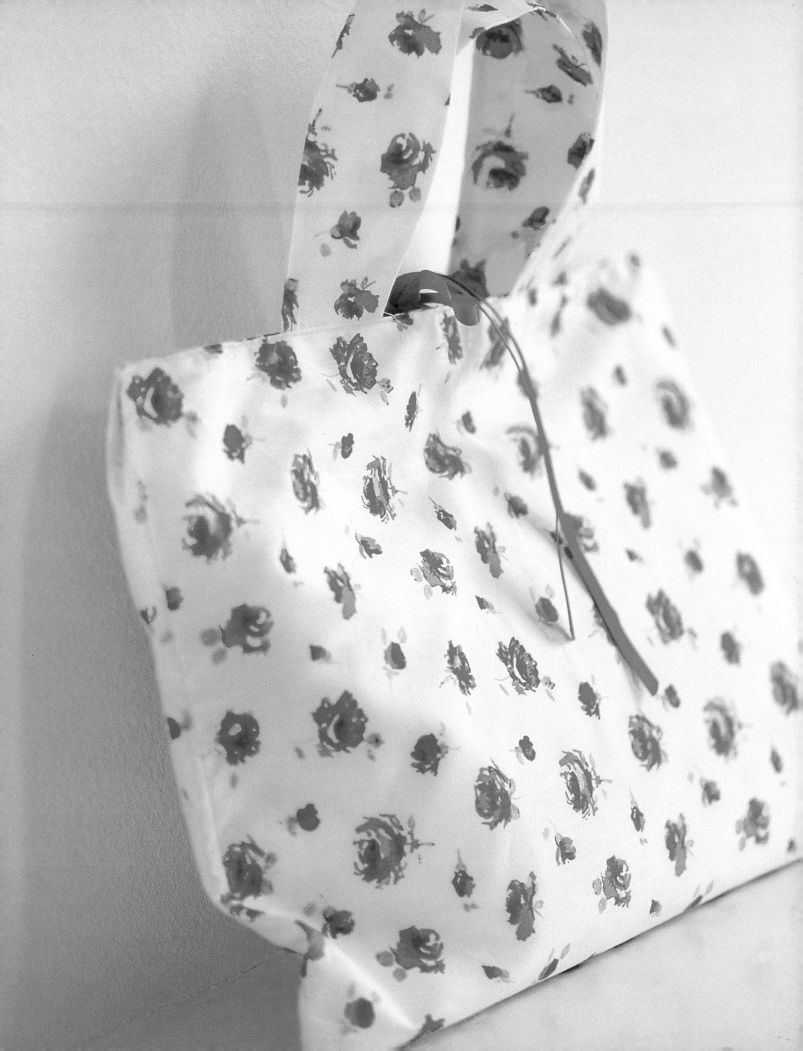

Colour

How do I choose the colours that I want to live with? I resist examining colour wheels or remembering which colours are supposed to go with each other. I use my **instinct** for colours that feel right – a **sentiment**, not borne of any particular logic, that is echoed by colour forecaster, Li Edelkoort, who predicts new trends in fashion and business. My instinct has no doubt been developed through being brought up in a drab English climate, where the very absence of colour during the winter months has stimulated my desire for it.

I look to **nature** for **inspiration** – the sea, the sky, plants and flowers – and, of course, **art** – the Scottish colourists and the Bloomsbury group of artists are favourites of mine. And two years ago, in rain-swept early new year Paris, I was lifted out of the gloom by the soft, luminous rectangles of colour on expansive canvases created by Mark Rothko.

I constantly **observe** and **appraise** colours around me – the **detail** of a cardigan trimming, or a painted door, or the colour of the fabric of a child's dress. I store these visual fragments in my mind like a mental pinboard of samples, to bring into my work as a stylist and as ideas for my home.

I prefer to live with a **backdrop of calm**, wrap-around colour –- such as white or a country cream – that serves as a **canvas** onto which I **inject colour** in the form of fabric – a bright throw or cushions or plants, a terracotta pot with blue hyacinths, or a jug of pink tulips.

white   Think of things that are white – a stark, snow-covered landscape, a smooth ovoid duck's egg, a worn and weathered creamy beach pebble, or a sun and saltwater-bleached clam shell. White is **pure**, **calming** and **soothing** to the soul. And white schemes are eminently liveable with, so white is eternally popular with architects and designers, who will use it in the simplest beach houses, as well as the hippest ultra-modern hotels. White is **light-reflecting** – the white huddled village houses of Andalucia and other hot zones are painted in white limewash because of this quality. If you adopt this principle in a grimy urban area, and paint a south-facing interior in white, the space will be infused with luminous light, even in the grey of winter. White is **rejuvenating** – think of freshly washed white linen flapping on a washing line – use it to spruce up tired pieces of junk furniture or for simple pull-on chair covers, and white is **seductive** – there's nothing more **cool** than white linen clothing against tanned summer skin, or a present simply wrapped in filmy layers of scrunchy white tissue.

earth colours in terracotta and various shades of brown are basic **back-to-nature** hues that evoke rural images – furrowed and ploughed fields, bare trees silhouetted against winter sky, **brown peaty earth floors**, rough hessian sacking stuffed with hay. In mediaeval England, the clay soil itself coloured mud-and-wattle huts a dull brown. And in parts of rural Spain today red oxide is still mixed with limewash to colour village barn or hut walls a pinky terracotta inside and out.

In the home **earth colours** and textures are **grounding** elements that add a certain **honesty** and down-to-earthness that makes an interior an **organic environment**. These can be **tough coir, and natural matting in brown shades**, natural wooden floorboards in scrubbed bare pine, or richly worn oak, or **linen in oatmeal or leather-brown** for slip covers and simple blinds. Roughly woven log baskets with cut logs for the fireside and irregular hand-thrown worn and weathered terracotta flowerpots planted with bulbs can bring nature in from the outside. If renovating an old house, search for suppliers of irregularly **brown and plum coloured handmade traditional bricks**, rather than the uniform textures and colours of mass-manufactured shapes.

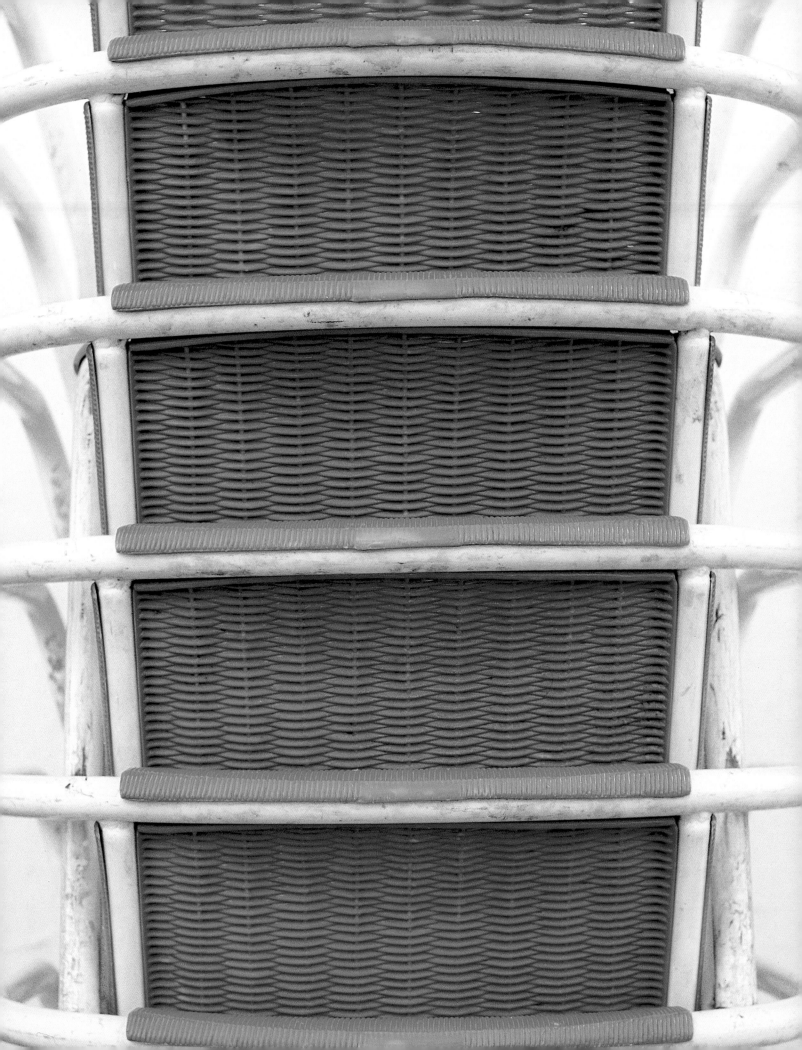

green is the colour of **new life** and growth, a **calming** colour which symbolizes **balance**. The greens of nature are diverse – take the **electric lime-green** stems of young shoots, fresh bright **spring-green** grass, silvery grey-green lavender, the green and yellow tightly packed layers of a fresh cabbage.

Soft greens for walls work all around the home, particularly in rooms that require **peace**, such as kitchens and bathrooms. In a wooden-panelled 18th-century house or other period interior, **sludgy grey-greens** in matt textures are appropriately **old-fashioned in feel**. For a modern look, a **lime-green cotton** in cushions or a blind set against white walls and neutral slipcovers **looks fresh**, and is also wonderfully **uplifting** in the dark winter months. **Timeless garden greens** inspired by the bean patch are just right for **painting sheds** and **outside furniture** to look at one with their natural surroundings. For inspiration, look at the vegetable plots and gardens of seasoned old gardeners who haven't been influenced by paint catalogues and continue to use traditional gardening practices that make their green spaces look as if they are part of the landscape.

blue   The colour blue evokes **serenity**. It's connotations with sea and sky are suggestive of **space** and **freedom**. Blue has been adopted as a **spiritual** colour too, and so the Virgin Mary is seen in flowing sky-blue robes in paintings, and when she is carried out on flower and candle-decked floats during the religious *paseos* of Spain and other fervently Catholic countries.

Blue shades belong to bathrooms and washrooms. I swim alongside artist Howard Hodgkin's giant **spuming and frothing wave mosaic mural** in various shades of tiny blue ceramic tiles which spans the length of the swimming pool at my fitness club and creates a **sense of calm** in this windowless underground site.

In the home, **paint walls in soft powder blues**; they are less cold than blue-grey shades. And **blue pigments added to limewash** create **luminous colour** for Mediterranean beach houses, or even a windswept English beach hut. **Blue-and-white striped ticking** or blue checked and striped cotton fabrics are **crisp and fresh**, and good for making into chair covers, blinds, table cloths, and cushions all around the home. And a jug full of heady-scented hyacinths in shades of blue are my favourite details at the table.

yellow is a **warm and positive** colour. It varies in hue from the **pale cream of straw** to the **brilliant yellow** in the petals of a **sunflower**. **Strong yellow** walls are **sunny** and **exuberant**, and are good for **enlivening** dark, north-facing rooms. Avoid using citrus-coloured yellows on walls; they are too harsh on the eye. The natural pigment **yellow ochre** is a wonderfully rich yellow for adding to **limewash** to make rich sandy colours — along with versions in white, green, and terracotta — and seen on the elegant, faded townhouses that line Seville's narrow streets. One of the most beautiful yellow-painted rooms that I have seen is in the sunny and airy drawing-room of the English architect Sir John Soane (1753–1837), at his house in Lincoln's Inn Fields in London. **Paler country cream colours** work in most interiors — they can **look really fresh in a modern apartment**, but also appropriately **authentic on old wooden panelling** in an 18th-century house or cottage. **Creamy yellow-coloured** pudding basins, **mixing bowls**, and dishes are an alternative to whiteware in the kitchen. A **sunny yellow-and-white checked chair cover** or blind is a good choice for brightening up a child's bedroom, painted in white. And what could be more spirit-lifting and cheap on the pocket than a bunch of daffodil buds from a flower stall for spring colour at the supper table.

pink and lavender colours are **inspired by the hedgerows** and garden borders. Purple **lavender**, scented heads of **lilac, foxglove** bells, dusky pink **roses**, and pinky **tulips** are nature's ideas that can be copied and translated to paint and furnishing colours. **Fuchsia-pink felt seat cushions** for a pair of recycled chairs, or a **fuchsia-pink wool throw**, are useful **colour injections** in an all-white interior. But such is the power of this colour that it would be a psychedelic experience to have to live with it as all-over room colour. **A bedroom painted in pale lilac** with white bedlinen and a jug of pink tulips, would be easier on the senses and look simple and fresh; it's a good choice for sitting rooms, too.

Sprigged and floral pink-printed cottons can also look clean and contemporary as slip covers, cushions, or a simple blind. And on a sartorial note, I love to wear pink. It looks great – a bright **rosy pink** scarf or shirt in winter when everyone is muffled up in winter browns and blacks, and in summer, strong **fuchsia pink** looks good against healthy tanned skin – a plain cardigan with jeans, a pair of silk fuchsia pink 50s-style cigarette pants, with an orange shirt, or a Liberty floral pink cotton skirt. Finally, for a cheap and colourful idea, wrap up your presents in bright pink tissue paper or use pink ribbon on lime-green tissue for a more contemporary look at Christmas time.

live

Eat

Work

Garden

Rest

Play

Wash

Sleep

Eat

Equip your kitchen with functional tools – heavy-based cooking pans, wooden spoons, pudding basins, plain white tableware, and so on. Buy the best ingredients you can afford – good cheese, fish, meat, fruit, vegetables, chocolate, and wine – and from local sources if you can. Make delicious food that is easy to prepare – hearty soups, crisp salads, fruit fools, homemade cakes and biscuits – and lay the table with fresh linen, simple glasses, and a jug of flowers.

seasonal produce   Buy fresh produce locally and in season for better taste and texture. **Savoy cabbage**, which is cheap and

plentiful, is a super vegetable that's packed with fibre and vitamin C (mostly in the dark green leaves), and is thought to have cancer-

preventing properties. The thick, curly green leaves should be lightly steamed, and covered with butter, pepper, and a little salt. **Quince**

is an old fruit (there are references to it as far back as Ancient Greece) that is still grown today; the Tudors made "marmlades" or sweet,

hardened pastes, which was a Portuguese idea (*marmelo* is Portuguese for quince). Golden yellow, with a furry coat and a sweet, slightly

cloying scent that permeates the air, I pick them from the garden to make slabs of sweet and sticky *membrillo*, the traditional Spanish

quince paste eaten with cheese. The children like to help shell **broad beans**. Picked young when still sweet and tender, they are best

served gently steamed with butter and a little chopped mint. They are packed full of fibre, vitamins, and minerals. A pinch of salt is all

that's needed to bring out the flavour of homegrown or local **tomatoes**. Cut into chunks and served with good bread, garlic, and olive oil they make a juicy, nutritious meal; tomatoes are a good source of vitamin C and lycopene (more potent in cooked than raw tomatoes), which is an antioxidant that may help to prevent certain cancers. I freeze and bottle homegrown tomatoes for winter needs. In Spain, after the rain, **wild mushrooms** magically spring up overnight. I pick chanterelles, ceps, and field mushrooms from the fields, always double-checking with an expert that they are edible. Cut up and fried with butter, garlic, and parsley, and spread on toast they make a little feast. In England, I look out for the big flat, dark-gilled field mushrooms that taste really earthy. Buy little bags of scalding roast **chestnuts** from street sellers or use peeled chestnuts to make a turkey stuffing or a rich chocolate and chestnut purée pudding. Chestnuts are very nourishing – some experts say more so than brown rice – being high in starches, fibre, and protein, with less than 5 per cent fat.

My ideal kitchen is one where an appearance of order can be maintained at the same time as cooking, eating, and dealing with the waves of everyday clutter – newspapers, toys, clothes, pencils, pens, and unwashed plates. I have no desire for a "dream fitted kitchen" with endless cupboards and drawers, and overhead contraptions hung with elaborate pots and pans and other decorative paraphernalia. My kitchen needs to be a **plain**, **functional backdrop**, where I can concentrate on family life and making good food.

I have always admired those gleaming institutional kitchens in factories and schools – all **white tiles and stainless steel**, with rows and rows of plate racks, industrial dishwashers, and streamlined surfaces (see p.90), where the process of preparation, cooking, and clearing up afterwards is a perfectly ergonomic sequence of events. My ideal kitchen has sun streaming through it at some point in the day, and decent-sized windows to let out the fug. There has to be enough space for a **big wooden table**, around which we all sit, eat, drink, chat, write, do homework, or read the papers. In my kitchen, surfaces, textures, and tools need to be there for a purpose and function, not because they are the latest state-of-the-art worktop or architect-designed gadget.

Within the confines of a tight budget and the limited space in my London flat, I think I have created a kitchen that is as near as possible to my perfect space (see pp.84–85). It comprises one row of **simple cupboards**, inherited from the previous owner and revamped with wooden doors. At eye level, there is a white chunky pine shelf for easy access to my key cooking ingredients and china. Beneath this is a metal rail with butcher's hooks for hanging sieves, scissors, colanders, graters, and other essential equipment – an idea borrowed from restaurant kitchens. The work surface is wooden, which is practical and tactile to work on, although if I had my time again I would choose stainless steel for its resilience and wipe-down quality. We also inherited a large **catering oven**, which I nearly sold, thinking it too big and cumbersome; in the event, we kept it and its capacious proportions have proved to be a tremendous advantage for cooking meat, vegetables, and a pudding all at once; the generous five-burner hob means there is plenty of space for the biggest pots and pans. There are now many places to buy redundant but perfectly good catering equipment, such as trolleys, storage racks, sink units, and tables, that can be given a new lease of life in a domestic setting.

When I married in the early 1980s, a **food processor** was a kitchen status symbol and was at the top of my wedding list. I used mine to rustle up many a delicate nouvelle cuisine sauce or fancy terrine – de rigueur at the time – for meals that went on into the early hours and were a feature of childless social life. Seventeen years or so later, it's still sitting on the worktop, a little battleworn perhaps, but it has never broken down, and is now used to help fill small, hungry tummies with quick-to-prepare hearty and wholesome soups, puddings, cakes, and pastry. My other long-standing kitchen companions are two **cast-iron enamelled saucepans** that my mother bought cheaply on a trip to France. After rigorous use for over fifteen years they have only a few chips. Even though they are heavy, I rely on them for stews, sauces, steaming vegetables, and countless other tasks. I've learnt through bad buys that cheap, light pans tip over, thin ones warp and cook unevenly, soldered handles fall off, and non-stick coatings eventually peel.

I am always on the look out for kitchen tool bargains in London markets or seaside junk shops; I keep my eyes open for items such as **old-fashioned** glass lemon squeezers, nicely worn breadboards, or green-and-cream ware pots, pans, and tins from the 1940s for storing dry ingredients.

New additions to my basic kitchen kit include a couple of rather good **shallow aluminium baking sheets** to bake shortbread, pizza, or chocolate brownies, and a **catering toaster** for thick slices of toast. I top up my supply of **creamy coloured pudding basins** (see p.91) because every now and then there's a breakage when the children are making one of their famous cakes or batches of biscuits. If anyone wants to give me a present, I would ask for another heavy kitchen **knife** with an excellent blade and well-designed handle.

making marmalade   The season for Seville oranges – the only oranges for making marmalade – lasts only a few weeks, from January to mid-February. Rows of stocky, bushy trees **laden with little orange orbs** can be seen on the huge estates around Seville in Spain. **Fragrant-skinned** but too bitter to eat raw, the fruit has been made into marmalade since the 18th century. I use my friend Emma's recipe, which, unusually, involves boiling whole oranges to make a rich, **aromatic**, tangy addition to the breakfast table.

1 Cover 1–1.5 kg of Seville oranges with water in a large saucepan and simmer with the lid on for up to 3 hours or until soft. If using a pressure cooker, reduce the cooking time to 1 hour. Seville oranges can be frozen if you want to make marmalade later in the year but defrost them before following the recipe.

2 Remove the oranges from the pan and put into a bowl; retain the liquid in the pan. Cut the oranges in half and remove the pips. Return pips to the pan, and boil rapidly for 10 minutes. Strain the liquid into another bowl and discard the pips.

3 Cut the peel up into pieces – the size depends on personal preference but I like my marmalade to be chunky. Use scissors rather than a knife to make cutting the squelchy oranges easier and less messy.

4 Measure the strained liquid and peel.
Add 500 g peel to 450 ml liquid and 750 g sugar.
Bring to the boil slowly, and then boil rapidly
until setting point is reached (see Step 5). (Any
liquid left over makes delicious orange jelly. Add
500 ml juice to 500 g sugar and boil until setting
point is reached.)

5 Test by pouring a spoonful onto a plate
that has been cooled in the freezer. If the
marmalade or jelly wrinkles when pushed with a
finger or spoon it is ready.

6 Leave to stand for l5 minutes, then stir
and pot into sterilized jars. Cover with waxed
paper and lids while the marmalade or jelly is still
hot. Makes about 2.5 kg of marmalade and a pot
or two of jelly. Customize with home-made sticky
labels – an idea that will appeal to children.

laying the table   In an age of snatched sandwich breaks and TV dinners, it is very important to sit down and appreciate good food when there is time available. An everyday meal of breakfast, lunch, or supper can become a feast with a **simply laid table**. I start by spreading an **ironed**, **white cotton or linen tablecloth** – a white cotton sheet will do. **Table components** include **simple tumblers** or plain wine glasses, **plain white china**, classic cutlery, and plain white or **blue-checked napkins**. I always put a jug or glass of **flowers** on the table. In Spain, they could be wild peonies, daisies, tuberoses, or herbs, and in London, tulips, narcissi, or sunflowers, depending on the season. **Hunks of bread** are cut to pacify the very hungry before plates of grilled fish or a simple salad arrive.

Plain, unfussy tableware and china lets the food speak for itself. Soup swirled with cream and scattered with a few chopped herbs looks magnificent in a shallow white bowl (see p.97); similarly, salad leaves, a batch of chocolate cup cakes, or even baked beans on toast are more inviting on a white plate. For daily use and eating outside, I have **basic white** plates and bowls from a department store or catering shop because they are cheap to replace. For suppers when friends come round, or weekends when the whole family sits down and eats together, I use my favourite large, white, bone china plates and bowls in a classic shape (see p.96). If I'm lucky, I can usually stock up on china during the sales in one of the large department stores because it's expensive when new. **Storage** for my linen and tableware is in slim, purpose-built cupboards – the width of the largest dinner plate – for which I designed versions for both my London flat and the house in Spain (see left and opposite).

making a table runner   A narrow table runner spread along **the length of the dining table** is a simple way to add texture and colour. I first came across the idea in **Sweden**, where freshly scrubbed tabletops have lengths of crisp linen – either plain or decorated with a plain stripe – placed along them. The runner shown below and opposite is made in a **straw-coloured**, **loose-weave cotton** and is trimmed with a pink, cotton **velvet ribbon**. Experiment with different colours and textures, but check that the fabrics are washable.

1 Measure the length of your table and add about 40 cm to give the length of fabric required for your runner. A suitable width for a runner is 35 cm, but bear in mind the table it is to go on – one-third of the table width is a good guide. The length of ribbon required is 2 x length plus 2 x width of the runner plus a bit extra for overlap. Overlock raw edges of the fabric, and hem about 1 cm all the way around.

2 Pin a piece of ribbon to the length of the runner. Turn the beginning of the ribbon under to make a hem, and cut the other end leaving a bit extra for the hem. Sew along the outer edge of the ribbon. Take one end, of the loose ribbon and tuck under the end of the length just sewn to make a neat corner. Pin this piece along the width of the runner, remembering to turn the far end over, and sew along the outer edge.

3 Continue to fix the ribbon until all four sides are trimmed. Tuck the final end under the first piece of ribbon and fasten. Now sew all the way round on the inside edge of the ribbon to finish off. Press flat, and place symmetrically along the length of your table (see opposite).

4 Matching napkins can be made in exactly the same way. For each napkin you will need a square piece of fabric measuring 35 x 35 cm, and 1.5 m of ribbon. Hem the napkins and attach the ribbon as described in Steps 1–3.

Small spaces When small kitchens in a flat or studio double up as eating areas, it is essential to keep clutter to a minimum and to use the maximum number of space-saving ideas.

Put up **shelving** so it almost reaches ceiling height; space the shelves so that they are further apart at the top to hold bigger and less frequently used items, such as a fish kettle or large meat dish. Have some lightweight folding aluminium steps so you can get at things up high. Stick to a **minimum number of essentials**; be strict and give gadgets or china you don't use to relatives, friends, or a charity shop. Likewise, **pare down your store cupboard** to necessities and don't hoard food you are unlikely to use. I couldn't live without black pepper, good sea salt, saffron, virgin olive oil, lemons, and garlic. My staples also include chickpeas for instant houmous; tinned tomatoes – good in winter when tomatoes are out of season; tins of tuna – for pasta and salads; tomato puree; pesto; rice – for risottos and paellas; couscous; pasta; and dried mushrooms for risottos and pasta sauces.

A built-in worktop with either integral cupboards and drawers beneath or space for **free-standing furniture**, such as a dishwasher, is practical. If money doesn't stretch beyond a worktop, a curtain can be hung to hide cleaning equipment and other kitchen paraphernalia beneath.

Buy a **narrow dishwasher** – 45 cm rather than 60 cm – and use it for storage as well as washing. There are even smaller machines designed to sit on a worktop. If you're not bothered about gadgets, a fold-up wooden draining rack does a pretty good job of storing the evening's washing up (see pp.84 and 87). Miniature electric cookers with one or two rings, a tiny oven, and grill have kept alive generations of hungry students in bedsits, and are brilliant for cramped kitchens. A tall larder fridge is a good way of storing food, and most have racks for holding bottles flat. Folding or stacking chairs are best in a small space. **Extra table space** can be created with two folding trestles and a top made from fibreboard, that can be stored flat against the wall when not in use.

Summer eating   Cook fish and meat on the barbecue, and prepare simple vegetables, salads, and puddings for low-maintenance

summer food that makes the most of what's in season. I enjoy **Spanish tapas** (which originated in Andalusian bars, where small dishes,

placed over glasses to ward off flies, were filled with olives and morsels of fish, ham, or sausage). At home we serve slices of jamon –

the rich Serrano ham from pigs fed on a natural diet of chestnuts, apples, and acorns; almonds toasted in the oven and rolled in salt;

olives; and anchovies marinated in olive oil. **Salads** are so much sweeter and crisper in summer when homegrown produce can be picked,

rinsed, chopped, dressed in something garlicky, and whisked to the table in minutes. Salad possibilities are endless, but you can't go

wrong with sweet cos lettuce leaves dressed with herbs, a little cucumber, and chopped carrot. Always prepare salads just before serving,

or they wilt. Summer is the season for barbecues. In Spain, we cook *solomillo* – **pork tenderloin** marinated in oil, lemon, and garlic for

a couple of hours before cooking; I prefer to barbecue it so that it's rare on the inside and crisply cooked on the outside. It is as tender as the most mouthwatering sirloin steak, and is delicious with boiled new potatoes and mint. Other barbecue possibilities include fish, steak, lamb chops, sausages, and vegetables. Buy meat that has been raised according to good farming practices, or better still, buy it direct from the farmer. Roughly chopped **homegrown tomatoes**, sprinkled with sea salt to help bring out the flavour, make a perfect accompaniment to barbecued meat. Over-ripe tomatoes are good to use for a chilled gazpacho soup. Serve a refreshing, nutrient-packed **mixed fruit salad** for pudding (chopped peaches, cherries, and melon mixed with a little orange juice, lemon juice, and dessert wine; chill for half an hour in the fridge before serving). **Orange and almond cake** is a sweet and aromatic pudding with Moorish origins; it is delicious sliced and served with the fruit salad and a dessert wine. As it is made without flour, it is good for people allergic to wheat.

When the temperatures rise and the days lengthen, it's time to head outside for **al fresco eating**; each hour of the day has its own special possibilities in the open air.

It is a **hit to the senses** to drag oneself from sleep and feel the grass bristling with dew in the cool of morning, a jersey tugged on over pyjamas for warmth, a cup of hot, steaming coffee clasped in one hand and a thick slice of buttered toast with honey in the other. Everything is hot and cold all at once, with the sun just warming up. Have lunch outside under a shady awning in the midday heat with a cold beer coursing through your limbs and munch a crisp, thirst-quenching, leafy summery salad, with the morning's fresh bread and slivers of salty, nutty cheese from a slab protected by a mesh net. At the end of the day, I sit with **bare feet** nuzzling warm stone, and nibble almonds with a glass of fino sherry as long shadows creep into the setting sunlight, and the air is **warm like velvet**. As night approaches, candles and nightlights flicker, and the heady fragrance of sweet jasmine wafts across from over the wall.

For the more practical aspects of **outdoor feasting**, use a table that can be left outside in the event of summer storms (see opposite). Better still, devise a collapsible eating surface from a piece of fibreboard, or even an old door or planks of pine stuck together, and rest it on a pair of folding trestles (see pp.104–105). The whole lot can be whisked away when the sky threatens. Spread a cloth in gingham, or white fabric for special meals, and buy some of those clips used by cafés for anchoring down tablecloths on windy days. **Candles and nightlights** can be contained in glass or metal lanterns so they don't blow out. For comfort, folding director's chairs are good for laying back in. Take out extra seat cushions, and blankets or throws if there's a nip in the night air.

making raspberry fool

In the cool of the evening after a hot summer's day, there's nothing more perfect than going out into the garden to pick a bowlful of **plump, juicy, fragrant** raspberries. The children love to eat them simply with a sprinkling of sugar and dollops of ice cream. I have a greedy liking for creamy raspberry fool – a **glorious concoction** of cream and raspberries – that makes a traditional summer pudding served in simple glasses, perhaps with some **homemade chunks of shortbread**.

1 Hull and wash 225 g fresh raspberries, or if they are out of season use frozen ones – defrosted – from the supermarket. Although not as flavoursome, I often use the frozen variety in winter for a taste of something summery.

2 Mash the berries with a fork in a pudding basin until they form a lumpy mess. My favourite mixing bowls are the good old-fashioned, cream ceramic ones that are found in most kitchen shops and hardware stores.

3 Stir 90 g of castor sugar into the mashed raspberries. If the berries are really sweet you will probably need less sugar and some fool lovers don't add any sugar at all. I think that a little sugar helps to bring out the flavour of the fruit.

4 Whip 225 ml double cream using a hand whisk until it makes soft peaks. For a slightly tart and less rich variation, you can use the same amount of crème fraîche, or for a healthier, low-fat version, use thick Greek yoghurt.

5 Add the mashed raspberries, a spoonful at a time, to the whipped cream. Wooden spoons are versatile tools and I have a large variety – new, slightly worn, very worn, short, long – to cater for different kitchen tasks.

6 Fold in the berries until the cream and fruit mixture has a uniform pink colour. Spoon it into small wine glasses or second-hand 1930s ice-cream glasses. Serve with shortbread and shots of sweet wine. This recipe feeds about four.

Lolling on the back seat of my dad's Ford Corsair, eating cold sausages, spreading breadcrumbs, and not being ticked off for it, was the highlight of the long, monotonous pre-radio car journeys of my childhood. **Eating on the move**, eating out of special lunch boxes, baskets, or carefully wrapped greaseproof paper packages, rather than sitting up straight at the table, and being correct with cutlery was bliss to a 7-year-old. I still **embrace the informality** of picnicking, tearing bread apart with hands, and then licking fingers clean afterwards.

I keep anticipatory **larder stocks** just in case. Slabs of chocolate, a few cans of soup, tins of sardines, tuna, and olives, plus jars of tapenade and grilled peppers. My kit includes a **plastic wine cooler** in the freezer, **thermoses** in the cupboard, and a **rucksack** with a permanent **corkscrew** in one pocket. Simple gutsy foods are best for **eating alfresco**, and the secret is to not take too many ingredients. What could be more comforting than a **picnic** of smoked salmon sandwiches and a bottle of ice-cold fizz (pour into small tumblers), especially when enduring the unpredictability of an English train journey?

In the winter, **slabs of fruitcake** and a thermos of hot chocolate warm everyone at teatime on a brisk walk. On the beach, sausages cooked up on a little barbecue to wedge between bread buns, with cups of hot soup, is the sort of nostalgic, sand in the sandwiches, **sand between the toes**, experience that is exhilarating for adults and kids alike – better than being shut in with the video and a sense of cabin fever on a dark winter's weekend afternoon.

In summer, I place a bottle of water in the freezer then add it to a cool bag with **bagels or bread buns** stuffed with slices of tomato, cucumber, tuna, mint, or basil to take to the beach. The buns are filling and tasty after a cooling dip in the sea, and drinking lots of water keeps dehydration at bay. Heat doesn't agree with sticky cake or chocolate, so we stop for ice creams on the trek back home.

camp-fire cooking   For my children, making a camp fire and cooking their own grub is a high spot of holidays in Spain. In summer, the fire risk is too great so our cook-ups are restricted to the cooler months. The children pick a spot and **make a circle of stones**, having cleared away any dry grass and leaves. Georgie is dispatched to **gather kindling**. Tom lays a few **dry logs** on the pile. Keeping a match alight is testing, but soon the adults get the blaze gets going. Once it has died down we start cooking. **Sausages** are all-time favourites, wedged hot-dog style between bread (the adults cook field mushrooms in garlic and butter). **Plastic plates**, kitchen paper, and tongs are useful. For a wickedly sweet treat, we lay bananas in the embers to soften, then slit and fill them with butter and brown sugar.

Homespun Christmas

By simplifying Christmas, I keep my sanity intact. The rule is not to start too early or to be too ambitious, and to **get key tasks done in advance**, such as stocking up on wine – we buy champagne, cava, lots of red and white riojas, plus some port and sweet dessert wine – buying olives, and ham for cutting in slivers for tapas; making and freezing stock for soup, and creating homemade ice cream to eat with puddings.

Stir-up Sunday in mid-November is traditionally the latest date for making the **Christmas pudding** so that it matures in time. Everyone in the family has a stir with the wooden spoon to mix the squelchy ingredients: raisins, suet (buy it fresh from the butcher or use the vegetarian version), figs, walnuts, and all the other fruity additions. Dark muscovado sugar will give the pudding a richer colour and flavour, and if you want to deepen it further, you can increase the quantity of stout. It doesn't matter if you throw the pud together at the last minute – steaming it for an hour or so longer than the normal 4–5 hours will help to give it more texture and taste. I also try and make **mincemeat** a couple of weeks beforehand, adding pine nuts, walnuts, orange liqueur, and orange peel, and stuff it into little mince pies to give as presents, or freeze to eat over Christmas, served with crème fraîche flavoured with vanilla sugar, or dollops of cream.

Table ingredients include candles in clear glass jars or plain candlesticks (see opposite) and, for scent, bowls of hyacinths, amaryllis, or white narcissi, which shoot up quickly and flower for a couple of weeks. Other essentials to get us in the Christmas mood are mounds of clementines with their citrus-smelling peel, walnuts to crack and eat with cheese and slabs of Spanish membrillo (quince paste), crackers, indoor fireworks, and chocolates wrapped in tissue paper.

I decorate my **Christmas tree** (see opposite) with iced biscuits in heart and star shapes, rag balls made from strips of fabric remnants (see p.198) – bright green is this year's theme, and white candles in cheap brass holders that have been camouflaged with white paint (the candles are lit only when adults are present and the tree is never left unguarded in case of fire). The black pot that the Christmas tree came in has been given a similar disguise with white emulsion. If the tree has roots and has been watered, it's worth planting in the garden for use again next Christmas.

Christmas food can be simple and quick to make, providing yummy treats for the festive table. **Potatoes and parsnips** are delicious roasted in olive oil. Peel, chop, and parboil before tossing in hot oil. Roast in a tin or place around the chicken or whatever meat is being cooked. Turn regularly to ensure even crisping. As an alternative to traditional Christmas goose or turkey, I like to serve **roast chicken** with the breast stuffed with lemon and herb butter, and trimmed with some sprigs of fresh rosemary. When the meat is finished, boil up the bones with bay leaves, onions, and carrots to make a delicious stock that could form the basis of a seasonal chestnut soup or be frozen for later use. Serve a big platter or dish of **mixed seasonal vegetables**, such as leeks lightly fried in butter; Brussels sprouts with bacon, shallots, and pine nuts; and carrots sautéed with the juice and grated rind of an orange for an aromatic twist. Other vegetables that might feature on my menu include steamed broccoli or cabbage, and roasted onions, peppers, aubergines, and whole garlic cloves

whole garlic cloves for a more Mediterranean flavour. Cut out star shapes with pastry cutters to make pretty **mince pies**, and finish with

a dusting of icing sugar. If you don't have time to make your own mincemeat, buy the luxury version from a supermarket and pep it up

with extra brandy, a little grated orange or lemon peel, or a few chopped almonds and walnuts. I find that the earthy, slightly tart flavour

of **walnuts** is perfect with cheese, fruit, fresh dates, or membrillo (quince paste) at the end of a meal. Invest in a good pair of nut crackers.

For the perfect finale to go with coffee, serve homemade chocolate **truffles**. Buy the best chocolate you can afford, melt and combine

with cream, butter, and rum or brandy, cool, and then roll teaspoonfuls in cocoa powder. Chill in the fridge and serve on small white

plates, or put in a little box lined with greaseproof or tissue paper, and wrap with a bright ribbon for an edible present idea.

Work

Create order in a home office or work space to help your thoughts flow. Find an area that is calm and peaceful, with adequate desk and shelf space, and invest in a comfortable chair and a good work light. Thank goodness for vacuum cleaners, dishwashers, and washing machines, that help to make light work of domestic chores. Cut back on chemical cleaners and detergents and use more eco-friendly ideas such as hanging the washing out on an old-fashioned airer, or cleaning surfaces with beeswax polish or plain hot water.

Home work

Now that e-mail, faxes, and computers enable us to work from home, **work space** and time vie with the needs of daily family life. Since giving up an office-based job as a design editor twelve years ago, to be **home-based** while the children are growing up, I have become expert at writing books on the kitchen table, jockeying for space with children's paintings, and working alongside the newspapers and clutter of everyday life. Despite the domestic pressures, I'd never go back to packed tube journeys or office politics.

My work room (see p.127), shared also by a husband and, after school, children doing their homework on the computer, has a **long work table** and **lots of shelves** for books and papers. It's small but **light and airy** and **quiet** (essential when living in a largely open-plan space). With a folding metal bed set up, it doubles as a spare room when friends come to stay.

Artists, and other small home-based businesses, need larger studios or office spaces. One way around this is to buy or rent a commercial property, such as shop premises with living quarters above or a large **loft-style space** in an industrial building, that can be **divided** into living and working areas. In the average home, the work space possibilities can be solved with a bit of **flexible thinking and planning**. A photographer friend of mine uses the ground floor of his house as a studio. It has a glass extension – housing the family's kitchen – overlooking the back garden. Another photographer I know works from a flat, using her kitchen/dining/sitting room by day as a **studio** (see p.126), and in the evening the big work table is pulled out and used for eating dinner.

My **dress designer** sister-in-law lives in a small terraced house, and has put aside the largest of the three bedrooms for her **work studio** (see pp.122–124), where she designs, makes, and fits her stylish creations. Most of the room is taken up with a **large cutting table**, which houses **tools, bolts of fabric,** and other **sewing paraphernalia** underneath.

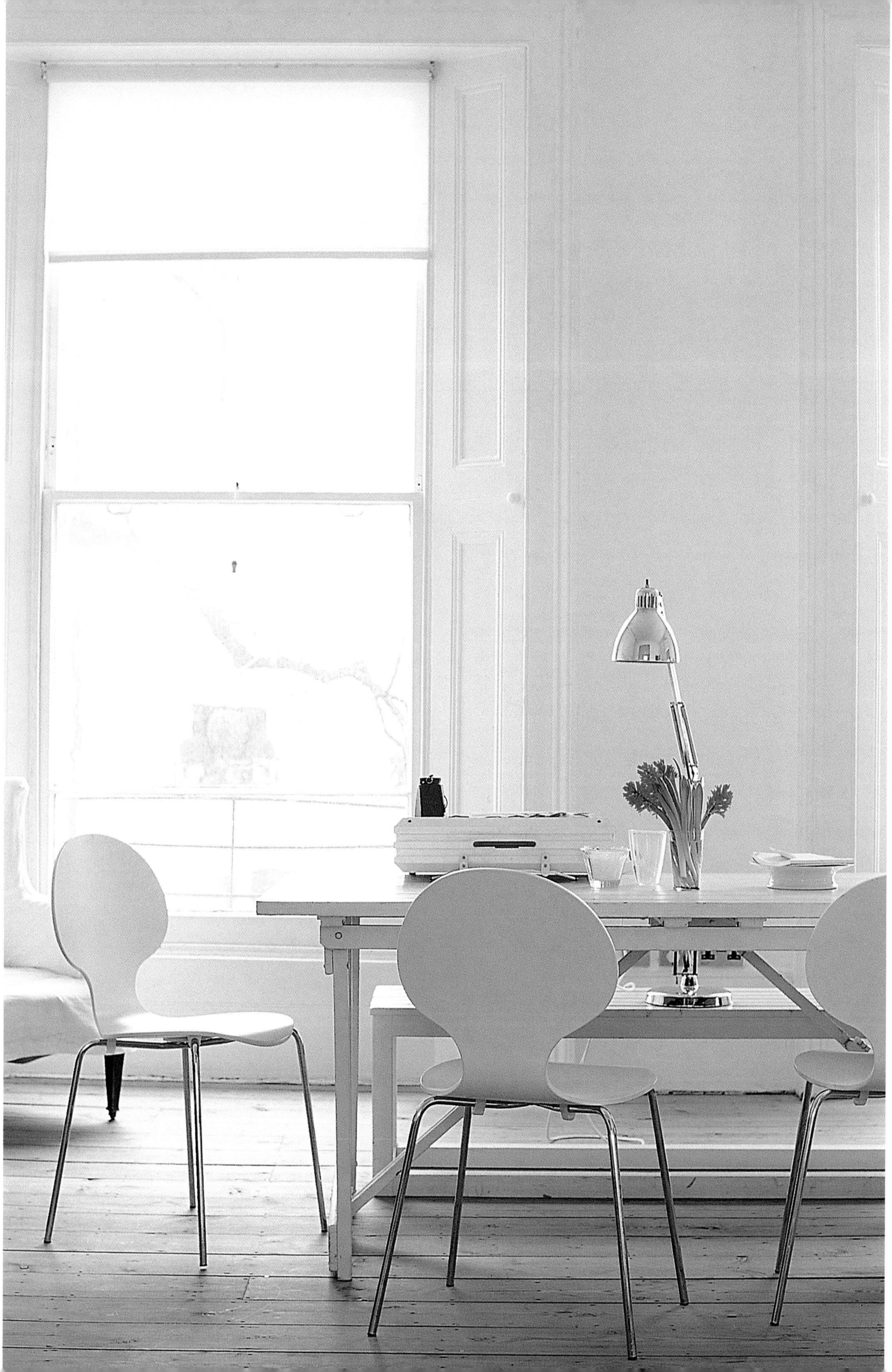

Practical, space-saving ideas

Practical, space-saving ideas for home work spaces (see pp.126–127, and above) should stay within arm's reach. Painted in smart colours, old **baked bean tins** are a good storage idea for pens, pencils, drawing pins, paper clips, and other office kit. A **slab of raw cork** is a new take on the traditional notice-board made from processed cork. Also, try covering a piece of fibreboard with felt for a new look (see the step-by-step instructions on pp.132–133). Push pins are best for securing things. **An angled desk lamp** will direct the light where it's needed, and stop shadows falling over work. Clip-on lights are useful when space is limited; most halogen bulbs are smaller, more efficient, and give off a bright white light compared to the standard yellow tungsten type. For work requiring realistic daylight, use special daylight bulbs, which give a near natural light; these can be sourced in art or lighting shops. **Make a notice-board** to run the length of a wall (the one above right is in plywood) and use it for cuttings, postcards, and inspirational

images. I have a notice-board made of white painted plywood in my office and another in the hallway created from stick-on cork tiles. The cork notice-board measures 3 m x 60 cm and is divided into sections for each child to pin up drawings, party invitations, and anything else they wish to stick up. Make full use of wall space with **overhead shelving**. I have lengths of painted pine, measuring 22 cm deep and 4.5 cm thick, that are wide enough to accommodate my magazines and box files. Shelving that is any deeper takes up unnecessary visual space. I have a lightweight folding stepladder to get at less-used folders that are out of arm's reach. There are many shops selling off cheap **office filing equipment** now that paper files are redundant in computerized companies. I bought two rather ugly grey metal ones that I revamped in white eggshell paint and they now look fresh and modern. Go to a good old-fashioned stationer and buy some **plain brown paper envelopes** in which you can store fabric samples, papers, photos, and other things that need to be filed.

Whatever type or size of space you set aside to work in, even if it's just a curtained-off alcove containing a desk with a phone and fax, it's important to make the area a **comfortable** and **pleasing environment** (see opposite).

Ideally, a work surface should be 150 cm long x 85 cm deep. If it is any deeper, things lurking at the back of the table won't be within easy reach. When considering **desk height**, make sure it is high enough so you **don't slouch** over it. There should be enough clearance underneath the desk for your legs when the chair is pulled up close.

The more time you spend sitting, the more adjustable the chair should be. A chair with adjustable height can be used by all the family. Your **feet** should be **flat on the floor** so that there is no pressure from the chair on the back of your knees. Also, make sure that the chair has adequate back support to avoid back problems in the future.

Choose your **workspace** to let in as much **natural daylight** as possible. Internal windows, glazed or open, between rooms can help spread the available light. However, working in bright sunlight is hard on the eyes and devices such as opaque white blinds can remove the glare.

The correct **temperature** (ideally between 18°C and 24°C) is essential for keeping the thought processes working. Trying to work in hot stuffy conditions is as bad as shivering in a draughty cold room. In summer, open windows for ventilation, and in winter, dress in warmer clothes to avoid having to turn the central heating up too far.

A **healthy body** helps to create a **stimulated mind** so avoid coffee and **drink plenty of water** to stop dehydration at your desk. When chained to a computer screen for long hours, it's sensible to take a break, and go for a walk or a swim. The fresh air and exercise will boost ideas. When energy levels run low, eat healthy snacks such as dried fruits and nuts, rather than reaching for crisps and chocolate bars. Bring nature into your work space with a jug of flowers, and make the place a little more sensual by burning a scented candle.

Making a notice-board A felt-covered notice-board is a **colourful and inexpensive** way of brightening up a home office. Felt is cheap and available in a **stunning array of colours** – try fuchsia pink, lavender, apple green, white, or the rich sky-blue shown below and opposite. Re-cover an existing cork notice-board or buy wood chip Sundela board from specialist DIY shops. Use your notice-board for **important dates** and telephone numbers, or make it more artistic with **favourite postcards** and children's drawings.

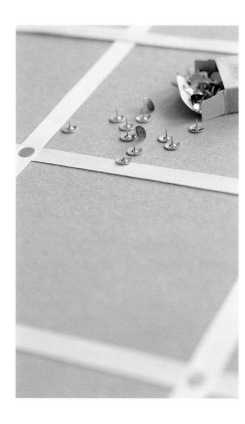

1 Assemble the materials: 59 cm x 78 cm board; 69 cm x 88 cm felt; 6 m cotton ribbon; scissors; staple gun; drawing pins; and string. Lay the board on the felt and cut around it to leave a 5 cm edge. Fold the felt around the board and staple, leaving the 5 cm edge behind the board.

2 Make sure the felt is pulled tight – not so tight that it stretches, but so there are no creases or wrinkles. Position the lengths of cotton ribbon every 20 cm in a checkerboard pattern.

3 Pin the cotton ribbons where they cross with the drawing pins or any other type of pins, such as map pins. Pull the ribbons taut as you secure each one. You could use pins of matching colours or a variety of colours to make a pattern.

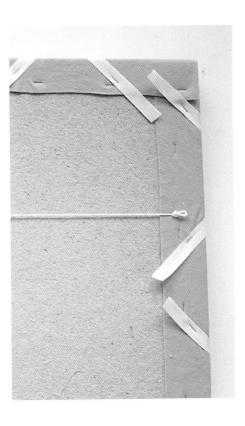

4 Turn the board over and attach the ends of the ribbon to the back using the staple gun. To attach a hanging cord, cut a length of string the same width as the board and tie a knot at each end. Measure 25 cm from the top of the board and fix the string across it using the staple gun. You may need a couple of staples at each end for added strength. Hang your board on a wall or leave it freestanding.

Laundry Gadgets such as washing machines make light work of domestic chores, but in order to be truly **efficient** I think it's important, even at the expense of kitchen space or other space in the house, to set aside a **utility** room – for washing, drying, and ironing. I also find that it is mentally important to be able to shut the door on demoralizing piles of laundry and dirty washing – a characteristic of family life.

Looking around preserved historic houses, one of the most architecturally plain and simple is Lutyens' Castle Drogo in Devon. It is inspiring to go below stairs and see the **functional** sculleries, washrooms, and laundry rooms with gleaming sinks and flagstoned floors. On a much humbler scale, I have borrowed some of these ideas, such as installing a ceramic butler's sink and an old-fashioned **clothes airer** (they are still manufactured today), in my flat in London (see opposite), where I have made a rectangular utility room, measuring 1.8 m wide x 6 m long.

My utility room can be described like this: along one wall there is a **butler's sink** on a stand, next to a 2 m x 1 m wide pine **work surface** (on which I pot plants, clean the shoes, and stack laundry); the washing machine, freezer, and an open space for storing laundry baskets are underneath this surface. Above the work surface there are two lengths of shelving that house extra washing powder, loo rolls, the iron, and other paraphernalia. There is plenty of space to set up the ironing board and do the ironing in front of the work surface, and above that the **clothes dry on the airer**. A radiator mounted on the wall helps speed up the drying process. To solve the problem of creating the utility room at the expense of a second bathroom, I have managed to squeeze a loo and a shower into a space at the far end of the room.

If you really have absolutely no space for a utility area, and you live in a tiny flat, plumb the washing machine into the kitchen, and store all your cleaning equipment in a bucket under the sink. Buy a folding wooden clothes airer that you can stand by a window in the sunlight during the day when you're out and about or at work, and you can plonk in the bath when the kitchen is needed in the evening.

It is tremendously useful to have a **utilitarian washing area** for heavy duty jobs such as removing mud from dirty boots, cleaning paintbrushes, and descaling fish. Plastic washing-up **bowls** in bright colours, and **metal buckets** are also useful for handwashing precious woollens, or scrubbing a bag of mussels for supper. One of the most practical shapes for a sink is the freestanding stone type with a built-in sloping ridged surface for scrubbing clothes on; you see these in the open courtyard wash areas in southern Spain and Portugal. Shallow stone sinks, or double **butler's sinks** can be bought new or picked up quite cheaply in reclamation yards and can be used in conjunction with either modern or old taps. I am particularly fond of the simple brass taps that can be fixed on the wall with their pipes exposed. Walls of **tongue-and-grooved** planks look basic and utilitarian in a washing area, and if painted with a durable eggshell finish will be quite waterproof. Floor surfaces should be equally durable and non-slip, with lino, rubber, wood, or stone being good choices.

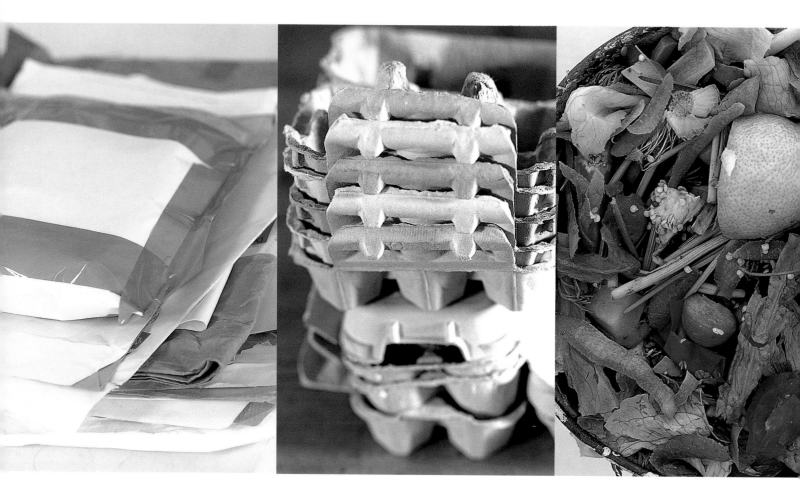

Recycling ideas   Think before you throw anything away. Be less wasteful around the house and recycle everything from vegetable peelings to jam jars and help take the pressure off the environment. **Recycle packaging** – make the most of reusable items, such as envelopes, which can be used again and again; I particularly like to keep those bulky padded bags for sending breakables as they are rather expensive to buy new. Cover old postmarks and addresses with a stick-on label or a piece of plain paper. This is also a good way to keep down costs if you're running an office from home. **Egg boxes** made out of recycled card can be saved and returned to the shop for further use or collected with your other recycled paper (or they can be used by children for cutting into creative shapes). Always try to avoid unnecessary packaging – especially goods like shrink-wrapped individual portions – and buy as many loose items as you can. Create **compost buckets** – save organic matter from kitchen tasks to put on a compost heap; this will make a nourishing compost that

will enrich the soil in the organic vegetable garden. Vegetable peelings, eggshells, bone, teabags, and small pieces of card are all good composters. **Build a compost heap** in the corner of the garden (see p.336). Surround the compost with wire or a wooden frame with holes for ventilation. Turn the compost regularly. **Sort recyclable materials** into different boxes and bins: glass, paper, metal (aluminium drinks cans are recyclable), organic matter, and plastic coke and lemonade bottles (reused to make fleece clothing) can all be recycled. Also, put old clothes into boxes and bin bags to send to a clothing bank or charity shop. **Save glass jars and wide-necked bottles** and re-use them for home-made jams, chutneys, and other preserves. Always clean out thoroughly before use, sterilize with boiling water or in a hot oven, and seal carefully. Also, keep plastic receptacles, such as fresh cream and soup containers, that can be used for all sorts of different things from freezing home-made soups and other foods, to holding sewing materials and pens and pencils.

Ecologically friendly Look for ecologically sound products and more **natural** ways to keep the home clean.

A little bit of dirt never did anybody any harm; in fact, some research suggests that children brought up in squeaky clean surroundings don't build up as much immunity against certain illnesses as their peers who live in homes that aren't kept clinically pristine. However, in our fussy, overprotected society we seem to be obsessed by cleanliness and germs, and so manufacturers cater for the popular demand for whiter- than-white whites or sparkly clean floors with chemical cleaning products that, while effective, have a high cost – that of damaging the environment.

For example, chlorinated bleaches and disinfectants certainly do their stuff, but they also disrupt the balance of micro-organisms in septic tanks and sewers. Equally damaging to the water supply are the enzymes, bleaches, whiteners, and abrasives contained in washing powders.

It's really important, therefore, to use products that are **phosphate-free** and chlorine-free from the growing ranges in organic shops and some forward-thinking supermarkets. There are also a number of more benign and natural ways to keep things clean. To **handwash the green way**, use bar soap and washing soda dissolved in hot water instead of detergent; and add a tablespoon of white vinegar to the rinsing water to prevent soap scum.

And if you want to **get rid of the limescale stain** in the lavatory, don't use one of those nasty chemical cleaners with bleach and caustic agents; instead try a strong solution of **vinegar** to remove it. Equally basic and natural is **beeswax** – unequivocally the best thing for **polishing** wood – rather than something that comes out of an aerosol can that calls itself furniture polish and is artificially perfumed and full of solvents and synthetic silicones.

The **control** of household **pests**, such as flies, ants, bugs, and mice, is another area where heavy-duty insecticides and rodent killers not only have unpleasant effects on the environment but can also cause serious damage to humans and pets. Spray insect killers are particularly unpleasant, and their chemical residues can be left on food and the skin. Eco-friendly ways to deal with pests include fly swats, electronic fly zappers, citronella candles to keep away mosquitoes, jars containing a tempting morsel and a makeshift ramp to lure cockroaches, and gruesome, but instantly effective, old-fashioned mousetraps. Remember, too, that adhering to **basic hygiene** rules, such as covering food and cleaning away food scraps, will deter many household predators.

Hanging out the washing to flap on the line is a wonderfully satisfying job, especially on a bright and **breezy** day. If it has been raining, I wipe the line before pegging out the clothes; I use either **plain wooden** or brightly coloured plastic pegs from the local hardware store. Whites – sheets, towels, underwear, and T-shirts – are **naturally whitened** and freshened by the effects of the sun. Remember to turn jeans and brightly coloured clothes inside out to prevent fading (even though I quite like the worn look of some of my favourite T-shirts). The summer sunshine is more efficient than any electric dryer and the whole wash is crisp and warm within a couple of hours. In **wintertime**, when there are long bouts of heavy rain, I often have to resort to drying things in front of the **fire**.

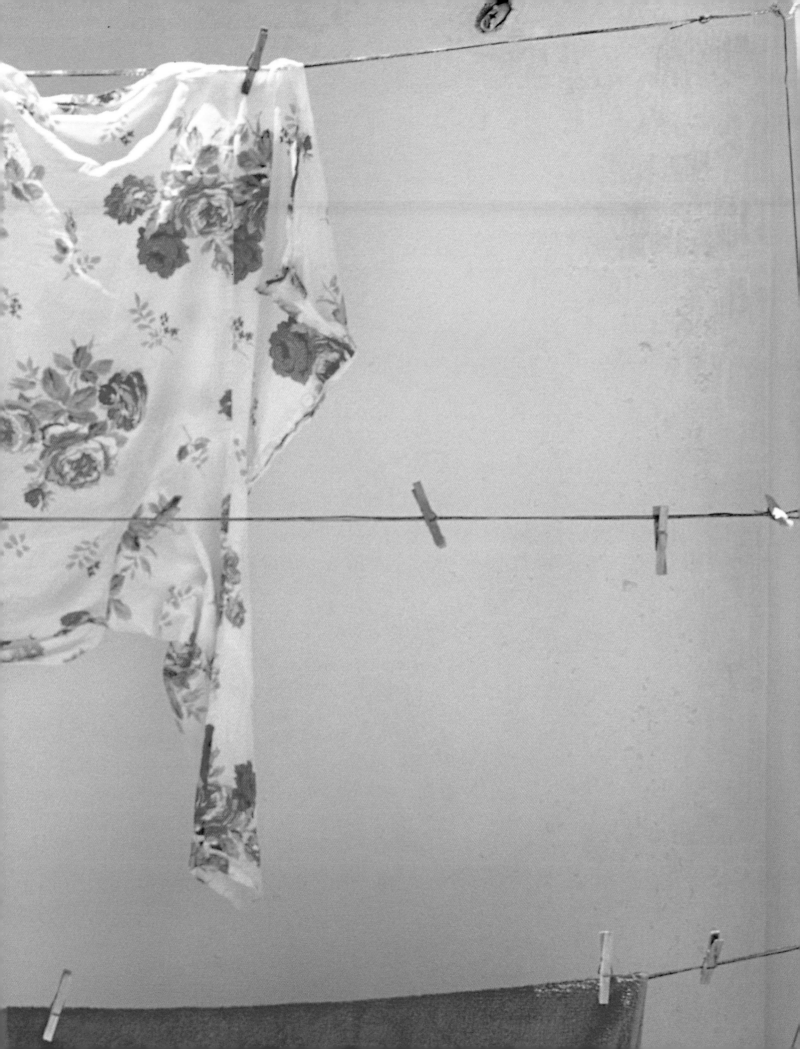

Garden

Make the most of your outside space, even if it's just a window box with herbs. Grow delicious scented roses, lavender or sunflowers for cut blooms in summer. Go back to nature and dig a vegetable patch, and garden organically with rich compost for home-grown produce – tomatoes, beans, peas, potatoes, courgettes, carrots, and other nourishing goodies – that taste sweeter and more delicious than anything bought in the shops.

Flowers   in brilliant colours, which grow from seeds or bulbs with little fuss, are enormously gratifying for any gardener. One small

packet of **nasturtium** seeds yields an amazing show of flowers. Plant the knobbly seeds straight into the ground, and remove dead

blooms regularly for repeat flowering. Nasturtiums can be grown up wigwams made of sticks, or allowed to free-fall from containers.

They look pretty in a vase, and the flowers and peppery leaves can be added to salads. Try Tom Thumb, a dwarf variety (height 30 cm) in

bright oranges, yellows, and reds, or Tall Mixed, a rapid climber (height 180 cm). **Tulips** look good planted randomly in clumps. Flowerpots

with five or six blue or white parrot tulips look great in the garden, or on a window-ledge or balcony. Plant bulbs in a well-drained, sunny

position sheltered from cold winds. If bulbs are left in the soil, as an alternative to lifting and replanting the following year, add bonemeal

to help further flowering. The trailing character of **convolvulus** is useful for disguising water tanks, outbuildings, or fences. Although

each voluptuous, trumpet-shaped flower lasts only a day, the various shades of pink, purple, and blue come in perennial as well as annual varieties. Try Heavenly Blue with sky-blue flowers (height 3–4 m). **Sunflowers** naturally turn their yellow heads to the sun. They can be grown straight from seeds planted in the ground, or potted singly and transplanted. Cut sunflowers in big jugs make good table decorations. Large-headed varieties, such as Russian Mammoth (height 240 cm) are the most dramatic; plant in a row in front of a fence. Or try Big Smile, a dwarf variety (height 40 cm), which is good for pots. The round fluffy heads of **allium** provide good architectural shapes for the garden. Members of the onion family, they like sun and well-drained soil. In pinks, purples, blues, and whites, they grow between 45 cm and 1 m high. Try Caerulum, a small hyacinth-blue variety (height 60 cm), or Globemaster, which sways on wiry stems at head height. **Narcissi** come in many varieties. I plant dwarf yellow tête-à-tête in pots and buy a forced white variety that flowers indoors in time for Christmas.

I find it deeply satisfying to **garden**, whether it's nurturing a few pots of herbs on the window-sill in my London flat, or digging up potatoes, pruning the roses, or planting bulbs in my garden in Spain. Trying to tame nature and be close to it is an innate part of our make-up, originating from a basic necessity to grow food for sustenance. In an increasingly frenetic and technological existence, having a vegetable plot or garden to tend is literally a **grounding experience**, giving us the opportunity to bring a little more order into a world that is largely out of our control. It allows us to experience the simple **pleasures** of being outside in the **open air**, cooking on a camp fire, or reading a book under a **scented**, climbing plant on a balmy evening.

You don't even need much space: some of the most sensual, **intimate**, and personal gardens that I have come across are little more than cultivated postage stamps. An example is transatlantic gardening pal Dean Riddle's **vegetable and flower plot**, which is a magical retreat from New York in the Catskill Mountains; it is surrounded by **stick fencing** and planted with a patchwork of ornamental cabbages, herbs, **marigolds**, and other everyday plants.

Neither do you have to be based in the country to enjoy the peace and tranquillity of a room outside, as in the secret leafy **urban oasis** (pp.150–151) where owner and artist Marianna Kennedy has painted her tiny, shady backyard in light-reflecting white, furnished it with textural **weathered York stone** flagstones and a nicely battered wooden garden table, and filled it with pretty, **low-maintenance** lilies, **nasturtiums**, and luxuriant, shade-loving **hostas**. This is a lush, still, **calm place** that belies its location just a few metres from the busy city street outside.

Making the most of even the tiniest **roof space** (see opposite) with sensible wooden decking and simple twig fencing for privacy and to support climbers, such as roses and honeysuckle, allows the busy owners of a food shop to escape from business and enjoy a quick rest in the sun on the roof.

Renovate junk chairs from a second-hand shop or market, and paint in a garden green eggshell to use around the table for outside feasts. I found four of the same chairs (see below and opposite) in a London junk shop, but it's not essential to have matching shapes. In fact, mismatched simple chairs painted in a unifying colour will look just as good and add a rustic touch. When the chairs are not being used outside, they can provide extra seating for parties and at other times when there are extra mouths to feed.

1 You will need newspaper to protect the floor, sandpaper of assorted grades, a small tin of wood primer, and a tin of eggshell paint in the colour of your choice. You will also need a 2–4 cm paintbrush, and, if your primer or paint is oil based, some white spirit or turpentine substitute to clean your brush. If you prefer, however, you can use a water-based eggshell and primer.

2 Sand down the chair to get rid of any loose flakes of old paint or varnish; start with a medium grade of sandpaper and finish with a fine grade. Wrapping the sandpaper around a block of wood will make it easier to apply pressure. Always try to sand along the grain of the wood and not across it. Once the chair has been sanded you will need to give it a good wipe to remove all the dust before applying the primer.

3 Apply a coat of the primer using plenty on the brush as it should not be spread too thinly. Allow the chair to dry if you have removed dust with a damp cloth) Try to coat the chair as evenly as possible, even though it will end up looking streaky. Always read the instructions on the tin and allow the primer to dry for the correct amount of time.

4 Apply the first coat of paint when the primer is dry. Try to follow the lines of the chair with your brush strokes. You may need to apply another coat once the first one has dried, depending on how even the finish is. Eggshell paint gives a durable matt/satin finish (see right).

Gardening in pots is a simple and effective way of bringing natural colour and scent to tiny patios and other small spaces where having flower-beds is not possible or desirable. Worn and weathered **terracotta flowerpots**, old ceramic kitchen sinks, wooden tubs, **galvanized buckets**, old tin cans, even old paint tins can all be put to use, and a surprising number of plants and flowers will flourish in such limited spaces provided they are fed and watered well. Create a miniature garden in pots on a window-sill or balcony; the **window garden** (see opposite) is a typical sight in the white villages of Andalucia and is an idea that could be transplanted anywhere. A traditional wooden **window box** always looks good whether planted with mixed herbs for the kitchen, with **bulbs** such as tulips, hyacinths, and narcissi, with a hedge of purple-headed **lavender**, or with bedding plants such as pinks, marigolds, and pretty, scented, **old-fashioned geraniums**.

Pots can be massed together and planted with a variety of annuals or bedding plants for colour in a back garden; or they can be arranged to look more **formal**, for example a pair of **leggy bay trees** or **box standards** in metal pots placed on either side of a doorway. Small orange or lemon trees grown in big terracotta pots are another favourite in my garden in Spain, where they can flower and fruit in sheltered spots without falling prey to frost. A row of containers holding the same plant can look dramatic. I tried it with twelve giant blue **agapanthus** that I planted in three wide, **shallow, terracotta** bowls on the edge of the sunny patio at my Spanish home. They flowered for months, growing to about 1.5 m. In my previous house in England, I achieved an equally successful visual effect using foxgloves and delphiniums planted in deep, terracotta pots on the roof terrace. On a smaller scale, a shallow, **stone sink** is a good container for miniature plants such as camomile, thyme, and small succulents.

The essential requirements for successful container gardening are **good drainage**, the right type of soil, and regular watering and feeding. Ensure that containers have a central drainage hole that is covered with a few stones before being filled with soil (see pp.160–161). For **a well-balanced potting medium**, use soil that is light, friable, and nourishing. You can mix heavy soil with sharp river sand to lighten it, and supplement light soil with rich loam and granulated peat to help retain moisture. With regular watering and additional nourishment in the form of compost, bonemeal, and other organic plant feeds, most potted plants, including climbers such as clematis, passionflower, honeysuckle, and some roses, will remain healthy in the same soil for years.

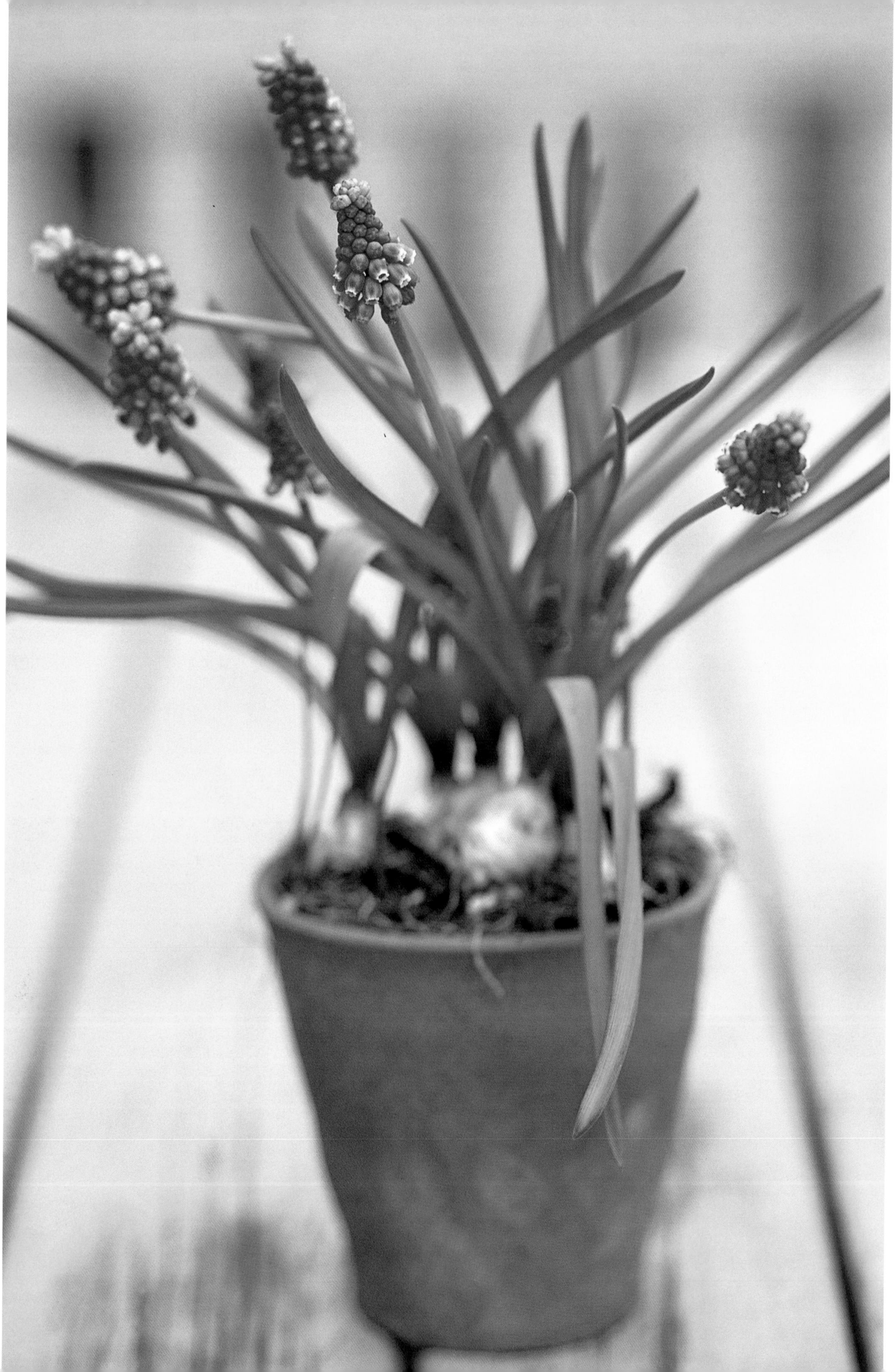

My **indispensable garden kit** starts with a pair of **well-worn boots** with a special thermal lining that are parked next to the front door. In **winter**, I also pull on **extra-thick socks**, and an old waterproof coat for garden tasks. In **summer**, there's no need to dress quite so defensively, but a large wide-brimmed **straw hat**, a long-sleeved T-shirt, and suncream (SPF 40) for the face are sensible measures against burning, especially in the intense Andalucian sun. Whatever time of year, I always make sure that there is a pair of really **tough gardening gloves** – thick rubber or tough cotton – lying about the place. I don't mind getting my hands dirty but unprotected they are prone to painful thorn pricks, allergic rashes from the leaves or sap of some plants, or insect bites from rummaging around in the bushy undergrowth.

I'd be lost without a pair of **secateurs** – for pruning, trimming, and cutting flowers and stems for decoration in the house. I keep these in a little **Sussex trug** – a functional wooden carrier used by many generations of English gardeners – along with a **trowel** (invaluable for digging and planting), a **little fork**, **string**, and **wire** for supporting and training plants, and a packet of bonemeal for top-up plant nourishment. I have two or three **watering cans**, of which a small, galvanized metal one with a short spout is the easiest to handle. I use a **hose-pipe** for the heavier watering jobs. Stored under the lean-to shed, along with the wood pile, are heftier tools including a couple of good **stiff brooms** for sweeping up dust, leaves, and other debris, and a **fork**, **spade**, and **wheelbarrow** for **weeding**, **digging**, and **planting** down at the vegetable patch.

In the **basement** of my Spanish house, along with the drying hams and jars of home-made jam, are numerous paper bags of **old bulbs and seeds** saved from previous years. I am very keen on the mouthwateringly sweet, local **Spanish tomatoes**, and since they're not available commercially I **dry the seeds** and keep them in foil in an airtight plastic box for sowing the following year. There are also stacks of old, worn, hand-thrown, **terracotta flowerpots** for bulbs, which were brought in the removal van from England.

Plant bulbs to create brilliant colour for pots and window boxes. Once a year, I make a pre-breakfast visit to the local Sunday morning flower market to buy **bulging bags of bulbs** – feathery white parrot tulips, scented white hyacinths, deep blue grape hyacinths, and delicate, miniature, yellow tête-à-tête narcissi. I plant these in old, weathered flowerpots rescued from the run-down potting sheds of country estates. Line the pot with **terracotta shards** or stones to help drainage. Fill half the pot with a **loam-based compost**. Sit the bulbs on a **layer of fine grit or sand** to improve drainage. **Evenly space about six bulbs** per 25 cm pot. **Cover with compost** about two to three times the height of the bulbs and then water. Continue to water sparingly to keep the bulb fibre moist.

Dig a vegetable patch in the garden for the simple and earthy delights of lifting **sweet**, **succulent carrots** to chop up and make into a crisp salad, or **new potatoes** that taste divine when **boiled with mint** and smothered with melting butter. If you don't have a garden, grow garlands of tiny tomatoes in growbags of organic compost in any available outside space, or plant up a box outside the kitchen window with **herbs** – tarragon, basil, thyme, and chives – for a permanent herb garden at arm's reach. **Urban gardeners** can feed their families with **fresh organic produce** by applying for a little growing plot in one of the communal vegetable gardens found in towns and cities or by being inventive with any outside space, even a tiny window-ledge. In the suburbs and countryside, however, there's much more scope for creating vegetable patches in the back garden.

A good example of organic vegetable gardening in **urban London** is John Matheson's vegetable and flower patch (see pp.164–165). This oasis is tucked away among a patchwork of communal allotments on a blowy hill; wedged between pylons, scrapyards, and factories, the plot boasts an unexpected view of a sliver of a tributary of the river Thames, where herons come to feed and frilly cow parsley grows head high in the summer. Only those with highly detailed instructions and a key are able to gain access to this little **inner city haven**, where retired publicans and rail employees tend their dahlias, feed the foxes, and offer gardening advice alongside families with young children who spend the weekends weeding, planting, watering, **manuring**, and harvesting homegrown produce. Like all good organic gardeners, John Matheson works with nature not against it, and so in the absence of harmful insecticides, his garden is **busy with wildlife** – bees, hoverflies, butterflies, scuttling beetles, and thrushes that tap snails out of their shells.

A thick **rosemary hedge** divides flowers off from vegetables; the flower garden is planted with **alliums**, **euphorbias**, and **lavender**, all good for attracting pest-eating insects. There is also a little **toolshed** for stowing garden kit and deckchairs for rest and relaxation. In late spring the vegetable garden bears the young leafy tips of **beetroots**, **swedes**, and **parsnips**. There are some good-looking shallots, climbing **white beans** that are starting to curl around the wigwam made of peasticks, and flowering **broad beans**, which will start to produce their crop in a few weeks' time. Throughout the growing season, Matheson's plot also yields an impressive six types of potato, three types of onion, three types of pumpkin, two types of French bean, broccoli, sweetcorn, rocket, mizuna, lettuce, and courgettes. One autumn day, John knocked at my door carrying a heap of tender **Jerusalem artichokes** fresh from the patch, which I chopped up and fried with butter to form the basis of a delicious, velvety, winter soup – this earthy offering from so local a source couldn't have been more appreciated.

Homegrown produce is fresher than anything you can buy and many herbs and vegetables are easy to grow. You don't need much room: reserve a small patch in the garden for herbs, or in a backyard raise a slab to grow courgettes, or on a balcony plant tomatoes in pots. **Lettuces** (see opposite), for vitamin-packed salads through the year, will even grow on a sunny window-sill. **Outside**, sow the seeds thinly in shallow troughs 30 cm apart, in the shade of another crop, such as peas, if possible. Water well for a good crop.

Young allotment crops raised in **rows from seed** under a **glass cloche** (from top: beetroot, spring onion, early little gem lettuce, leek, early carrots, mature little gem lettuce, early carrots, and calebrese). Forced under a terracotta cloche, **rhubarb** is delicious in fools and fruit crumbles, but remember that the leaves are poisonous. A single packet of seeds can give you basketfuls of **climbing beans** that will grow in any good garden soil. Dig a trench before planting and fill with organic matter – my grandmother has used seaweed for decades. Grow in a double line supported by canes or climbing up a wigwam made out of sticks.

Rest

We live such a stressed existence that it's important to rest and relax. On long hot summer days flop under shady trees, doze, or read a book. Inside, use light-reflecting whites to create a light and airy sitting room. Furnish with a well-upholstered sofa, the largest you can afford, and soft feather cushions. In winter, build a blazing log fire, light candles, and keep draughts at bay with woolly throws in checks and stripes.

Bundled up in layers to protect winter chapped skin, I look forward to summer days in the fresh air on a beach or under the dappled shade of a tree in the park as the ultimate way to relax and let worries drift away. I am all in favour of the **siesta** – still a feature of life in the hot Andalusian summer, where between the hours of 2 and 5 every afternoon, very little human or animal life stirs, the sheer ferocity of the heat sending everybody to the nearest horizontal surface. Daily, during our holidays at the *finca*, I drift into afternoon sleep in the cool of a shuttered room, lulled by the bees humming in the eucalyptus tree and the smell of hot, dry grass outside.

Practical, **hard-working fabrics** are vital for making cool furnishings on which to flake out. Tough **cotton** is useful for a **shady**, **collapsible canopy**, to be used either on the beach (see pp.170–171) or at the park. Constructed on the tent principle with a cover, poles, nylon guy ropes, and wooden tent pegs, the canopy can be folded up and carried under the arm or in a lightweight basket or bag.

Also easy to make are **cotton-covered mattresses**, stuffed with foam (which dries more easily than feathers) to lie on or sit on by a swimming pool or on a patio (see pp.172–173). Use bright stripes or plain colours in green, orange, or hot pink and make **removable covers** for the mattresses in different sizes suitable for adults and children.

One of my most exciting fabric discoveries recently has been **sea-green**, **heavy**, **waterproof canvas**, the sort used for old-fashioned tents; this has been made into **awnings** at the front and back of my Spanish house (see opposite). The fabric is thick and the amounts required are bulky to work with on a normal sewing machine, so it is best to use a curtain or blind specialist to make up your awnings. For easy removal if it starts to rain, mine were constructed with hook and loop fastenings. Also, note that it's wise to **choose dark colours for shade**; I once made the mistake of making awnings in thin, pale creamy calico which let the sun through and caused burning to bare skin beneath.

Blues, **greens**, **and whites** are cool, relaxing colours for summer rooms inside and outside. With little spare time, and practicality at the top of my list of priorities, I used ordinary exterior **white paint** for our patios in Spain (see pp.172–173 and 175), but purists are likely to choose traditional paints. For example, our friends Nick and Hermione Tudor used **traditional limewash** at their seaside retreat in Southern Portugal (see opposite). Organizing a supply of limewash is time-consuming, but worth it for the **matt**, **chalky texture** that you can't achieve with other types of paint.

Limewash – or *cal* – is still made in the traditional way in the village where the Tudors live, by boiling marble chips and pig fat in outside ovens for 24 hours; this technique dates from Roman times. After being cooled for 24 hours, the calcified chips are then added to water and mixed to give the thin white liquid typical of old-fashioned limewash. The chips are caustic and, therefore, they should be handled carefully and always be stored in metal containers.

Stirring a very small amount of *azul-oscuro* – a **blue pigment** – to metal bucketfuls of wash, Nick and Hermione mix up varying shades of blue from a very pale lavender for the walls, to darker shades for door frames, benches, and skirtings. Depending on how much the rain has damaged the surfaces in winter, the Tudors revamp the house with fresh coats of limewash at the beginning of each summer.

Other elements to make an outside space **textural and sensual** are rough **terracotta** or **ceramic tiles** underfoot, and **light**, **floaty fabrics**, such as **muslin**, hung in a doorway to draw in a cooling breeze. **Plants** are key ingredients in my view: **climbing jasmine** grows in most conditions, and the white flowers release their headiest scent in the night air; passionflower is a fast grower, and, although unscented, produces extraordinary flowers; and **architectural agapanthus** – tall green stems carrying white or blue flowers – is my favourite summer bloom. Finally, **candles** burning in **lanterns** on the table or strung on a wire are best for natural lighting.

Making a curtain   A basic curtain with looped headings can be simply made in any kind of fabric – lightweight muslin, heavier canvas, or wool. The curtain width should be 1.25–1.5 times the width of the window depending on how full you want it to be. Striped patterns (see below and right) look fresh and work well in bedrooms and sitting rooms. This curtain design also looks good across alcoves used for clothes storage. Hang the curtain on a wooden pole bought in kit form or made out of dowelling from a builder's merchant.

  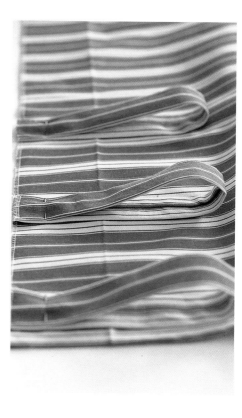

1 Cut fabric to required length, allowing an extra 15–20 cm for top and bottom hems. Measure and cut the curtain to the required width, allowing 2 cm for side hems. If your windows are very wide you may need to join two widths (take care to match pattern repeats). Overlock or zig-zag stitch the raw edges. Cut a strip of iron-on interlining, about 5–10 cm wide and as long as the curtain width. Iron the strip onto the back of the top edge of the curtain.

2 To make the tabs, cut strips twice the width and length that you require the finished tabs to be. Our finished tabs measured 4 x 18 cm, so we cut strips that were 8.5 x 36 cm. Fold each one in half lengthways with the right sides facing and sew the long edges together. Turn each one inside out and press flat so that the seam is in the centre at the back. Now fold to form a loop making sure that the seam is on the inside, and stitch the two ends together.

3 Position the tabs at regular intervals along the top edge of the curtain on the right side, with the edge of the tab level with the edge of the curtain. Pin and then sew along about 1 cm from the edge, fixing the tabs into position.

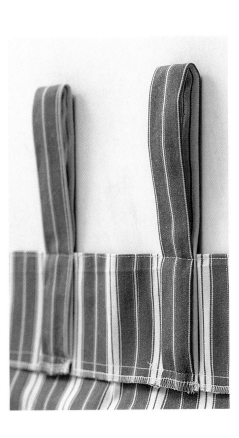

4 Turn a hem at the top edge the depth of
the interlining and press flat. Now sew along the
fold, fixing the tabs into position. At either end
of the curtain sew down the depth of the hem.
Hang the curtain and pin up the bottom hem to
make sure the length is correct. Remove the
curtain, sew the pinned hem, and press. The
curtain is now ready for hanging (see right).

Keeping **cool** inside in summer isn't easy when it's hot and sticky outside and there's barely a breath of wind in the air. It helps to have **light-coloured natural cotton or linen fabrics**, which can be whisked off sofas and chairs and given a wash to keep them fresh and crisp. Remember that strong sunlight fades fabrics ruthlessly; I have found that cushions brought to Spain from England have become much paler than their original colour, so it might be worth having one set of **pale slip covers** for summer and another set in brighter colours for winter. Invest in a portable electric fan – they can be enormously effective. When the temperatures begin to soar, it's wise to **close the shutters** during the day and open them as night falls; in this way, the strong heat of the day is kept at bay. Our sitting room in Spain (see opposite) also has a **lofty ceiling**, which helps to keep it cool in summer. In winter, the underfloor heating is kept turned on to maintain a comfortable temperature.

Although I have written about the damaging effects of sunlight and how we keep it out of the house in summer in Spain (see p.181), at home in London I am grateful for the **enormous warehouse windows** that allow sun and **natural daylight** to flood in (see pp.182–183). Living in a space with plenty of natural daylight is **uplifting to the spirits**, and I consider it a feature more important than the number of rooms or even the location of a property. When house hunting, it is sensible to determine whether rooms in which you plan to spend a lot of time **face south or south-west**. If you are seeking the perfect country retreat, cottages with roses climbing round the door are certainly romantic, but the down side is likely to be a dark interior with poky windows. Instead, look for barns and agricultural buildings that have been converted using large expanses of window – a device used by architects to bring light into period rural buildings.

Ways to **improve light quality** in a room include **painting an outside yard** a light colour to reflect light back into the room and inserting a **skylight** to let in the late afternoon sun. As well as natural light, I find the airy and spacious qualities of a living room help to make it a calm and relaxing place. Therefore, keeping it **simply furnished and uncluttered** is the aim – obviously this is not always possible with the debris of family life. Ways to create a sense of spaciousness include painting the walls in a **light colour**, making built-in cupboards, and painting furniture in the same colour as the walls. Using the same paint colour throughout a room has a wonderful **unifying effect**, as in the sitting area in my London flat (see pp.182–183). To match the walls, I have used white eggshell to paint a couple of folding card tables from a junk shop and a basic fold-up coffee table bought very cheaply from a large furniture superstore.

Natural textures in **pale colours** accentuate a sense of **light and spaciousness**. The colour of flooring is a particularly important factor: choosing a dark oak or a highly varnished finish doesn't give the same sense of space as a paler surface, such as the **solid natural oak** strip flooring (see opposite) that has been treated with an environmentally friendly matt sealant. Cream and oatmeal-coloured throws, blankets, or cushions in linen or wool add **sensual layering** to chairs and sofas, which I like to cover in white, calico, cotton or linen covers (see left, and p.184). **Plain white cotton roller blinds** are an economical, simple, and stylish window idea, and unless you're expert at fitting them, it's far cheaper in terms of time and hassle to let the supplier come along and put them up. White blinds can also help to **diffuse the light** on a particularly bright day (see left).

One chair, four looks

For centuries, loose covers have been used to protect upholstery. In the **pure style** home, unfitted covers are the key to revamping junk chairs and updating upholstery. My preference is for white covers – I choose robust, machine-washable textures to cope with the frequent washing. An old armchair (opposite and below) has been dressed in four easily-made covers for different effects. To make, allow about 4 m of pre-shrunk fabric per chair; if necessary, add 5–10 per cent for shrinkage.

A pretty, vintage-style floral cotton cover with side pleats and ties creates colourful detail in simple white decorating schemes – good for bedrooms and sitting rooms. Striped cotton ticking with side pleats and stitched bands is stylish and classic, and suits both traditional and modern interiors. A soft green cotton cover has pleated sides and button detailing. Green is calming and looks good with pink details, such as flowers or cushions – try it in a conservatory or bedroom. A plain white cotton cover with a side zip is suitable for any room in the Pure Style home. With white or pale colours, make sure the material is thick enough to conceal darker upholstery beneath.

Laying a fire For a glowing retreat on damp, blustery days at my Spanish *finca*, I make a fire first thing in the morning that burns all day. **Logs of encina-scrub oak and chestnut** are kept under cover and we collect kindling that has fallen from the cork trees. Combustible pine cones are gathered from nearby trees and bundled into sacks. I clean out the grate and scatter the nutritious ashes around the young fruit trees in the garden. I lay two largish logs 50 cm apart and parallel to the sides of the grate with four or five **balls of newspaper**, three or four **pine cones**, and a **bundle of kindling** in between. On top of this pile I lay five or six logs wig-wam style. If the wood is dry, a lit match produces **roaring flames** that catch the logs to produce a warm and comforting focus to the house.

Even on the most foul wind- and rain-swept day, a **blazing log fire** warms and revives flagging spirits. We crowd around our Spanish fire (see opposite) to dry off damp feet, **roast chestnuts**, and **toast marshmallows**. In cities with smokeless zones, for example London since the Clean Air Act of 1955, you must burn a **smokeless fuel**, such as **anthracite**. Alternatively, although they can't recreate the heat and energy of a real fire, flame-effect gas fires are worth considering, and modern types with no grate or obvious gas source are more stylish-looking than the kitsch log-effect fires from the 1970s. Multi-fuel **cast-iron** and **aluminium stoves** in plain shapes for burning wood briquettes, logs, and smokeless fuels, or gas versions if you don't have a chimney, are easy to maintain and a good substitute for a real fire.

Being someone who much prefers bare floors with **rugs and mats** to the more insulating qualities of deep-pile wall-to- wall carpeting, it has been exciting to experience the warming benefits of **underfloor heating**, which we have installed in our house in Spain. Laid underneath the terracotta floor, the heating system circulates hot water through a series of plastic pipes to create an even temperature over the whole surface of the floor. It produces a very pleasant sensation, which enables us to walk over the tiles with bare feet. In our previous home, we used the same underfloor heating system below the wooden floorboards, but it wasn't nearly as effective because gaps beneath the boards and a poorly insulated house led to heat loss and barely warm floors.

Another comfort factor for surviving long winter nights **curled up on the sofa with a book** is a collection of plump feather-filled cushions and woolly rugs to tuck up in when it's really chilly (see pp.190-191). **Soft pools of light** from table lamps are more moody and easier on the eye than harsh overhead lighting. Dark nights are good times for sticking all those photos from last year's summer holiday into an album, or listening to music, or watching the videos that you didn't have time for when the days were longer.

Bring nature   and its tactile, organic qualities into the home with collections of shells picked up on beach-combing expeditions. Pebbles have wonderful organic shapes, as beautiful to look at, if not more so, than many works of art (see opposite). We have a collection of old plant specimen jars from a botanical garden that we bought from a local reclamation specialist; the children fill these up with their nature finds: pieces of cork, acorns, lichen, seeds, shiny black stag beetles, a silvery snake skin, a dragonfly for an unusual display.

Stick **shells** with extra-strong adhesive glue in **shadow-box frames** and mount on the walls, or leave flat, museum style, to look at on a table. Razor shells also look good displayed in this way.
Old botanical specimen jars filled with nature finds can be grouped together for an eye-catching and educational exhibit.
Uninhabited bird's nests are simple, twiggy sculptures that provide an original and natural arrangement when stacked in a simple white bowl.

Play

We're only young once so childhood should be a time to have fun – adults can join in as well! Don't rely on TV and video games for entertainment, but get out the paintbrushes and crayons to create colourful artworks. Read, run, jump, dance, and play imaginary games to stimulate young bodies and minds.

Inspiring children to choose **creative play** activities, such as painting, reading a book, doing a puzzle, or play-acting can be a battle, especially with older children who have to be steered away from television and computer games. It really pays to be **organized** and to have a good stock of **materials** immediately to hand. I save fabric cuttings for collages and dolls' house furnishings; cardboard boxes for numerous imaginary homes; and I ensure that there is a good supply of **plain white paper**, coloured sugar paper, and bottles of poster paints. A small chest of drawers on a shelf in the kitchen is completely stuffed with pens, **crayons**, **glue**, **scissors**, pencil sharpeners, rubbers, and other equipment. Projects with edible incentives, such as chocolate prizes, are popular; you could try an **art competition** with subjects such as vegetables or flowers from the garden (see left and opposite), or the family cat or dog. Asking children to make things for a special occasion is a good way of attracting interest, for example **baking a birthday cake**, making tissue-paper bunting for a party (see pp.200–201), or preparing biscuits, mince pies, and tree decorations at Christmas (see pp.216–217).

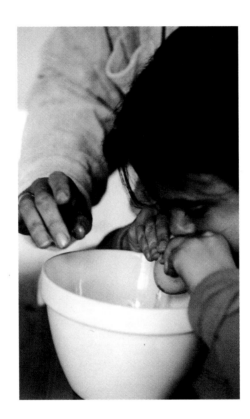

Painting eggs   for the Easter breakfast table is a tradition my children look forward to each year. **Pierce a small hole with a pin** at either end of an egg, making one hole slightly larger than the other (this is tricky and requires a steady adult hand). Holding the egg over a bowl, **Gracie blows through the smaller hole** so the yolk and white slip out of the other end (use later for a tortilla, omelette, or scrambled eggs). Gently rinse the empty shell in water and leave to dry. With **poster paints** or **watercolours, paint a design** on each egg – **spots and stripes in bright pinks, blues, and greens** are good combinations (see pp.204–205). To dry the paint, put the eggs in a low oven. When dry, pile them into a **basket with straw**, tiny **foil-wrapped chocolate eggs**, and chicks for **Easter Sunday**.

Making space for children to **paint and play** doesn't mean you need a separate playroom. Even though we were lucky to have a lot of space in our previous house, I found that my children literally played under my feet whether I was at the sink or working at my desk. Despite the sophistications of modern life, it seems that humans, especially young ones – although I am not so sure about bolshie teenagers – have the in-built herding instinct of our cave-dwelling ancestors who all squashed together under one roof. We muddle along in a communal way in our London flat, where there is one large **kitchen/eating/sitting space** in which everyone congregates. One child might be playing with the dolls' house on the floor, the others reading, or doing homework at the **big kitchen table**, while I am cooking. My only irritations about this arrangement are the noise levels – whether it's high-spirited yelling, the television, or one child's latest music craze. When I get my way, I like the comforting tones of news and reviews on the radio.

Practical ideas to accommodate children's toys and materials in an open play/living area are essential. One example is making a **blackboard** area for messages and artwork: buy special blackboard paint and apply to a flat, emulsioned wall; the area can be left open, or framed in painted wood with a useful shelf for chalk and a blackboard rubber below (see right). Notice-boards made out of cork tiles or painted plywood (see pp.128, 132–133) are also useful for displaying paintings, pinning up invitations, school telephone lists, and other day-to-day information. Allow small children a corner for a **child-sized table and chairs**, and a couple of baskets filled with toys or dressing-up clothes. A few cushions on the floor and a rug are also a good idea if the children want to read, sprawl out, or have a nap.

Dressing up   Weary with the routine of wearing school uniform all week and jeans at the weekend, Georgie and Gracie are always keen to experiment with the **dressing-up box**. The gypsy theme is their favourite and they love to dress up in authentic **frilly and flouncy flamenco dresses** (*trajes flamencas*). Georgie has one in bright pink and yellow (see pp.210–211) – genuine bull-fighting cape colours – and Gracie's is blue with white spots. We bought them from one of the many flamenco shops in Seville. **Ironed and pristine**, this gorgeous finery is normally reserved for **Spanish fiestas, ferias, and romerias**, but my daughters can't resist putting them on to **swish, twirl, and stamp their feet** when they hear the strains of a *gitano sevillana* dance on the compact disc player.

Potato cuts are fun for adults as well as children; they are an easy way to make prints on paper for **stylish wrapping ideas, cards, and labels**. Cut a potato in half – the size depends on your design, but we used a medium-sized one (see opposite). Outline the design on the cut surface of the potato with a pencil; cut away the potato with a kitchen knife outside the outline to a depth of about 5 mm. **Soak the stamp in poster paint**, not too thick or runny, on a plate for a few seconds and start printing onto paper, card, or even paper bags.

Two potato halves ready for printing. For design ideas use **trees** and **stars** for Christmas, **hearts** for **Valentine's day**, and **pumpkins** at **Halloween**. Stamp out the initial of the person receiving the present for a really individual touch. Single motifs printed on pieces of paper or card for labels. Small paper carrier bags printed to make unusual packing; print rows of the same motif on plain paper for wrapping paper. Take it a stage further and **decorate** printed cards.

Homespun Christmas decorations are so much cheaper and more original than shop-bought baubles. Children can take part in dressing a tree with offerings such as **fabric balls** (see opposite). Decide on your colour theme and **cut strips of fabric** from a remnant bag; checked and striped patterns in blues and greens look good, or experiment with your own colour and print ideas. **Wrap the strips** of material around a florist's oasis ball or a plain polystyrene ball that you can buy from a haberdashery. Secure the fabric with a pin at the top of the ball, and add a ribbon or string loop, secured in the same way, to hang the ball on the tree (see p.198). **Iced biscuits** decorated with tiny silver balls (see right) have a **fairy-like quality** as they dangle from the branches of a twinkling tree. Their tempting aroma means they won't last long, but they can easily be replaced with a fresh batch as they are eaten. Make them speedily with ready-made pastry or prepare a delicious buttery version yourself (see p.393). Roll out the pastry and cut out the **heart shapes** with a pastry cutter, which you can buy from a kitchen shop or supermarket; pierce a hole at the top for a hanging ribbon or piece of wool. After baking, let the biscuits cool, then ice, decorate, thread with a ribbon, and hang on the tree.

Wash

Washing is both cleansing and rejuvenating. Bathrooms with efficient delivery of hot and cold water, waterproof and wipe-down surfaces, and warmth to keep towels dry are key features in the contemporary bathroom. Bolster your mood at bath time with scented soaps, moisturizing lotions, and potions.

Water is essential for life, but its sensual aspects – water cooling hot skin, the freedom of floating weightlessly in a limpid, eau de nil sea, plunging into an **ice-cold pool**, soaking tired limbs in a **hot, steamy bath**, or rinsing prickly sea-salty skin under a gushing, freshwater hose – are also basic human needs. Happily, as a reflection of the current mood and trend for ritual and a more **natural approach to life**, bathing is considered much more than a basic hygienic necessity (I shiver at the thought of the arctic school showers and dank bathrooms of my childhood). No longer is the bathroom just a clinical space or poky, avocado-hued nightmare.

My ideal bathroom combines efficient **plumbing** with simplicity and natural **textures** – wood, stone, terracotta, rough loofahs, soft cotton, and **scented soaps** and lotions. It is a visually calm, warm retreat, just like the **blue ceramic-tiled bathroom and walk-in shower** that belongs to food writer Alastair Hendy (see this page and opposite). While also being **practical and easy to clean,** this bathing haven, filled during the day with soft, muted light from the skylight above, is a joy to use at any time.

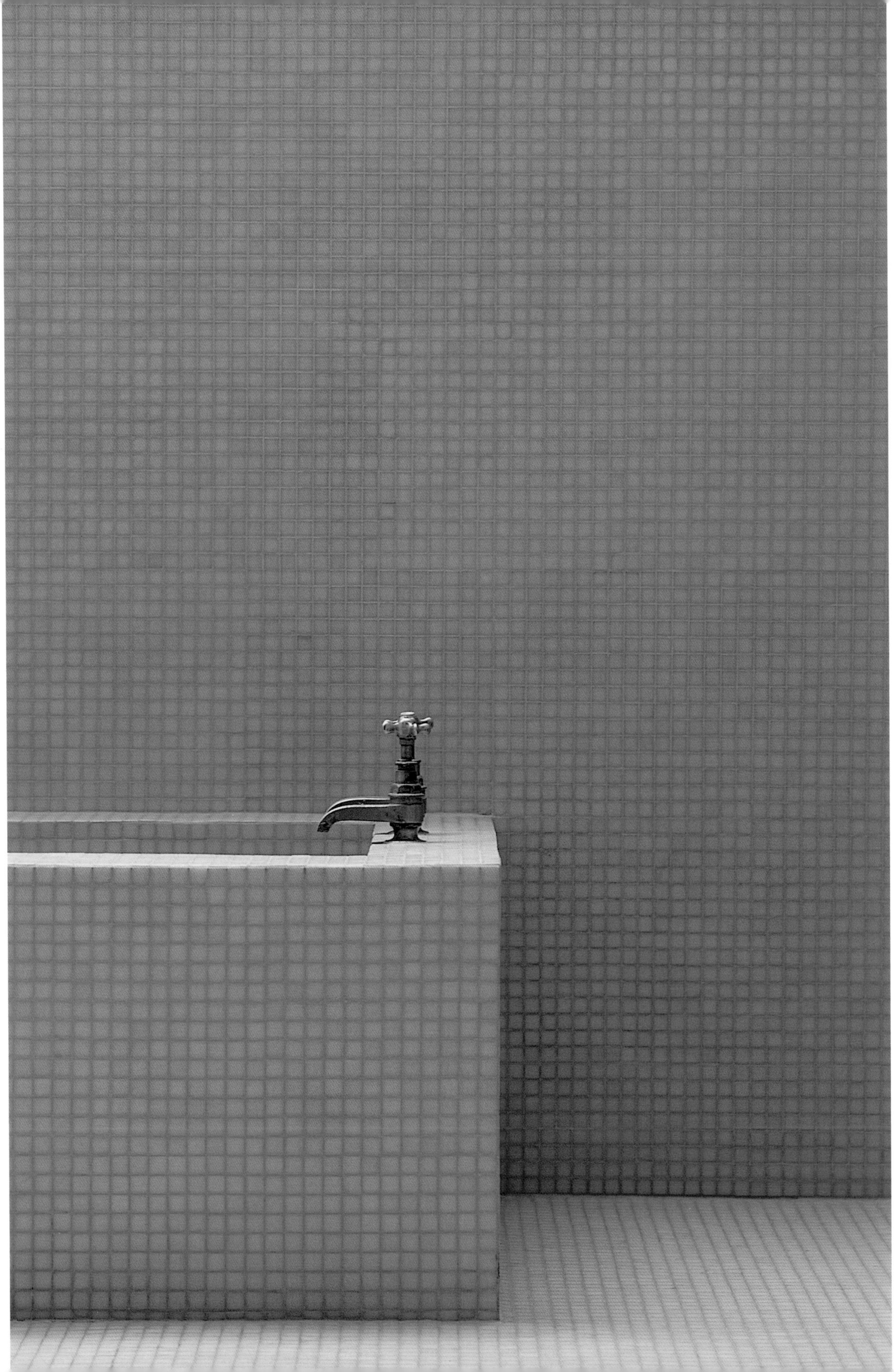

Plain tiling, useful for its waterproofing and hygienic qualities, has long been standard issue in institutional and public baths. Despite their clinical associations, I love the simplicity of **gleaming white tiles** and purchased them cheaply in huge quantities to line the walls and sides of the baths in the three simple bathrooms in our Spanish house (see the guest bathroom, this page and opposite). White tiles are **light-reflecting** and make the room feel **airy and spacious**; they are deliciously cool during the long, hot summer in Spain. I think **natural textures** can help to counteract the bleak look that is a danger with such a large expanse of whiteness – try **terracotta flooring**, made warmer with underfloor heating, crisp white cotton towels, fresh flowers, the odd piece of old, painted shelving, or a woven basket for laundry.

Making a laundry bag Use a heavy cotton canvas or calico to make a functional laundry bag. Trim with a contrasting band of fabric or ribbon, and make a drawstring with rope, cord, or a strip of the same fabric folded in half, sewn along the length, and turned inside out. Make a bag as big or as small as your household needs, or maybe have two or three for different members of the family or for different coloured clothes. To personalize the bags, sew in name tapes or write names on the front with a fabric pen.

1 Materials for a finished bag measuring 64 cm x 85 cm: 2 pieces pre-shrunk canvas or calico, each 66 cm x 90 cm; 2 strips striped cotton ticking for band, each 10 cm x 68 cm; 2 m rope from a ship-chandler.

2 Take the two pieces of fabric and overlock or zigzag stitch any raw edges. Place fabric with right sides together and sew around three edges, leaving the top edge open. Fold over 3 cm at the top edge, press, and hem.

3 Overlock or zigzag along the edges of the ticking bands. On each band, fold the long edges 2 cm towards the centre and press flat. Fold over 2 cm at each of the short edges, press flat, and hem.

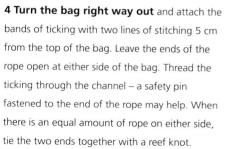

4 Turn the bag right way out and attach the bands of ticking with two lines of stitching 5 cm from the top of the bag. Leave the ends of the rope open at either side of the bag. Thread the ticking through the channel – a safety pin fastened to the end of the rope may help. When there is an equal amount of rope on either side, tie the two ends together with a reef knot.

Wood is a texture perfectly suited to the bathroom environment: wooden floors are warm to the touch, and wooden-panelled walls and baths look natural whether painted in white eggshell, as in my bathroom in London (see this page and opposite), or left as **sealed pine planks** and battened to the walls, as in the cosy **cabin-style** bathroom (see p.237) in the windswept and romantic Scottish castle belonging to Lachie and Annie Stewart. Panelling walls and boxing-in baths is a useful way to hide ugly plumbing, and it can also be used to create cupboards and storage space for potions and lotions.

The **clean and functional** look of a simple bathroom is also determined by its fixtures and fittings. I find that standard **plain white ceramic** basins and loos, and enamelled steel baths (that can be boxed in) are more stylish and functional than flashy marble baths with glitzy gold-trimmed taps, or other over-the-top celebrity-status-symbol plumbing. Plain bathroom fittings are available from good builders' merchants or bathroom shops.

Recycled or **reclaimed** 19th- or early 20th-century **bathroom equipment** can be found in architectural salvage yards; such fittings are **utilitarian** and tend to be solidly made. A pair of old-fashioned Victorian brass taps, an old sink on a pedestal, or a huge hotel-style shower head can add interesting detail to the plainest bathroom interior, whether it is contemporary in mood or more **traditional** like the bathroom, right, and the bathroom in my previous house (pp.234–235), both in restored Georgian terraced houses in London's Spitalfields. I miss the old **cast-iron, roll-top bath** that we found in a salvage yard that needed six men to carry it upstairs. It sat rather regally on a wooden plinth, and I remember many blissful hours spent soaking in its **deep and curvaceous** proportions while looking out onto the Dickensian rooftops. Note that old taps generally need new washers, and might not deliver such an efficient flow as modern ones. You will probably need to re-enamel most period cast-iron baths.

Planners have established minimum bathroom dimensions, but it's important to create a bathroom that suits your **individual needs**. Existing plumbing arrangements, such as the soil stack and water supply, can be determining features. It is usually the case that a **family** desires a **larger space for bathing** than a one-person household. In our home, everyone piles into the bathroom for a chat, or to sit down and read by the bath. If space is at a premium, a **small walk-in shower room** might be all that is practicable. However, if fitted with an efficient shower, lined with beautiful tiles, and decked with **slatted teak**, it can be as sensual a washing retreat as a bigger bathroom.

White is an obvious and practical **colour** for the bathroom, useful because of its **light-enhancing** qualities, but **blues** and **greens** inspired by the **sea** and **sky**, are also great for creating **serene** bathing retreats. The cool blue tiles in Alastair Hendy's bath and shower room (see pp.220–221) show the use of colour to perfection.

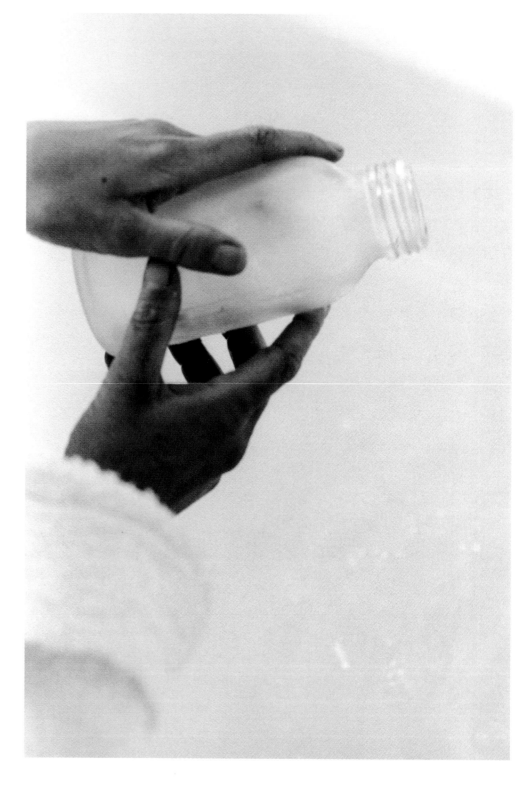

Having a bath   I am a complete **bath addict** and couldn't imagine a day without taking at least one **hot, steamy soak** in the tub. The ritual begins when I put in the plug and twiddle the hot tap to release a gush of water. This signals the suspension of domestic duties for as long as I can wangle. I pour in some spicy **orange cologne** to scent the water and swish it about. When the water is just below overfill level, I ease myself into its inviting depths and submerge the day's tensions and **relax body and mind**. There I lie – contrary to sensible advice – for at least half an hour, topping up the water from time to time. I might read a **glossy magazine**, or light **candles** if there's no one else at home. **Wrapping** myself in **a warm towel** and heading for bed is the ideal way to round off the experience.

The **sensual bathroom** needs to be warm and draught free, especially in winter, and it must have a plentiful supply of **hot running water**.

A **light and airy** space is a **healthy** environment. A dank, dark bathroom will not produce an invigorating or rejuvenating experience. Don't worry about creating lots of steam – it's all part of enjoying the sensual aspects of bathing, but open the window afterwards to aid the airing process.

When taking a bath note that **hot** water **relaxes muscles** and **relieves stiffness** but it also expands blood vessels. A long, hot bath (over 40°C) is not generally a good idea as it tends to be exhausting, and it dries out the skin by drawing out natural oils.

After a bath or shower, be inspired by the sauna ritual, which culminates in jumping into **ice-cold water** or snow, and finish off with a shower of cold water; or sponge cold water over your body to **stimulate** the circulation, close pores, tone, and **invigorate**.

Use **natural** soaps and lotions, and **flower water** such as lavender or rose to splash on and energize skin after a bath, and almond oil for moisturizing dry skin. Basic **mud** face packs are good **skin cleansers** and can be applied while enjoying a long, relaxing soak. **Olive oil** is a great natural conditioner: massage a tablespoon into damp hair and leave for half an hour then rinse out.

Good-quality **soaps** that soften the skin contain fats and oils, rather than harsh artificial detergents. Look for **palm-oil** soap – mild, creamy, and good for the face and dry or sensitive skin; **almond-meal** soap – a good body or face scrub; **oatmeal** soap - an old-fashioned skin cleanser, which is soothing to irritated skin; and **rosemary** soap – slightly astringent and good for oily skin.

Use a few drops of natural fragrant **essential oil** in the bath and choose a particular scent to suit your mood – lavender, melissa, and ylang ylang are **soothing**, while rosemary, lemon grass, and grapefruit are **uplifting and invigorating**.

Your bathroom kit should also feature a hairy mitt **loofah** or **rough linen towel** to tone and exfoliate skin, and a good long-handled scrubbing **brush** for backs.

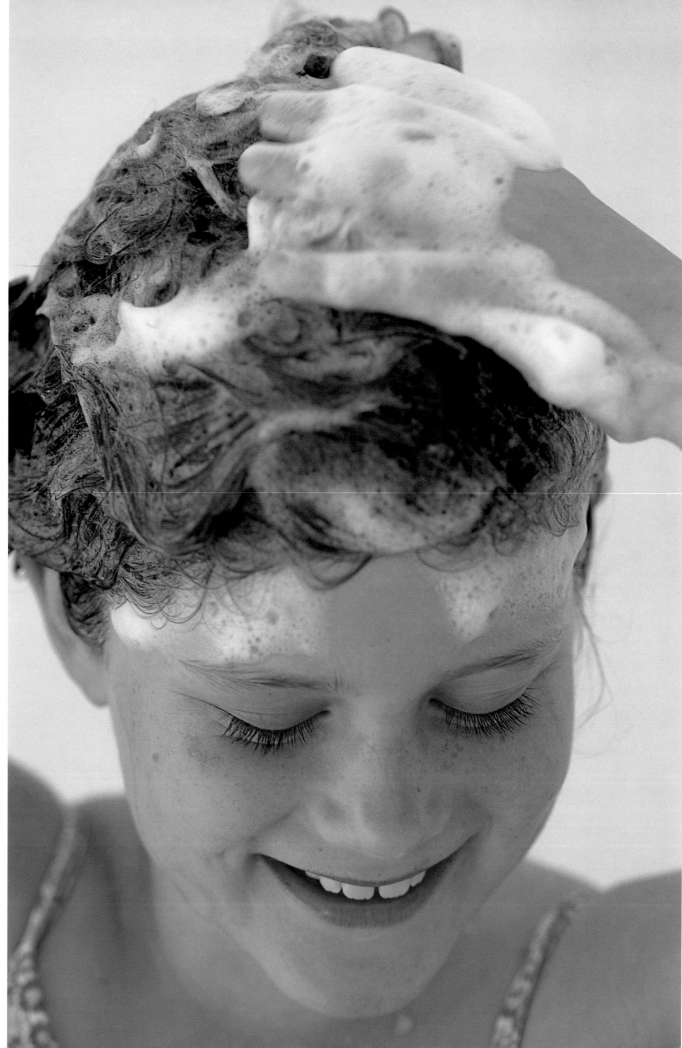

Wash basics Twenty five years ago, on a gruelling overland trip from England to Morocco, I know that I only survived weeks of heat and cramped living conditions in the knowledge that there'd be a reviving shower at the end of each day. When travelling today (older, but still seduced by new places), I equip myself with a basic wash kit of cotton towel, toothbrush, toothpaste, and cologne.

Essential bathroom ingredients, whether on the move or staying at home, include lashings of hot water on demand, practical and durable washable surfaces and accessories, ceramic sinks, wipe-down flooring, and towels in linen and cotton textures.

Sleep

Make the bedroom an oasis away from the demands of everyday domestic life. Choose a good firm mattress for your bed and tuck up with crisp cotton sheets and warm woollen blankets, or the lightest of light and cosy goose-down duvets. Get a good night's sleep in a ventilated room, and tuck a cotton bag filled with sleep-inducing dried lavender under your pillow.

Nowadays, we live in a 24-hour society where **sleep** is an increasingly prized necessity. Phone calls at all hours, small children crying in the night, and early rising for work all chip away at the eight hours or so of restoring slumber that is essential to keep us in good mental and physical health. It's no wonder that half the population are supposed to suffer from some form of sleep deprivation.

The bedroom, therefore, should be a **retreat** and a **calm oasis** away from daily demands with **beds** that are nests of **soft pillows, crunchy linens, and warm blankets**. Light and airy spaces with good ventilation are also essential bedroom ingredients. At night, sleep with the central heating turned down or off altogether – if it's too high, it's drying to the skin and makes the air stuffy – and with a **window open** enough to let in a **cool breeze**.

To make your bedroom a comfort zone, it's worth investing in the best linen you can afford – crisp, cotton sheets, light goose-down duvets, and wool blankets. Outlaw the television and listen to the radio instead – it's much more relaxing for the brain and calming to the soul. If space is not at a premium, introduce a small sofa or armchair for extra seating or for feeding a baby at night.

If you have children, buy a big bed with a good mattress so that everyone can tuck in together to eat jammy toast and read the papers at weekends.

Paint bedroom walls in light-reflecting white or calming, soft lilacs or greens. A vibrantly painted bedroom is not the most restful environment to sleep in, but I do find that **shots of bright colour** work well in a white scheme; for example, in my Spanish bedroom (see pp.242–243), the **orange cotton** throw, **pink-checked**, **floaty**, **muslin** curtain, and **crimson roses fresh from the garden** seem to heighten and intensify the bright light and airiness, especially in the summer.

Basic window treatments for bedrooms include **simple blinds** and looped or tie-on curtains; internal or external **wooden shutters** are also useful for blocking out early morning light, which may disturb light sleepers, or for keeping a bedroom cool and shady during the heat of the day.

Making a bed for a good night's slumber. I aim for a weekly change of crisp, ironed **white cotton bedlinen.** I don't battle with fitted sheets – flat ones tucked in at the corners are smoother and more luxurious to slide into. In the heat of summer, a top sheet and light blanket suffice; otherwise, I prefer the warm, enveloping qualities of a **light goose-down duvet,** which I **shake and air out of the window** every few days. In Spain, the duvet is hung out in the morning sun, especially in winter when dampness permeates the house. I always plump up **pillows** that have been flattened overnight. Light goose-down pillows are expensive but they're especially inviting. For an extra layer of warmth and visual appeal, I fold and lay a **big white cotton bed cover** across the bottom of the bed.

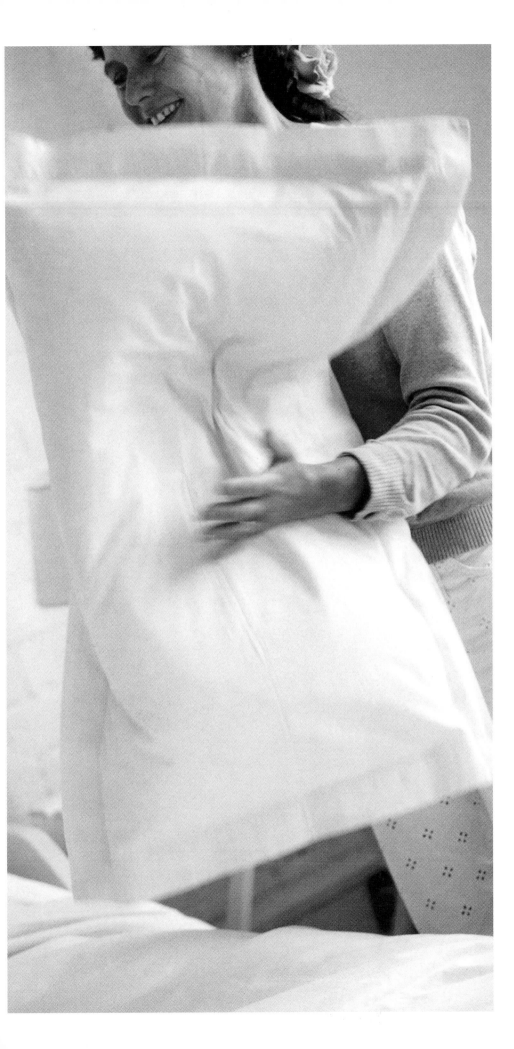

Even if a bed is used for only one night by an **overnight guest** who tucks up in a duvet or a sleeping bag, it should be **comfortable and functional**. Although a feature of Japanese sleeping arrangements for centuries, roll-up, cotton-padded futon mattresses are the new, laid-back sleeping idea for cool urbanites; they **create flexible sleeping** when space is limited, such as in a cramped studio flat or small apartment, and, being inexpensive, are accessible for students and others on tight budgets. This type of bedding **needs very little effort** and can be rolled up during the day and used as a seating surface when not in use as a bed. A traditional folding bed with a mattress on a metal frame is another cheap, **temporary sleeping solution**; it provides a firm surface and, being above the ground, is particularly suitable for elderly guests who may not be keen to rough it on the floor.

A divan bed with a mattress and a box base is a **traditional bed shape** that can be used in any bedroom as a **basic sleeping** surface and then covered with layers of bedding as desired. In the lilac bedroom (see p.256), a plain double divan has been dressed in simple white bedlinen to create an inviting, completely pared-down sleeping idea. A single divan is a good idea for creating **extra sleeping space** in a small area; pushed against a wall and covered with throws and cushions to function as a sofa for daytime use, it can be turned back into a fully-fledged bed with sheets, pillows, blankets, and a duvet at night.

I think that understated **wooden bed frames** are honest and **functional shapes**. They look neat and have a **visual lightness**. Old school dormitory single beds painted in a soft, powdery blue eggshell and made up with **cosy flannel bedlinen** and checked wool blankets look stylish as well as homely (see opposite). Basic metal hospital-style beds or old brass bedsteads – better than new brass, which looks too flashy – also have a similar feel.

Making a duvet cover   As a cheaper alternative to buying a ready-made cover, buy white cotton sheeting by the metre and dye it the **colour** of your choice. Although dyeing in the washing machine is easier, results are unpredictable as it is difficult to work out how much dye to use. **Hand dyeing** in the bath is more reliable. Dyeing can also revive an old, unpatterned duvet cover. After dyeing, cut the material to size and make up. Simple ties, button-holes, or hook and loop fastenings can be added to the open end.

1 Assemble the materials: 4.5 m of white cotton sheeting to fit a large bed (220 x 400 cm) (pre-wash the material to remove fabric dressing); pair of rubber gloves; bucket; old wooden or plastic spoon; dye; salt; fixative; 1 m of 3-cm-wide heavy-duty hook and loop fastening strip.

2 Weigh the fabric to assess how much dye is needed. One pot of standard dye is sufficient to dye 1 kg dry weight of fabric. You will also need to add table salt and soda ash dye fixer to the quantity specified (with some dyes this may not be necessary; check the instructions on the packet).

3 Mix the dye ingredients in a bucket following the instructions on the packet and pour into the bath. Add the fabric, keeping it fully submerged. Move the fabric around to ensure an even finish. When the dyeing time is complete, rinse the material and wash and dry it. Wash out the bath straight away to avoid discolouring.

4 Cut the fabric in half to make two equal lengths. Overlock or zig-zag stitch the raw edges, place the two pieces together, then sew three sides together 1 cm from the edge. Fold back the edges of the open side and stitch a 5 cm hem. Cut the hook-and-loop fastening strip into 25 cm pieces and stitch them at regular intervals along the open edge of the cover (making sure that the two halves meet when the fabric is closed together). Turn the finished duvet the right way round and press. The cover is now ready to be put onto a duvet (see right). Wash separately the first time you use it.

Childrens' bedrooms demand their own set of priorities: a large enough space to accommodate **beds, toys, books, and a desk or table**, and floor space to sprawl out on.

Space-saving **bunk beds** are a brilliant idea for housing several children in one room. Flatpack versions in pine are cheap and stocked by most large furniture superstores; they can be **painted** in white, blue, or your child's favourite colour. There are also raised beds that have a **built-in work space** below with a ladder to reach the bed above; these are good for squeezing into the smallest box room. Junk shops and salvage yards are good hunting grounds for old-fashioned metal beds from hospitals and school dormitories, which are generally robust and neat in proportion (see p.248).

If you have to give in to lurid cartoon prints for walls, curtains, and duvet covers, it isn't the end of the world; however, **duvets and sheets in stripes, checks, or plain colours** (see the home-made, dyed duvet cover on p.252) are more appealing as far as most adults are concerned.

When **children have to share a room**, it's important that they each have **individual cupboard space**. I chose floor-to-ceiling built-in cupboards along the length of one wall in my children's room; divided into three sections – one for each child – the cupboards house child-height hanging space for clothes, and shelving, with more shelves higher up for toys and games that are less frequently needed (which are reached by a lightweight, folding, aluminium ladder).

It is good to encourage individual creative talents by allowing children **wall space for their artworks** (see my children's room in our London flat, p.252), together with a working surface, such as a wooden trestle table (also in my children's bedroom, see p.253), which is like the one in our office space. We have put a piano in the children's bedroom to encourage on-the-spot practice. Although my children spend most of their time in the main living area, it is always good to know that they can retreat to **the sanctuary of their bedroom** if they want to – a relief for the parents, too.

Keep bedroom clutter to a minimum to maintain a sense of calm in your sleeping oasis. **Built-in cupboards** (see right) are the neatest solution for stowing away clothes and linen. At the most basic level, you can simply curtain off an alcove and fix up some shelves and a hanging rail. Small **bedside tables** and chests of drawers (see left) can accommodate small pieces of clothing and other bedroom paraphernalia, such as bedside reading matter. Be inventive and **recycle furniture** designed for other purposes; for example, in one bedroom a **1960s dining-room cabinet** has been given a new lease of life as a storage space to hold socks and underwear (see p.257). Owners of large shoe collections might find it tidier to stow them away in plain boxes under the bed; this is also a useful idea for keeping jumpers, blankets, and other bulky items hidden when they are not in use.

Making a slip-on chair cover   Every bedroom needs a chair, and even the most basic fold-up chair can be transformed by dressing it in a removable cover. A neutral calico or linen will soften the edges of the bedroom environment, and add to the feeling of calm and repose. To achieve a really smart, clean look, the bottom edge of the cover can be defined with a band of contrast colour trimming; blue always goes well with neutrals. This simple shape can be run up quickly and easily, even for those inexperienced at sewing.

1 Measure the chair to calculate fabric requirements. For the length of fabric, add the depth of the seat to twice the height of the back plus an extra 10 cm. The width of material is the chair width plus 3 cm. For our chair, the seat depth was 32 cm, back height 36 cm, and width 43 cm so the piece of fabric required was 114 x 46 cm. When cut to size, overlock or zig-zag stitch the raw edges. You will need the same length of trimming as the skirt length (see Step 3).

2 Place the fabric on the chair so that the seat edge is overlapped by about 1 cm on three sides and the extra length hangs down at the back. Pin the edges together at either side of the seat back, noting with a pin or dressmaker's chalk the point where the seat meets the back of the chair. Take the fabric off the chair and sew two vertical seams where you have pinned. This makes the main part of the slip that covers the back and seat of the chair.

3 To make the skirt, you need to cut a strip of fabric that in length is twice the depth of the seat plus the width plus 2 cm, and 10 cm wide. So for our chair, the strip was 109 x 10 cm. Overlock or zig-zag stitch the raw edges. Turn a 1-cm hem along the length on one side only, then do the same for the short ends. Put the cover back onto the chair, still inside out, and pin the skirt into place, leaving a 1-cm seam. Make sure that all the hems and seams are facing outwards.

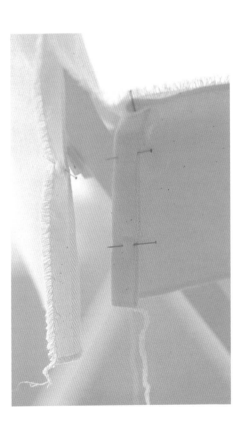

4 Remove the cover and sew where you have just pinned. Hem the back edge of the cover so that it is the same length as the skirt using a 1-cm hem. When all the edges are hemmed, turn the cover the right way round and you can apply the trim. Simply place your chosen ribbon or trim about 1 cm from the bottom of the side and front edges of the cover, pin, and sew using thread in a matching colour. Press to flatten the trim, and slip onto the chair (see right).

Tactile, **natural fabrics** are the most **luxurious** bedroom textures; wear nothing at all between the sheets or loose cotton pyjamas, a big, white T-shirt, or a simple cotton night-dress – beautiful, embroidered Victorian night-dresses can be picked up quite cheaply. When you clamber out of bed in the morning, wrap up in a deliciously soft, over-sized **cotton robe**. Warm your feet with **woolly slippers** or thick bedsocks when the temperature drops.

Soft cotton **rugs** are welcome underfoot when you are springing out of bed on a cold morning; if they are not too large, they can be cleaned in a washing machine.

Classic cream **wool blankets** with a satin trim, which are central to traditional English bedroom decor, are warm and sensual in the contemporary bedroom. **Slip-on covers** soften the edges of bedroom chairs and can be easily made to disguise a folding chair (see pp.260–261). I like creamy calico or linen fabrics, which can also be used for **blinds** or **simple curtains** to create a unifying effect through the room.

Washed **antique** bedlinens are soft and have a lovely worn, faded quality that can add to the serenity of a bedroom environment. I have mounds of old, white cotton sheets and pillowcases handed down through the family, and I am a collector of old **pretty quilts** with delicate **floral patterns**. One of my favourites is the 18th-century, lavender-striped quilt that covers the white cotton linen and blankets on my box bed – painted a deliciously soft and soporific green eggshell – in our London flat (see opposite).

If money were no object, I think we should all sleep only in **linen sheets**; spun and woven from flax, linen doesn't retain moisture like cotton and has a cooling effect that makes it ideal for the summer. Two sets of fine linen sheets used alternately can easily last twenty-five years.

directory

Paint

Fabric

Flooring

Eat

Work

Garden

Rest

Play

Wash

Sleep

Paint

white

cream and yellow

terracotta

green

blue

pink

Paint data

Paint is one of the **simplest and most effective ways** to transform our living space and the objects in it. How we paint our homes is intrinsic to establishing who we are, what we feel, and what we aspire to. Scientists have known for years that **different colours trigger** different **emotional responses**: children paint with black to express unhappiness; **white is uplifting**; **red is exciting and eyecatching** (traffic lights the world over are red); **yellows and oranges are optimistic**; **blue is cool and calming**; and **green** – at the centre of the colour spectrum – represents **balance**.

The choice of colours and textures today has never been so wide and confusing. Don't get stressed looking for shades that have to be exactly right. Paint samples on cards are unlikely to match exactly with the real stuff on the walls as colour *in situ* is affected by wall texture, the amount of light in a room, and the colour of surrounding floors and furniture.

Be true to your individual needs. A decade or so ago, when I restored our early Georgian house in Spitalfields, London, there was pressure from traditionalists to use **authentic colours**, most of which were dull and sombre. Being housebound with babies and in need of light and airy surroundings, I did not want my house to be gloomy and depressing. Ignoring the "tut-tuts" of the conservationist brigade, I stuck to my gut feelings and painted the panelled rooms in **matt eggshell country creams, whites, and greens**. The resulting look was **fresh and modern** but not at all out of place in its historic context.

Be aware of the effects that different colours have on our **perception of space**: **warm colours**, such as **deep creams, yellows, and terracottas, advance** and make a room appear smaller and cosier; **cool colours**, such as **white, slate grey, and blues recede** and have the opposite effect, enlarging the room and making it feel light and airy.

Think about the colours that you like and see in your immediate **environment**; colour doesn't always travel – seductive hot Mediterranean pinks, blues, and yellows can fall flat without the sunshine in cool northern light.

Many different **colours and contrasts** throughout a house or in one room are unharmonious and can be stressful. I now live very happily with **calming white wraparound colour** in our London flat and our house in Spain. To prevent the whole look from being too clinical, I have introduced **shots of brilliant colour** in throws, **cushions**, painted pots, and a **jug of bright flowers**.

Textures

For walls and ceilings, a water-based paint, such as **emulsion**, is best. An **oil-based eggshell**, with mid to low sheen, is good for protection against moisture; I use it on woodwork and for painting furniture. **Water-based eggshell** – a more environmentally friendly eggshell – provides a tough washable surface for interiors, although it's not so good for hard-wearing surfaces, such as shelves or worktops. **Exterior masonry paint** is a water-based paint for exterior cement, stone, and brickwork. **Floor paint** is oil based with an eggshell finish and can be used for wood and concrete floors. **Flat oil paint** used on wood, plaster, and metal is a good traditional finish for period interiors. **Limewash** is a traditional matt-textured paint based on chalk and water and coloured with artists' pigments – limewashed houses in white, blue, green, and terracotta are typical in Mediterranean countries such as Greece and Spain. Its high alkalinity – it was once used to disinfect hospitals – can cause problems and users are advised to wear gloves and goggles when mixing it up and painting with it.

Eco-notes

There is an increase in environmentally friendly paint formulas, and products are now made with fewer solvents, fungicides, chemical preservatives, and toxic volatile organic compounds (VOCs) that contribute to low-level pollution. **Natural paints** contain **organic**, **renewable**, **and biodegradable ingredients** such as orange-peel oil or binder derived from resin that is harvested in a non-destructive, sustainable way from the dammar tree, which grows in tropical rainforests. **Traditional distemper** or **casein paint** (based on a milk-derived protein) and limewash are also less destructive to the environment. **Recycle**, and take care to dispose of **unwanted paint** in an ecologically responsible manner. Countless half-finished paint cans are thrown away with the household rubbish only to end up contaminating landfill tips, or unwanted paint is poured down the drain to pollute water supplies. To remove the last dregs in a can, pour onto absorbent paper and allow it to dry. **Dry paint** can be disposed of with the household garbage. Use recycling centres to find a source for empty steel paint cans, and contact your local council to dispose of liquid paint.

white

the huge variety of white paints available allows me to experiment with tones and textures for painting walls, floors, and furniture

1

2

1 **clay emulsion**
A water-based paint that is perfect for calm, understated neutral walls in any interior.

2 **chalk emulsion**
Easy to apply, this creates a light, modern, and unifying effect if used throughout a flat or apartment.

3 **neutral eggshell**
The hardwearing finish of this paint adds practicality as well as style to a basic chain-store pine kitchen table.

4 **paper eggshell**
This has an easy-to-clean finish that is ideal for wooden shelving or cupboard doors.

5 **cowparsley floor paint**
Heavy-duty paint that can smarten up even the most worn wooden floorboards.

6 **weathered white eggshell**
Eco-friendly water-based eggshell is used to transform a battered side table from a market (see opposite).

3

4

5

6

7 **pebble eggshell**
An oil-based paint that gives
a matt covering suitable for
wood panelling or tongue-
and-groove lined walls.

8 **calico exterior eggshell**
A more durable paint that is
ideal for painting junk
garden tables and chairs.

9 **ice-cream emulsion**
For customizing flower pots,
which can then be filled with
plants for indoor use.

cream and yellow

I find inspiration for creams and yellows from sunburnt fields, sunflowers, straw, and sandy beaches

1 **caramel eggshell**
Could be used as a wood-effect paint to revamp a plain wooden lamp base.

2 **beeswax eggshell**
A country colour that I used to good effect in the hall and stairways of our 18th-century house in London.

3 **sand emulsion**
For a warm covering that would suit a south-facing sitting room with blue-checked fabrics.

4 **toffee eggshell**
Gives a warm sheen and a hardwearing finish to woodwork and panelling in a period house.

5 **butter eggshell**
A tough paint in creamy yellow to jazz up a wooden crate for colourful kitchen storage (see opposite).

6 **honey eggshell**
Cream paint with a warm feel to liven up plain kitchen cupboards.

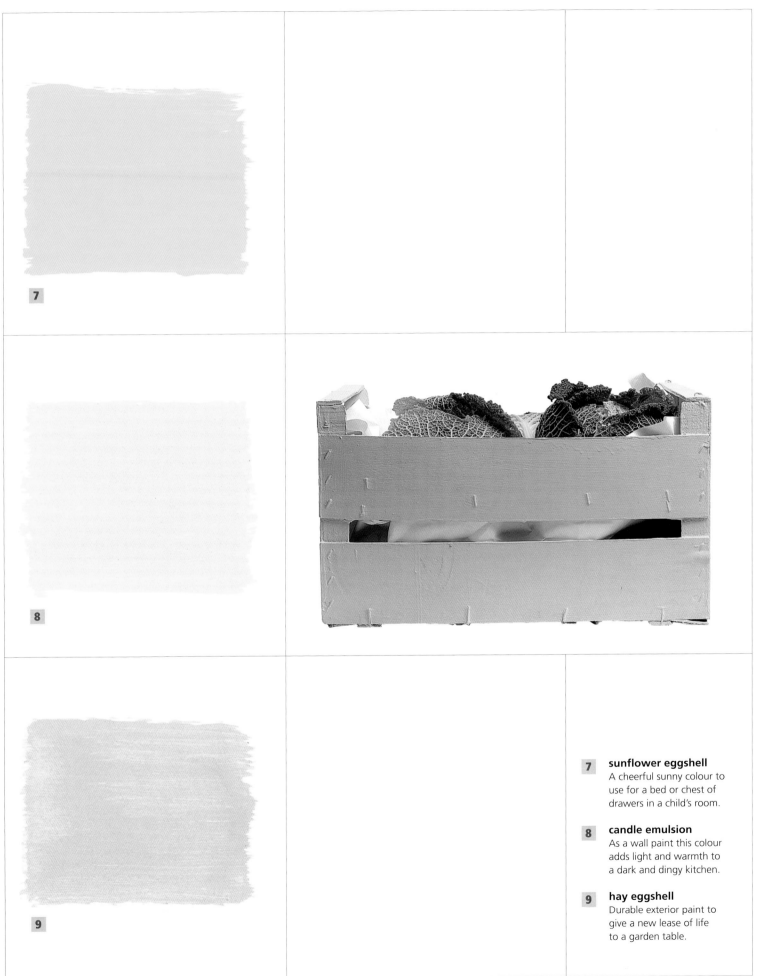

7

8

9

7 **sunflower eggshell**
A cheerful sunny colour to
use for a bed or chest of
drawers in a child's room.

8 **candle emulsion**
As a wall paint this colour
adds light and warmth to
a dark and dingy kitchen.

9 **hay eggshell**
Durable exterior paint to
give a new lease of life
to a garden table.

terracotta

good old-fashioned earthy colours for use in kitchens, gardens, and on exterior walls

1 **flowerpot emulsion**
A rich, clay colour for the walls to give warmth and intimacy in a small room.

2 **earthenware eggshell**
Just the job for disguising cheap plastic flowerpots as the real thing, and it makes them sturdier, too.

3 **pumpkin eggshell**
Brighten up and protect garden pots with earthy paint and place on a white patio for a Spanish look.

4 **brick exterior eggshell**
Paint a garden shed in this natural shade that will blend beautifully with garden hues.

5 **conker eggshell**
A paler terracotta that looks good on a side table placed in a room with whites and neutrals (see opposite).

6 **pantile eggshell**
A pink-toned paint that is used to best effect in small doses – for example, to unify a display of cheap wooden photograph frames.

1

2

3

4

5

6

7

7 chestnut exterior eggshell
Hardwearing with a matt finish, this warm colour would look good on a country house front door.

8

8 potato masonry paint or limewash
Typically used for Spanish fincas and village houses, this colour and finish could work in most rural settings.

9

9 twig emulsion
The colour of natural wood, this shade would go well in a utility room or larder in an old house.

green

garden-green shades that
can be used inside and out

1

2

3

4

1 **fig leaf emulsion**
A bold, bright colour that
will uplift a sitting room.

2 **lime-green emulsion**
To perk up a pot for interior
display (see opposite).

3 **asparagus eggshell**
A subtle shade for junk
garden chairs and tables.

4 **apple eggshell**
Gives a flat covering that
complements Georgian
wood panelling.

5 **grass exterior eggshell**
This would be suitable for a
country cottage front door.

6 **broad bean emulsion**
A matt finish that lifts the
appearance of garden trellis;
it may wash off in the rain
but can be repainted yearly.

5

6

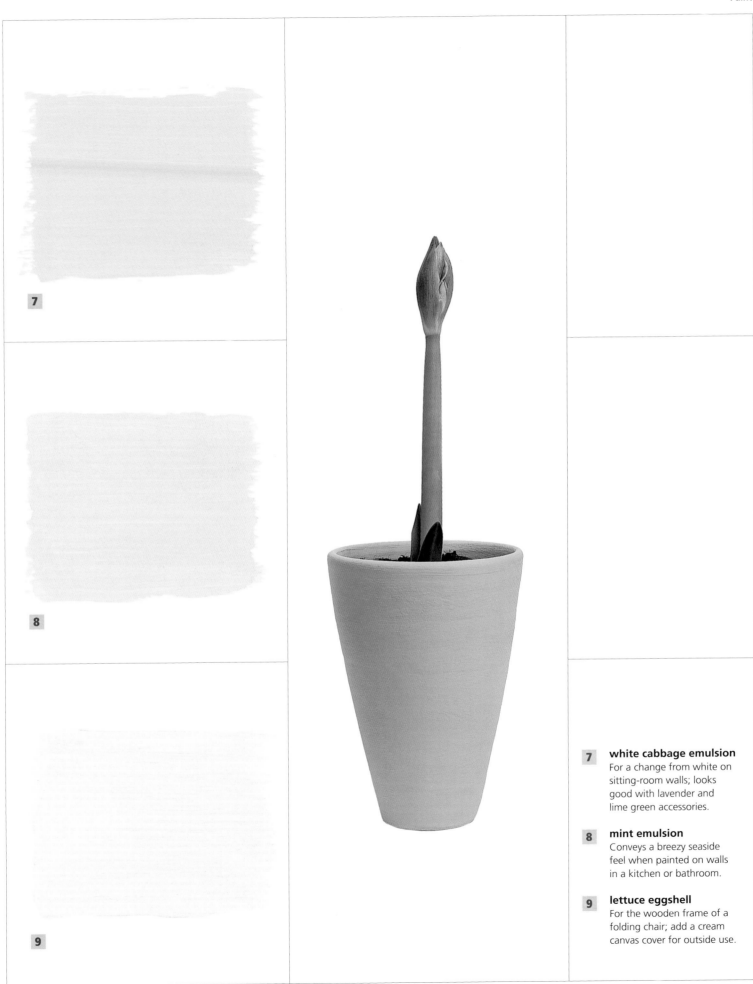

7 **white cabbage emulsion**
For a change from white on sitting-room walls; looks good with lavender and lime green accessories.

8 **mint emulsion**
Conveys a breezy seaside feel when painted on walls in a kitchen or bathroom.

9 **lettuce eggshell**
For the wooden frame of a folding chair; add a cream canvas cover for outside use.

blue

my favourite blues come
from observations of sea,
sky, and swimming pools

1 **beach hut eggshell**
An ideal summery colour
to paint patio and garden
tables and chairs.

2 **pale denim eggshell**
A lively shade to brighten
up a set of wooden kitchen
drawers (see opposite).

3 **wave eggshell**
For shelving and cabinets;
provides contrast in a white
painted bathroom.

4 **pool exterior eggshell**
If you don't want your
garden shed to fade into its
surroundings, try painting it
this delicious blue.

5 **sea eggshell**
A calming colour that is
good for wooden bunkbeds
in the children's bedroom.

6 **cloud emulsion**
For coolness without the chill
factor; team with crisp white
bedlinen in the bedroom.

7

8

9

7 **boat exterior eggshell**
To update a wooden folding chair, paint the frame in this colour and dress with a neutral canvas cotton cover.

8 **surf exterior eggshell**
A turquoise blue to enhance the front door and shutters of a seaside cottage.

9 **tide eggshell**
Paint old tins with this uplifting colour, line with tissue paper, and fill with homemade biscuits.

pink

shocking and pale pinks, mauves, and lilacs from garden borders brimming with foxgloves, lavender, and other flowers are reinterpreted in the home

1 **fuchsia eggshell**
Great for jazzing up old food cans for use as kitchen or workroom containers (see opposite).

2 **rose emulsion**
A pretty shade to paint bedroom walls.

3 **hyacinth emulsion**
A warm colour suitable for sitting-room walls that looks especially good with green.

4 **pale lavender eggshell**
Painted wooden frames in this colour will complement children's drawings.

5 **petal exterior masonry paint or limewash**
For the outside walls of a country cottage by the sea.

6 **lilac emulsion**
A pretty bedroom in this pale hue would be further enhanced by floral bedlinen.

7

7 tulip eggshell
A good colour with a matt finish to update an old chest of drawers or cupboard in a feminine room.

8

8 bud eggshell
Brighten up patio flowerpots with a lick of pastel paint.

9

9 foxglove emulsion
For a version of white with just a hint of pink, use on walls for warmth and light.

Fabric

neutral fabrics

plain colours

checks and stripes

floral fabrics

Fabric data

Natural fabrics are sensual and tactile. **Linen sheets are deliciously smooth** on the skin; **floaty muslin curtains** catch the breeze on a searing hot day; **wool is beautifully soft and hardwearing**, and makes tough, upholstered surfaces – snuggle up with warm woolly throws in checks or plain colours, or sprawl outside on a soft picnic rug.

It's not necessary to splash out large sums of money for good quality and great colours. Try **old-fashioned haberdashers** or **traditional hardware shops** for **basic blue-and-white ticking**, cotton, and strong canvas. There are also **wholesale companies** that sell **muslin**, cotton, **canvas**, and **other basic fabrics** for theatre backdrops, artists' studios, and other commercial outlets, who will sell small quantities to individuals. I buy durable cotton for loose covers, and bright muslin for children's dressing-up clothes from a local wholesaler. Washroom linen normally supplied to hospitals and schools comes by the thick roll to make up into cushions, loose covers, and simple table runners. It is also worth scouring the fabric sections of **large department stores** for **cheap silk**, **plastic-coated cotton**, **ticking**, and **muslin**. And of course, **sale time** is ideal for picking up **bargains**.

Cotton

The white downy fibrous balls that enclose the seeds of the cotton plant are woven into cloth and thread of various weights and weaves: **calico** – unbleached cotton cloth; I use the heaviest weights for loose covers; **chintz** – printed, and usually glazed, cotton; tiny traditional floral prints are my favourites; **drill** – coarse, twilled cotton (with a diagonal weave); **denim** – extremely hardwearing, twilled cotton, usually dyed indigo; **duck or canvas** – strong, untwilled cotton; good for garden chairs, awnings, and heavy-duty laundry bags; **gingham** – checked cotton cloth, usually of one colour on a white background; comes in many different sizes of check; **muslin** – loosely woven, very fine, cotton fabric; makes floaty curtains; **ticking** – stout twilled cotton, closely woven in one-colour stripes on a cream or white background, traditionally used for covering mattresses; makes good chair covers and curtains; also pretty when old and faded; **voile** – a thin semi-transparent material; good for fine curtains or blinds.

Linen

A durable material with many uses that is derived from **flax** – a blue-flowered plant also cultivated for its seeds (linseed). There are many different weights of linen ranging from **cambric** – fine white linen used for handkerchiefs – to heavyweight upholstery quality. Linen sheets must be one of life's great luxuries. There are other textural and tough linen-type fabrics cultivated from plants: **hemp** – a herbaceous plant from India used mainly for rope; **jute** – plant fibre used for sacking, carpeting, and mats; **hessian** – strong coarse cloth made from hemp or jute; it was fashionable in the 1960s for covering walls; now useful for bags and noticeboards; **sackcloth** – coarse fabric woven from flax or hemp; **canvas** – strong, unbleached cloth of hemp or flax.

Silk

Fine, soft thread harvested from the cocoons of specially raised silkworms that feed on a diet of mulberry leaves, silk is warm and luxurious to wear. No longer prohibitively costly, silk comes in many different weights and qualities to suit requirements: **velvet** – luxurious, closely woven fabric with a thick short pile on one side; **dupion** – heavy silk with a textured weave; **tussah** – cloth with a linen-look weave; **saraburi** – heavy, flat-look, Thai silk; **parachute silk** – very lightweight silk for making billowy curtains.

Wool

Hair from sheep, alpaca, and goat that is spun into yarn for knitting or weaving. Wool is warm in winter, cool in summer, water-resistant on the outside, and absorbent on the inside. It is woven into many different textures: **flannel** – woven woollen fabric, usually without a nap; **alpaca** – luxuriously soft fabric made from the long, woolly hair of the alpaca llama; **cashmere** – fine, soft, but expensive, wool from the Kashmir goat; if you can afford it, it's worth the investment of at least one throw; **mohair** – fine, hairy yarn from the angora goat; makes great shawls and beautifully warm throws; **felt** – matted, woollen material that is non-fraying and easy to cut; comes in a great range of colours for noticeboards, chair pads, and children's art projects.

neutral fabrics

I choose bone, cream, stone, and other earth colours for rooms with natural textures

1

2

3

4

1   white cotton muslin
Makes translucent curtains and blinds for windows that need minimal covering.

2   cream cotton calico
is great for loose covers but preshrink before making up.

3   white cotton
A loosely woven fabric that makes nice, easily washed chair and sofa covers.

4   heavy brown linen
Roughly woven cloth with a utilitarian feel that makes it ideal for pinboards and chair cushions.

5   sand wool/polyester mix
A soft, yet tough, texture for a sensual upholstery covering.

6   cream cotton duck
Once used for making sails, a strong, hardwearing fabric that is just right for awnings and garden chair covers.

5

6

7 earth brown silk muslin
Ideal for a simple blind or lightweight bed throw.

8 cream wool mix
A luxurious upholstery fabric that should be restricted to child-free zones.

9 stone-brown jute
Sackcloth for fashioning into lightweight curtains, bags, and cushions.

10 fine white linen
A light weave for napkins, tablecloths, and bedlinen.

11 medium-brown linen
A mid-weight texture suitable for roman blinds and bedcovers.

12 egg-white ribbed cotton
To make a beautiful set of pull-on chair covers.

plain colours

use fabrics in strong
shades of green, blue,
and pink to bring colour
detail into the house

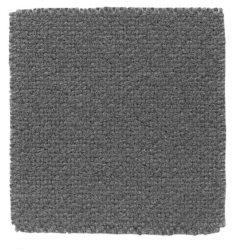

1   **blue wool mix**
Use to cover an armchair to
brighten up a neutral room.

2   **bright pink cotton drill**
Hardwearing fabric suitable
for a roller blind, roman
blind, or a simple curtain.

3   **pink cotton muslin**
Perfect for lightweight floaty
curtains that introduce a
splash of colour.

4   **spring-green felt**
For covering noticeboards,
and making handmade
Christmas stockings.

5   **sky-blue wool**
Hardwearing, soft, and
warm upholstery covering
to curl up on.

6   **pale violet cotton muslin**
Ideal for running up flower
and herb bags for scented
drawers and gifts.

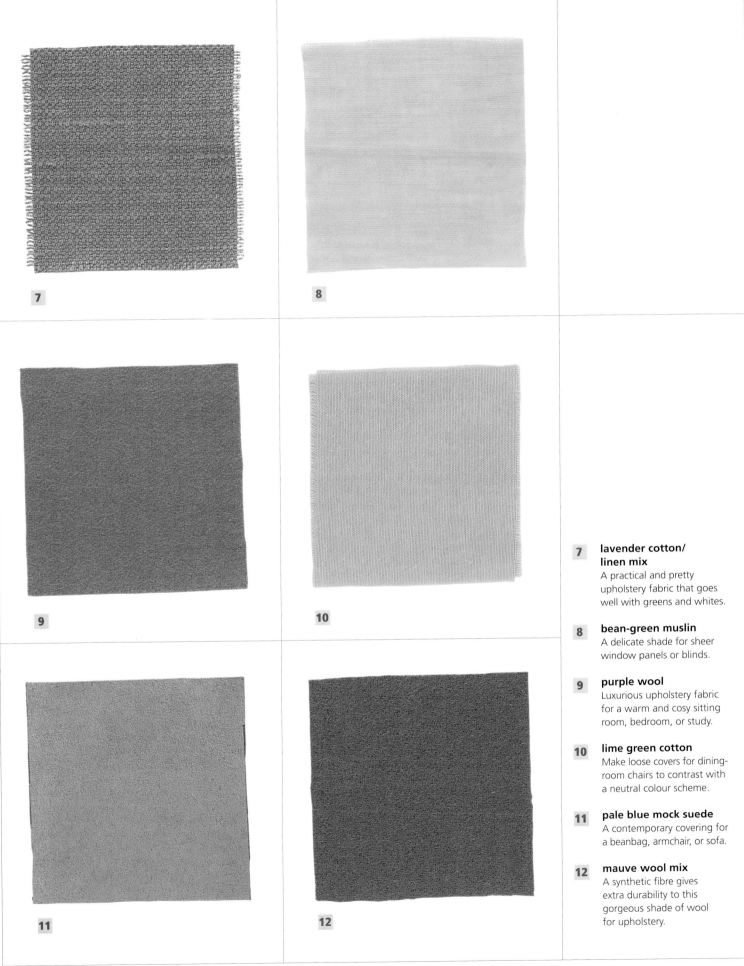

7

8

9

10

7 lavender cotton/ linen mix
A practical and pretty upholstery fabric that goes well with greens and whites.

8 bean-green muslin
A delicate shade for sheer window panels or blinds.

9 purple wool
Luxurious upholstery fabric for a warm and cosy sitting room, bedroom, or study.

10 lime green cotton
Make loose covers for dining-room chairs to contrast with a neutral colour scheme.

11 pale blue mock suede
A contemporary covering for a beanbag, armchair, or sofa.

12 mauve wool mix
A synthetic fibre gives extra durability to this gorgeous shade of wool for upholstery.

11

12

checks and stripes

I like the simplicity, timeless style, and sense of order found in these patterns

1

2

3

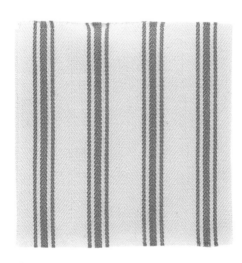

4

1 **green cotton check**
Ideal made into cushion covers for a fresh, summery addition to garden chairs.

2 **stone cotton check**
Will add subtle interest for covers or cushions in neutral-coloured rooms.

3 **yellow cotton check**
To make a bright and sunny roller blind for the kitchen.

4 **red cotton ticking**
This classic mattress covering can be used to transform a bedroom bolster.

5 **green PVC check**
No-sew, instant wipedown tablecloth that is a boon with children, whether used in the garden or kitchen.

6 **yellow cotton/polyester gingham**
Easily washed and dried, makes cheerful cushions for a child's bedroom.

5

6

7

8

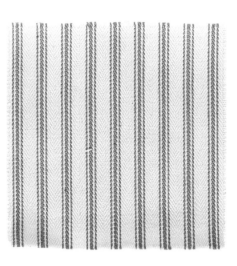

9

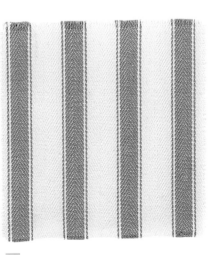

10

11

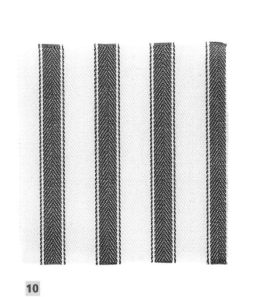

12

7 powder-blue cotton check
Creates freshness in any room; use for cushions, curtains, or loose covers.

8 blue cotton check
A lightweight cloth for creating a basic looped curtain (see how to make pp.178–179).

9 brick-striped cotton ticking
Use for a roomy laundry bag for all the family or make smaller ones for individual use (see how to make pp.226–227).

10 blue striped cotton ticking
A good buy for homemade loose covers (see p.189).

11 blue variable striped cotton ticking
A variation on plain stripes, this is a great choice for smart pull-on loose covers or roman blinds.

12 green cotton ticking
Makes lovely cushions with self-coloured, tie fastenings to throw onto a white sofa.

floral fabrics

cotton prints in spriggy
buds and blooms for floral
interest around the house

1 **spotty print**
For cushions, curtains,
or blinds in a room with
pistachio-painted walls.

2 **tiny bud print**
Perfect for small-scale items,
such as a bag or a child's
elasticated summer skirt.

3 **old-fashioned print**
With its contemporary white
background, this is my
favourite fabric design for
loose chair covers (see p.188).

4 **deep pink print**
A bold design for bed linen
in a room with white walls
and plain furniture.

5 **blue and lavender print**
Add style to alfresco eating
with a tablecloth made out
of this summery material.

6 **cream and pink print**
Use this delicate, classic print
to run up a loose cover and
revamp an old armchair.

7

8

9

10

11

12

7 **rosy sprig print**
The subtlety of the pattern allows abundant use in the bedroom for sheets, curtains, and matching chair cover.

8 **border print**
A striking design with a defined edge – perfect for roller or roman blinds.

9 **buds and hearts print**
This print's strong pink background and bold design will work well in a neutral colour scheme.

10 **crisp multi-coloured print**
A timeless design to use for cushions; combine with an old, faded quilt throw for a stronger floral look.

11 **buds and roses print**
Use this fine lawn for scented lavender bags, pillowcases, children's headscarves, or a bag (see p.51).

12 **retro rose print**
A 1950s-style pattern suitable for an ironing board cover or a laundry bag (see how to make pp.226–227).

Flooring

hard flooring

soft flooring

Flooring data

Choose floor surfaces in sensual textures such as **wood, rubber, cork, and terracotta**. Wall-to-wall, deep-pile carpeting is out of place when the aim is to create feelings of space, light, and airiness. **Opt for wooden boards spread with cotton rugs or big sisal mats**, and if you really have to have the fitted look (compulsory under some flat leases) use coir, sisal, or seagrass. For **noise insulation**, choose textures such as cork or rubber. For **heat insulation**, install low-energy, underfloor heating if you have stone floors or tightly packed wooden boards (heat is lost between gaps). Select your floor textures according to your needs and budget.

Wood

Pine is relatively inexpensive, and can be waxed, varnished, stained, or painted. Other woods for floors include maple, ash, beech, cherry, and black walnut. **Reclaimed pine or oak boards** have a lovely worn quality, and come in wider widths than new boards; it's possible to find 23-cm wide 18th-century floorboards in specialist reclamation shops. **Narrow strips** of light-coloured oak or maple flooring look more modern. Use natural oil sealants rather than glossy varnishes, which look horribly shiny and artificial. **Sanding** – prepare wooden boards with a sander (remember to wear goggles and a face mask); hammer in protruding nails and tacks; run the sander along the grain until the surface is even; start with coarse sandpaper, then medium, and finish with a fine grade; vacuum; then apply one of the following finishes. **Liming** – produces a lovely, whiteish finish that picks out the wood grain; damp the wood with a cloth and rake out the grain with a wire brush; apply liming paste and allow to dry; gently rub off the excess paste with medium-grade wire wool; clean off any powder with a damp sponge; seal the boards (see below). **Staining** – colours boards without concealing the grain; test the colour on a sample area; apply stain to one board at a time with a lint-free rag, building up the layers to get the right colour. **Sealing** – for a totally natural look, use Swedish floor soap; scrub the floor with the solution up to three times to seal it properly; the floor can be kept clean by scrubbing it with a weaker solution of the floor soap; an alternative matt sealant is **natural oil sealer** – apply to bare or newly prepared wood; the more layers you apply, the tougher the result; the finished floor can be mopped or wiped to keep clean; **water-based varnishes** are another option, but try to find one with a satin or matt finish to avoid a shiny look; apply in layers for the required toughness. **Painting** – wall paints, such as emulsion or eggshell can be used, but must be sealed with varnish once dry; specialist floor paints are more hardwearing and don't need to be varnished; all paints are liable to chip and flake in areas of heavy use.

Terracotta

Seal terracotta and quarry tiles with linseed oil. Although lovely and cool in summer, terracotta can be cold and uncomfortable in winter. The solution in our Spanish house was to install low-energy, underfloor heating, which keeps the terracotta floors toasty. To keep clean, sweep or hose down with water. Remove cooking stains with a clean cloth dampened with water or white spirit.

Cork

Tiles made of cork are resilient, and insulating against heat loss and sound. Good for all around the home, including the bathroom. Cork is environmentally friendly: the bark of the cork tree is harvested every nine years and removing the bark doesn't harm the tree – it just grows a replacement layer. Leave tiles for 48 hours in warm, dry conditions before laying. Set out the tiles before fixing to the floor in order to get a good mix of the natural variations in shade.

Rubber

Synthetic rubber floor tiles are unbreakable, anti-slip, and noise and water resistant; in addition they are warm to the feet and easy to clean. They are, therefore, ideal for every room in the house, including the kitchen and bathroom. Rubber tiles come in a huge range of colours, as well as in black and white, so will blend into any colour scheme.

Matting and rugs

I once had some authentic mediaeval matting that needed to be watered daily in order to keep it moist. At the time the labour was worth the aesthetic experience, but I now to stick to more basic, low-maintenance natural mats and rugs in cotton, seagrass, and sisal, which are all tough enough to deal with spillages, for example red wine (cover with salt to soak it up), and mud from children and dogs. Choose a natural fibre according to your needs. **Coir** – a naturally golden fibre that comes from the outer husks of coconuts; first softened in water, it is then beaten, spun, and woven; tough, practical, and good for busier areas of the home. **Jute** – grown in India, it has tall stems that are processed in a similar way to coir; a softer material, suitable for less heavily trafficked areas. **Sisal** – grows in East Africa and produces a tough shiny fibre that is very suitable for heavy use. **Seagrass** – from mainland China, where it grows in coastal salt marshes; a fibre with a slightly waxy finish that makes it resistant to stains.

hard flooring

wood, cork, rubber, terracotta, and stone floor surfaces to suit individual needs and budgets

1 **reclaimed oak boards**
These are nicely worn, textural, and hardwearing; alternatively, use new oak sealed with a matt varnish for a paler, more modern look that will weather with age.

2 **waxed pine boards**
Unbeatable basic, practical, and affordable flooring; sand and scrub with soap for a Scandinavian look, or apply paint or lime paste.

3 **hardwood parquet**
Reminiscent of polished floors in Parisian apartments, this floor covering works well in modern and period homes alike.

4 **cork tiles**
A 1970s revival that is also ecological – cork is harvested from the same tree every nine years. Insulating and warm, it can be used in hallways, workrooms, and playrooms.

5
6 **rubber tiles**
7 Modern, warm, and easy-to-clean flooring for most areas of the home; comes in a range of colours, including white.

1

2

3

4

5

7

8

9

10

11

8   **terracotta tiles**
     In Spain, I have terracotta
     tiles throughout the house,
     bought cheaply from the
     local builder's merchant;
     they are sealed with linseed
     oil for a flat, unglossy finish.

9   **limestone tiles**
     Natural and hardwearing,
10   limestone comes in a range
     of colours and looks modern
11   and streamlined in the
     kitchen and conservatory.

soft flooring

tactile surfaces for underfoot to add warmth and texture

1 mat in seagrass squares
Flooring from the 1960s (I grew up with them) that has seen a revival with the current trend for more natural-looking floors.

2 herringbone coir
A rough-textured covering derived from coconut husks. Useful in heavily trafficked areas such as stairs and halls.

3 basketweave seagrass
Grown in salt marshes, this fibre looks good woven into large mats bordered with neutral or contrast-coloured cotton webbing.

4 bouclé sisal
A tough, lustrous fibre from East Africa; soft on bare feet, it is a good choice for bedrooms.

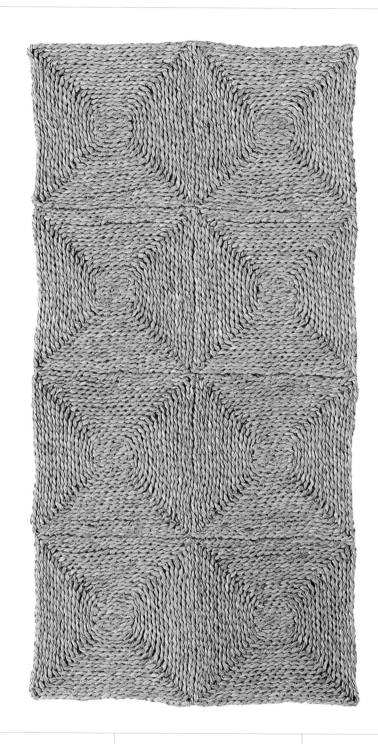

1

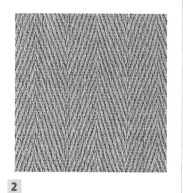
2

3

4

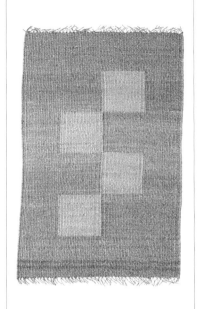

5

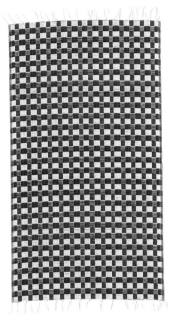

6

7

8

5 fine seagrass rug
Practical and softer than
some seagrass (see 1 and 3),
this is ideal as a hearth rug.

6 woven plastic mat
A tough, washable mat
from Africa that makes
perfect sense in kitchens
and bathrooms.

7 cream rag rug
Made from old bits of fabric,
this softly textured rug looks
great on painted or bare,
scrubbed floorboards.

8 cotton check rug
I have several of these
rugs in different colours
bought from chain stores;
immensely practical, they
can be rejuvenated in the
washing machine.

Eat

Healthy eating data

Fuel your body with good food to keep healthy. All food and drink can supply you with energy, which is measured in calories: the current recommended daily averages are 1,940 calories for women, 2,550 for men, and over 3,000 for children. For good health, it is important that these calories are made up of the right proportions of the three main food groups and the recommendations for a balanced diet are roughly: 50 per cent carbohydrates; 35 per cent fat; and 15 per cent protein.

Carbohydrates

There are two types of carbohydrate: simple and complex. **Simple carbohydrates** are sugary foods, such as biscuits, cakes, and sweets, and although they can give you a quick burst of energy they are bad for your teeth and can lead to weight gain. **Complex carbohydrates** are starchy foods and include bread, pulses, pasta, rice, breakfast cereals, and some vegetables; these are digested slowly and provide sustained energy. Eat more **unrefined carbohydrates** – for example, brown rice, wholemeal bread, nuts, and seeds, which along with fruit and vegetables will also provide your body with **fibre**. Indigestible fibre has no energy value but is important because it helps to prevent constipation and other bowel problems, including cancer of the colon.

Fat

Although fats are essential for energy and vitamin absorption, it is important that you eat the right sort. There are two main types: saturated and unsaturated (divided into monounsaturated and polyunsaturated). **Saturated** fats occur in animal products, such as meat, cheese, cream, butter, milk, eggs, and lard, and also in refined cakes, biscuits, and pies. **Monounsaturated** fats are found in olive oil, rapeseed oil, nuts, seeds, houmous, and avocado. **Polyunsaturated** fats are found in safflower oil, sunflower oil, and corn oil, and in oily fish, such as sardines, mackerel, and tuna. **Diets high in saturated fat** are bad for the waistline and the heart. **Unsaturated fats** are thought to give some protection against heart disease (polyunsaturates having a greater effect than monounsaturates), and are associated generally with good health, as seen in people who eat a Mediterranean-style diet.

Protein

Essential for growth, development, and repair, much protein comes from **animal sources** – meat, fish, eggs, cheese, and milk – but it is also found in **plants** – pulses, wheat and other grains, nuts, and seeds. A **healthy diet** should contain more protein from fish, white meat, vegetables, and cereals, and less from red meat and dairy products.

Alcohol

Although alcohol contains calories it is by no means an essential part of the diet; however, many of us drink it daily as part of our lifestyle. To avoid alcohol-related health problems – weight gain, liver damage, heart problems – there are recommended safe drinking limits: 14 units a week for women, and 21 for men, where 1 unit = 100 ml wine; 25 ml spirit; 250 ml lager or beer. Needless to say, a week's units should not be taken in one sitting, and one or two days per week should be kept free of alcohol.

Good eating habits

If possible, **buy organic** fruit, vegetables, and meat. **Buy seasonal** and local produce – there are many organic farmers' markets springing up so check to see if there's one near you. If you have garden space, make a **vegetable patch**, or rent an allotment to grow your own nutritious fruits and vegetables. **Buy the best-quality** food you can afford – I couldn't live without decent cheese, reasonable wine, fresh fish, or chocolate high in cocoa solids, and would rather consume them sparingly than pay less for inferior mass-produced and processed stuff. **Eat more fruit and vegetables** – five portions a day is the official advice. I have fruit juice at breakfast, a handful of dried fruit (figs, dates, prunes) mid-morning, salad with soup and bread at lunch-time (I make leek and potato or mixed vegetable soup from leftovers blended with homemade chicken stock), and carrots and broccoli with meat or fish in the evening. I also make a big salad with raw carrots, onions, sunflower seeds, lettuce, or whatever is in the fridge to eat with supper every day. Try to eat a wide range of fruit and vegetables to incorporate varying nutrients – for example, avocados are high in fat and vitamin E, while cabbage is low in fat and high in vitamin C. **Steam vegetables lightly** and don't boil them to death (vitamins C and B are depleted in cooking). **Grill, don't fry** meat and fish to keep fat levels down. Season with herbs rather than salt – sprigs of rosemary and garlic stuffed in lamb, mackerel stuffed with lemon, chopped parsley, and garlic, or chicken breasts marinated in lemon juice and tarragon. **Start the day** with a good breakfast to keep hunger at bay. Try a big bowl of milk and muesli with a low sugar and high fruit, nut, and seed content (I add oatmeal as it is thought to lower cholesterol), and a glass of fresh orange juice. **A handful** of dried fruit, nuts, or seeds is a good stomach-filler and a source of protein, minerals, and fibre, and makes a healthier snack than chocolate bars or biscuits. **Drink more water** (we should drink 2 litres of water a day to maintain health) and less tea and coffee. **Healthy children's food** – mine like hot porridge for breakfast; fish pie; pasta with meat and tomato sauce; grilled cod, plaice, salmon; baked beans on toast; vegetables; potatoes (mashed, boiled, roasted in olive oil); frozen peas (full of fibre); sticks of raw carrot and cucumber (good for teeth); oranges, apples, peaches, pears cut into slices; bowls of mixed berries; fruit crumbles with oat and almond topping (goes well with ice cream); and homemade flapjacks.

kitchen tools

basic kit for routine kitchen and cooking activities

1 **wooden spoon**
I have a collection picked up very cheaply from hardware shops all over the world. Useful for stirring stews, fools, and soups, a wooden spoon is simple, functional, and satisfying to hold.

2 **pudding basin**
Cream-coloured ceramic mixing bowls have been around for years. I use them for making sponge puddings, mixing chocolate cake, as salad bowls, and even plant spring bulbs in them.

3 **sharp knife**
I find that a small, good quality stainless steel knife is invaluable for chopping herbs, garlic, fruit for jam, and slicing bread, cake, or oranges for school lunches.

4 **balloon whisk**
This style of whisk is good for small-scale cooking jobs such as whipping cream, pancake mix, mayonnaise, and salad dressing (my favourite is made of olive oil, lemon juice, Dijon mustard, and garlic).

5 **metal colander**
Mine hangs strategically above the sink and I like the ritual of rinsing earthy potatoes and watching the water drain through the holes. Metal is more durable than plastic and can cope with greater heat.

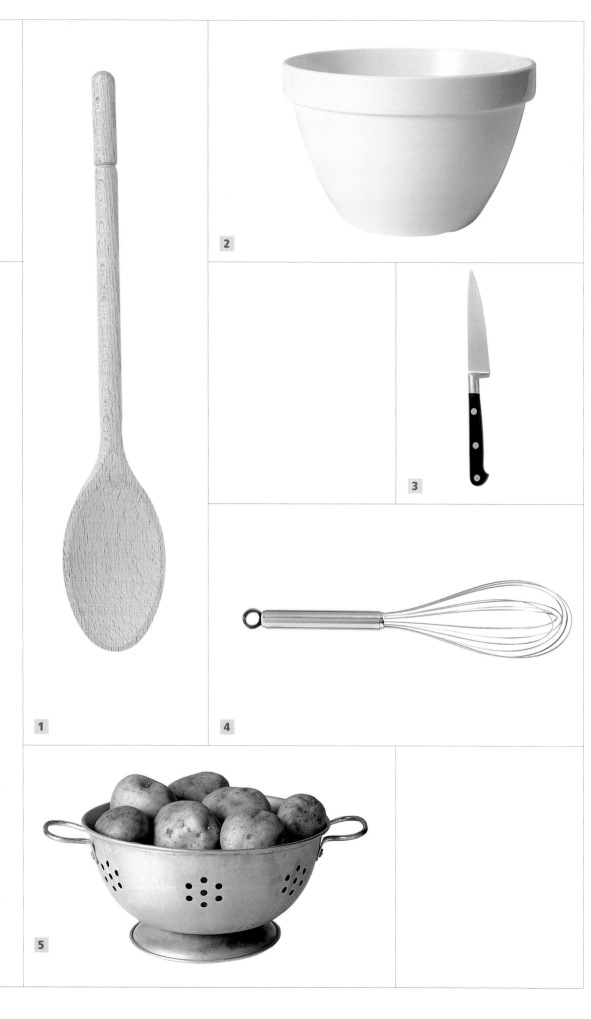

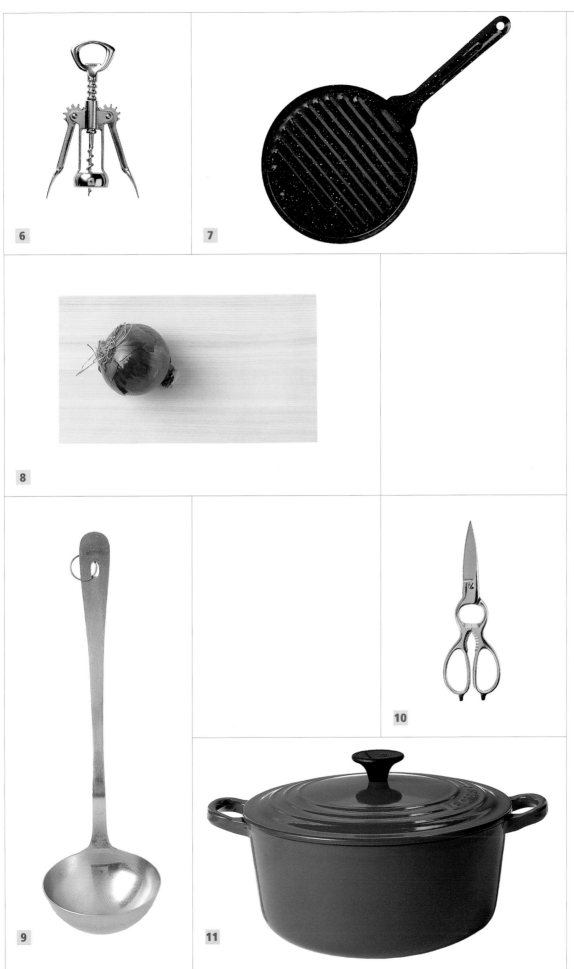

6 **lever-type corkscrew**
The easiest corkscrew to use – once screwed into the cork, minimal effort is required to lever it out. Panic breaks out in my household when it's mislaid, so I advise keeping it in a safe place.

7 **metal griddle pan**
A cheap find from a Spanish market, it produces perfectly seared swordfish or tuna steaks (marinated in olive oil, freshly chopped parsley, garlic, and lemon juice).

8 **wooden chopping board**
I have several boards in different sizes for different uses. Keep colour-coded plastic boards that are used only for raw meat and fish.

9 **stainless steel ladle**
Indispensable for stirring jams and marmalades, and dishing up homemade soups in the winter – leek and potato, Jerusalem artichoke, chicken and vegetable, mushroom, and chestnut.

10 **kitchen scissors**
These have endless uses; they are particularly handy for topping and tailing beans, cutting up squid, or gutting sardines and mackerel.

11 **blue, oval enamelled cast-iron casserole**
A heavy-based pan is ideal for slowly cooking juicy stews. Rabbit with tomatoes and rosemary is my favourite.

food cupboard

edible essentials for my
kitchen. See also store
cupboard ingredients
on p.102.

1

2

1 **good quality chocolate**
I buy bars with 70 per cent
cocoa solids for chocolate
mousse, chocolate and
chestnut cake, and for
tucking inside hunks of
bread for a tea-time snack.

2 **homemade Seville
orange marmalade**
Prepared in Spain each
February during the half-
term holiday for spreading
on breakfast toast (see
pp.92–93). Other preserves
easily made include apricot,
strawberry, and plum jams.

3 **organic fresh bread**
Made with unbleached white
flour, and great for thick
slices of toast with melted
butter and jam. I also like to
buy wholemeal loaves and
French sticks for picnics.

3

4 **real Cheddar cheese**
I select one with a strong
flavour and crumbly texture
from a local cheese shop to
eat with bread and soup at
lunch-time, or at supper with
crisp, crunchy apples or
slivers of my homemade
membrillo (quince paste).

4

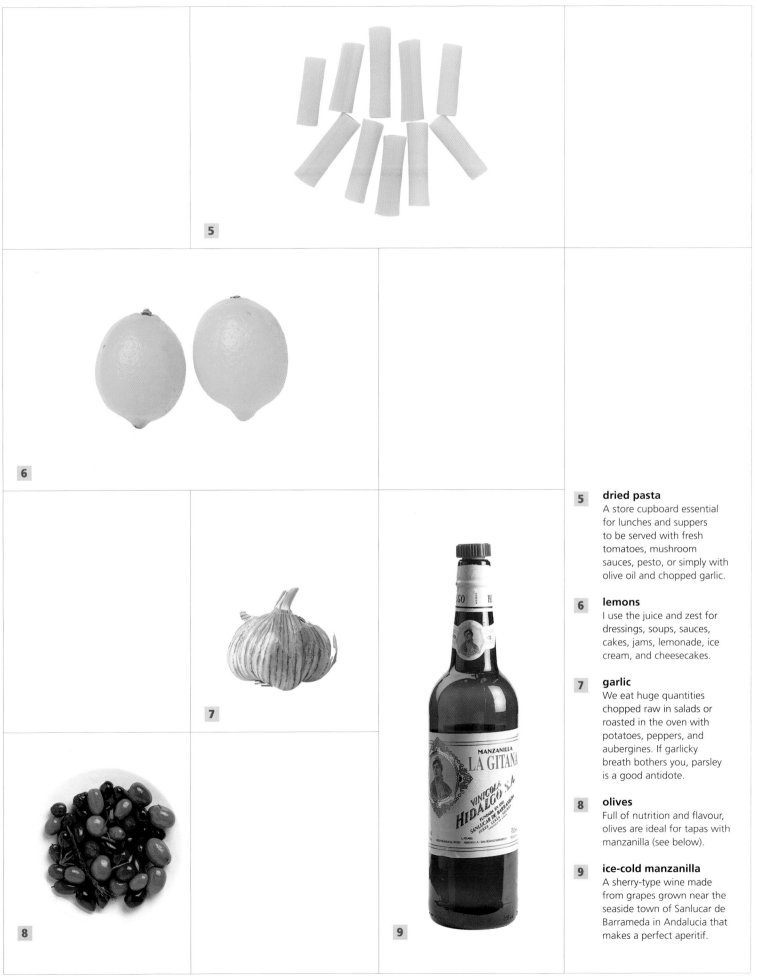

5 **dried pasta**
A store cupboard essential for lunches and suppers to be served with fresh tomatoes, mushroom sauces, pesto, or simply with olive oil and chopped garlic.

6 **lemons**
I use the juice and zest for dressings, soups, sauces, cakes, jams, lemonade, ice cream, and cheesecakes.

7 **garlic**
We eat huge quantities chopped raw in salads or roasted in the oven with potatoes, peppers, and aubergines. If garlicky breath bothers you, parsley is a good antidote.

8 **olives**
Full of nutrition and flavour, olives are ideal for tapas with manzanilla (see below).

9 **ice-cold manzanilla**
A sherry-type wine made from grapes grown near the seaside town of Sanlucar de Barrameda in Andalucia that makes a perfect aperitif.

kitchen storage

functional ideas for storing food, cutlery, china, linen, and other kitchen items

1

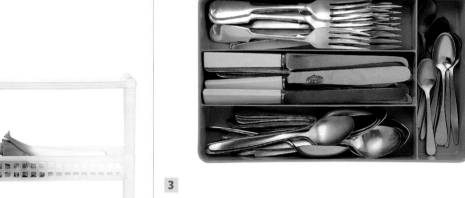

2

3

4

5

1 **mesh food net**
A useful device for covering cooked meat before it is put in the refrigerator, or for protecting plates of cheese from flies and wasps.

2 **plastic trolley**
A portable idea for storing vegetables, linen, and other kitchen kit.

3 **1950s Bakelite® cutlery tray**
Found on a market stall and bought for its pea-green colour.

4 **1950s enamelled stacking tin**
A junk shop find, I store cake in the bottom part and layers of biscuits above. Also available is a modern version in stainless steel.

5 **stainless steel tin**
With a plastic lid – a simple camping-style idea for packed lunches, picnics, and general food storage.

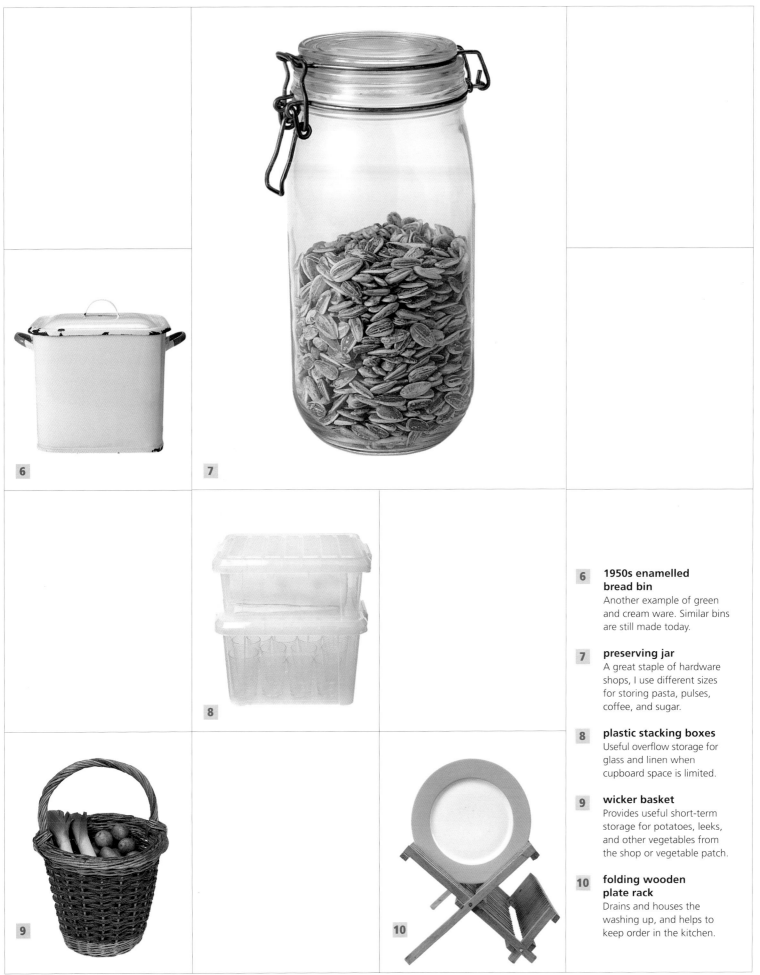

6

7

8

9

10

6 **1950s enamelled bread bin**
Another example of green and cream ware. Similar bins are still made today.

7 **preserving jar**
A great staple of hardware shops, I use different sizes for storing pasta, pulses, coffee, and sugar.

8 **plastic stacking boxes**
Useful overflow storage for glass and linen when cupboard space is limited.

9 **wicker basket**
Provides useful short-term storage for potatoes, leeks, and other vegetables from the shop or vegetable patch.

10 **folding wooden plate rack**
Drains and houses the washing up, and helps to keep order in the kitchen.

functional tableware

ideas borrowed from utilitarian cafés and institutional canteens

1

2

4

3

1 white-handled stainless steel cutlery
Bistro-style cutlery that goes in the dishwasher.

2 stainless steel cutlery
Solid, formal cutlery that can be buffed up with a linen tea towel for a gleaming shine.

3 robust glass
Unbreakable glassware available in a range of sizes and shapes for orange juice, water, or any other drink.

4 espresso maker
I have a small two-cup size for weekdays and a large eight-cup model for large numbers at the weekend.

5 **salt and pepper shakers**
6 A plain and simple idea borrowed from café tables.

5

6

7

9

8

10

11

12

7   1930s ice-cream bowl
Perfect for portions of home-made ice cream, served sundae style with a delicious biscuit; equally good for raspberry fool.

8   robust tumbler
A good-sized tumbler is perfect for breakfast milk, lunch-time lemonade, or a cool beer in the evening.

9   sugar shaker
Another sturdy café detail that keeps the sugar dry and away from little hands.

10   silver fork and bone-handled knife
Buy beautiful cutlery second-hand, to team with a crisp white cotton cloth and napkins.

11   simple wine glass
Can be bought cheaply in boxes of 12 from kitchen shops or department stores.

12   glass water jug
As used in canteens. Buy from hardware shops.

basic china and linen

plain white china and linen,
with a splash of blue,
for everyday eating and
special occasions

1

2

3

1 **white mug**
Easy to replace and looks
good in my white kitchen.

2 **white dinner plate**
I buy this classic design in
bone china in the sales at
department stores.

3 **pale blue-and-white
striped table linen**
For a fresh feel to the
table. Always iron linen
when damp.

4 **white mug edged in
dark blue**
Hang a row of these
from cup hooks.

5 **plastic checked cloth**
Easily wiped down, this is
a practical table covering
for everyday use. I buy it
by the metre from a
hardware shop.

4

5

6 blue-and-white checked cotton table linen
As seen in cafés; works well at home as a simple, stylish backdrop to white china.

7 white cup and saucer
An old-fahioned shape for steaming cups of ground coffee or Earl Grey tea.

8 plain white bowl
I use for vegetables, salads, or, lined with a white or checked cotton napkin, for serving fresh bread.

9 traditional milk jug
Equally useful for juice, cream, or even a bunch of spring flowers.

10 blue-and-white striped Cornishware mug
Originally made in the 1930s; a modern version of this utilitarian shape is still in production today.

11 crisp white table linen
transforms the most basic table and gives even simple meals a sense of occasion.

12 basic white egg cup
for holding a freshly-laid egg at breakfast.

tables

multi-functional surfaces on which to prepare food, and to eat and work

1

1. **second-hand oak desk**
   Doubles as a dining table. Here laid with white plates, simple glasses, cutlery, and a single potted hyacinth.

2. **lightweight folding metal table**
   Easily carried, this table is really useful for picnics and other outdoor eating ideas.

3. **fold-up wooden table**
   A simple, small, slatted table painted in white eggshell can be put to use all around the house.

4. **limed pine kitchen table**
   Used for food preparation, family meals, and as a surface for my children to work on, too.

2

3

4

5 folding hardboard table
A basic shape that has been painted in two coats of white eggshell and can be used to eat at or as a stylish side table.

6 hardboard table top on wooden trestles
I have several of these "instant tables" in Spain for setting up when needed – for example, for dinner parties or eating outside.

7 1950s-style plywood and metal table
The neat proportions of this design are practical in a small kitchen.

8 beech zinc-topped table
A sreamlined shape with modern proportions and a durable, easy-to-clean top.

picnic

just add ice-cold wine, good cheese, and some bread to the items shown here for a perfect picnic

1

2

3

1 **floppy straw sunhat**
A wide-brimmed hat is essential for beach picnics or whenever shade is minimal.

2 **small camping kettle**
To boil water for coffee or tea on a camp fire or portable gas ring.

3 **Spanish grass basket**
My favourite picnic basket – generally stuffed with a rug, suncream, a corkscrew, and a good book.

4 **portable barbecue**
Big enough for sausages or skewered chicken, and easily carried to the beach or countryside picnic area.

5 **re-freezable water packs**
I keep loads in the freezer, and use them to pack around food in the picnic basket, or place in a rigid cool box or bag to keep food and drinks cool in high summer.

4

5

6

7

8

9

10

6 plastic mugs
Indestructible, stackable, and perfect for all picnic drinks. Also include plastic picnic plates and cutlery.

7 folding deckchair
A staple of parks, the seaside, and back gardens, it is a great portable picnic idea.

8 tartan wool rug
Nothing beats lying on a rug staring up at the sky. The type with a waterproof back that folds up into a holdall is more practical.

9 storm kettle
Use when windy, or at other times when open fires are hazardous. Filll base with paper and twigs, and light. Boils about 1 litre of water.

10 fold-up cutlery/can opener
The tools fold down Swiss army knife-style and then both pieces slide together to make a compact pocket-sized gadget.

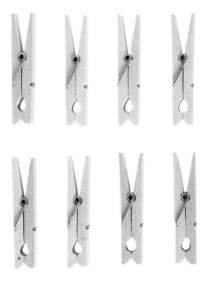

Work

household

eco-friendly

storage

seating

Work data

In the new millennium, mothers like myself do not expect to be domestic saints – we realized long ago that the odds are stacked against us.

Consider one of my typical domestic scenarios – squealing children, a hamster with a gungy eye that needs to be rushed to the vet, a broken dishwasher, pasta sauce boiling and bubbling, and a work deadline to be met – all to be dealt with before I allow myself a pampering trip to the swimming pool.

Efficiency

I have found that the following **solutions** help to keep imminent insanity at bay: **domestic cleaner** – when I am working, Sandra takes the strain off me by washing up last night's dishes and tidying up the bomb site that is the childrens' room; **laundry baskets** – I have one for dirty clothes, one for stuff waiting to be ironed, and one for ironed laundry that is ready to be put away; **clothes airer** – good for small spaces, and a neat, eco-friendly way of hanging washing; **damp mop and duster** – for whizzing around the flat and cleaning up dust and dirt efficiently; **linen tea towels** – the only way to dry glasses; **take the weight off your feet** – some people I know do the ironing while sitting down; **notebook** – for copious lists; **computer** with e-mail facility, **and mobile phone** – indispensable items; **anglepoise desk lamps** – for spotlighting work tasks on gloomy days and at night; **open shelving** above my desk, lined with filing boxes for all work cuttings and research material; **ex-office filing cabinets** – painted white for all personal filing; **big notice-board** – for displaying all the family's social commitments.

Eco-office

Help to take the pressure off the environment by being eco-conscious around the house: **use recycled paper** and write notes on both sides; keep a pile of scrap paper and ultimately recycle; **recycle old computer equipment**, and printer, fax, and photocopier toner cartridges can be sent to developing countries; **save envelopes** for reuse; **stop junk mail** by removing your name from mailing lists (contact the mailing preference service).

Eco-household

Buy household cleaning products with only natural botanical and mineral ingredients, with no petrochemical detergents, phosphates, optical brighteners, bleaches, synthetic perfumes, or colourings; **buy recycled** loo and kitchen paper; **choose products with reusable packaging**, for example, jam jars and ice-cream cartons can be used for storage around the house, and glass milk bottles can be reused up to 100 times; **use recycling points** supplied by the council for newspapers, glass and plastic bottles, jars, and aluminium cans; **recycle old clothes** and take them to a charity shop; those not good enough to sell can be recycled to make blankets; **use washable nappies** as disposable ones make up 4 per cent of household waste; new styles have velcro and popper fastenings and some have biodegradable liners that can be flushed down the loo; **use cooler wash temperatures** and full loads in the washing machine (the average wash uses 95 litres of water, and a full load uses less water than two half loads), and let clothes dry naturally; **replace washers** in dripping taps – one dripping tap could waste 90 litres of water in one week; **insulate** the attic and lag the hot water tank and pipes to save heat and money; **boil only as much water** as you need in the kettle; **cool water** kept in the fridge is more refreshing and you don't have to run the tap for ages to get a cold drink; **install a water meter** to monitor how much water you use; **turn down the heating** thermostat by 1°C or use 1 hour less heating a day to cut household CO_2 emissions by 5–10 per cent; **salt** will soak up fruit juice, urine, and red wine – pour a large mugful onto the spillage, leave for several hours to absorb, and vacuum or shake out; **borax** (an alkaline mineral salt) loosens dirt and grease and works as an antiseptic; add 1 tablespoon of borax to 5.5 litres water to soak stained clothes and linens, and use half a cup in a bucket of hot water for kitchen cleaning; **a vinegar and water solution** can be used for cleaning the loo; **castor oil** conditions leather boots, saddles, and bags; **citric acid** (found in lemon juice) removes hard-water limescale from the bath and loo, and cleans brass; **a moth deterrent** can be made by putting lavender, cloves, cinnamon, black pepper, and orris root in a muslin bag and placing among clothes; **baking powder** (sodium bicarbonate) removes stains from china, glass, tiles, and the fridge (use as a paste mixed with water); **washing soda** (sodium carbonate) is useful for cleaning and clearing drains; **DIY beeswax polish** is sold in blocks and can be bought from chemists and hardware shops; to make the polish, scrape or grate 30 g beeswax into 140 ml turpentine and leave to dissolve for several days; shake before using and wear gloves when applying; **to restore whiteness** to white cotton socks and other small, white items boil for 5 minutes in water containing a slice of lemon.

household

basic kit for an efficient home

1 wooden airer
Great for flats and other small areas; laundry can dry naturally without taking up too much valuable space.

2 candles
Keep a supply handy in case of power cuts.

3 cotton duster
Can be dampened to whizz round dusty surfaces.

4 doormat
A must for wiping muddy shoes and boots.

5 wicker basket
A rustic-textured and practical laundry room staple.

6 ball of string
An indispensable item that I rate alongside my corkscrew.

7 folding wood and calico laundry basket
Simple, practical, and can easily be carried to and from the washing machine.

8 cotton tea towel
Keep at least half a dozen ready for use.

9 galvanized dustbin
A utilitarian idea for garden or household rubbish.

10 wood and bristle broom
Use to sweep both inside and outside the house.

eco-friendly

recycled, resourceful, and
energy-saving ideas

1

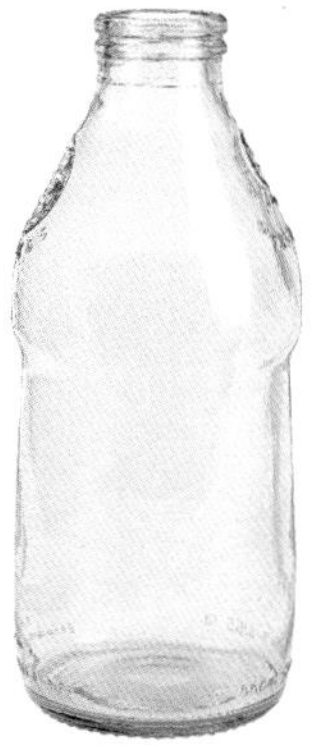

2

3

1 **washing-up brush**
Use brushes with replaceable
heads to save on materials.

2 **milk bottles**
Glass bottles can be recycled
up to 100 times. Return to
the milkman or local shop.

3 **clockwork and solar-
powered radio**
This ingenious design
negates the need for
batteries or electricity.

4 **old newspapers**
Keep old papers for covering
surfaces when painting,
polishing shoes, and lighting
fires. Dispose of them in the
paper recycling bank.

4

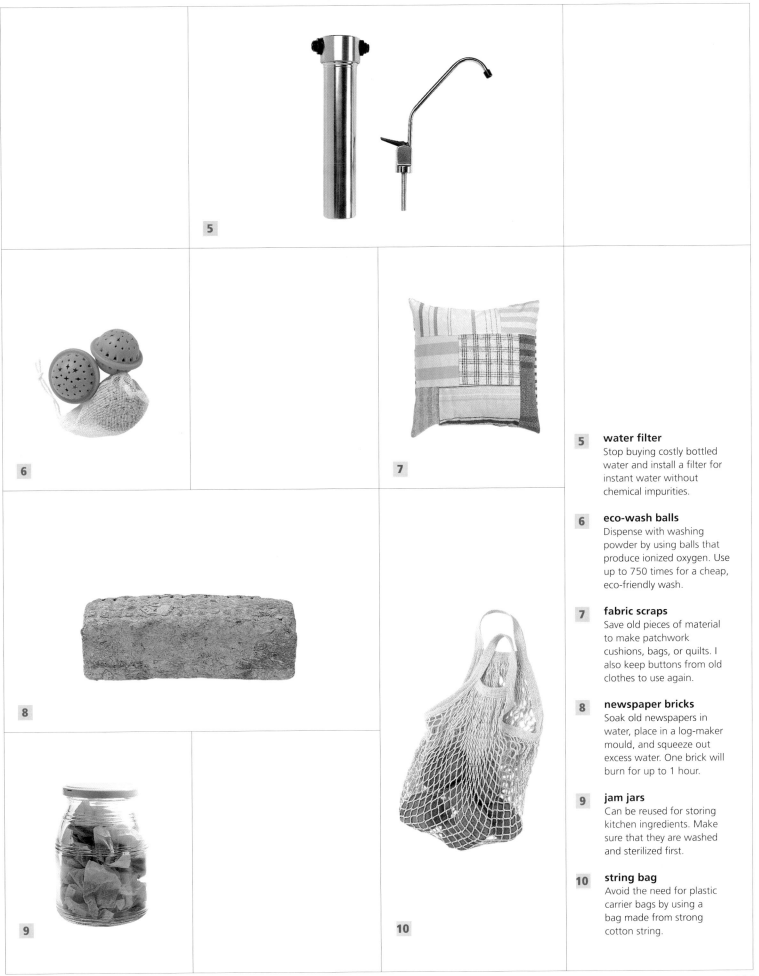

5

6

7

8

9

10

5 **water filter**
Stop buying costly bottled water and install a filter for instant water without chemical impurities.

6 **eco-wash balls**
Dispense with washing powder by using balls that produce ionized oxygen. Use up to 750 times for a cheap, eco-friendly wash.

7 **fabric scraps**
Save old pieces of material to make patchwork cushions, bags, or quilts. I also keep buttons from old clothes to use again.

8 **newspaper bricks**
Soak old newspapers in water, place in a log-maker mould, and squeeze out excess water. One brick will burn for up to 1 hour.

9 **jam jars**
Can be reused for storing kitchen ingredients. Make sure that they are washed and sterilized first.

10 **string bag**
Avoid the need for plastic carrier bags by using a bag made from strong cotton string.

storage

multi-functional crates,
baskets, and shelves

1

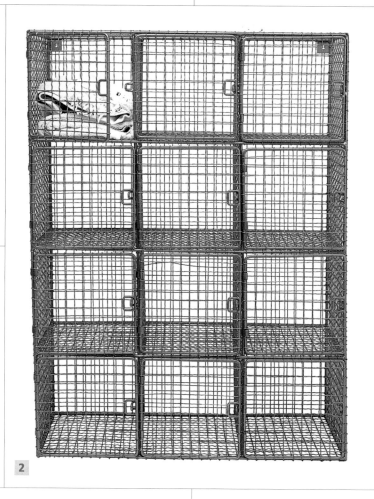

2

1 **collapsible canvas bag**
Pack with bulky jumpers or
extra bedlinen to store out
of sight under a bed.

2 **utilitarian steel mesh
lockers**
Remember these from the
local swimming baths? If you
can find some, they are
excellent for linen, kitchen,
or office storage.

3 **old schoolroom
pigeon-hole unit**
Provides an ideal storage
space for books or files.

3

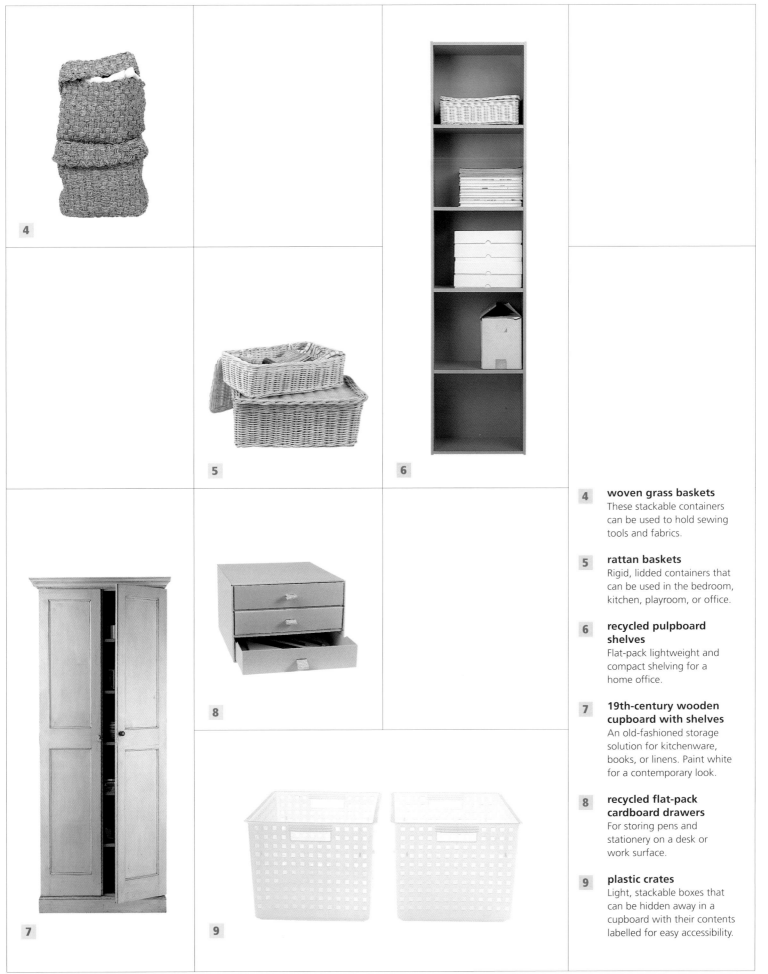

4 **woven grass baskets**
These stackable containers can be used to hold sewing tools and fabrics.

5 **rattan baskets**
Rigid, lidded containers that can be used in the bedroom, kitchen, playroom, or office.

6 **recycled pulpboard shelves**
Flat-pack lightweight and compact shelving for a home office.

7 **19th-century wooden cupboard with shelves**
An old-fashioned storage solution for kitchenware, books, or linens. Paint white for a contemporary look.

8 **recycled flat-pack cardboard drawers**
For storing pens and stationery on a desk or work surface.

9 **plastic crates**
Light, stackable boxes that can be hidden away in a cupboard with their contents labelled for easy accessibility.

seating

flexible shapes for all
around the house

1

3

4

5

1 **metal mesh 1950s chair**
Designed by an Italian, Harry
Bertoia, this is a classic
retro-style chair picked up
in a local second-hand shop.
Its curved back and seat are
really comfortable and it fits
in with both old and new
pieces of furniture.

2 **second-hand country
chair**
An unpretentious chair that
looks at home in both urban
and country spaces.

3 **wooden folding chair**
A traditional village hall and
café design, this seat is great
for work rooms or kitchens.

4 **folding wood/metal
chair**
My favourite shape for
inside and outside eating,
this chair can be folded up
and stored when not in use.

5 **wooden stool**
A versatile piece of domestic
furniture for perching on
while you work, eat, or chat.

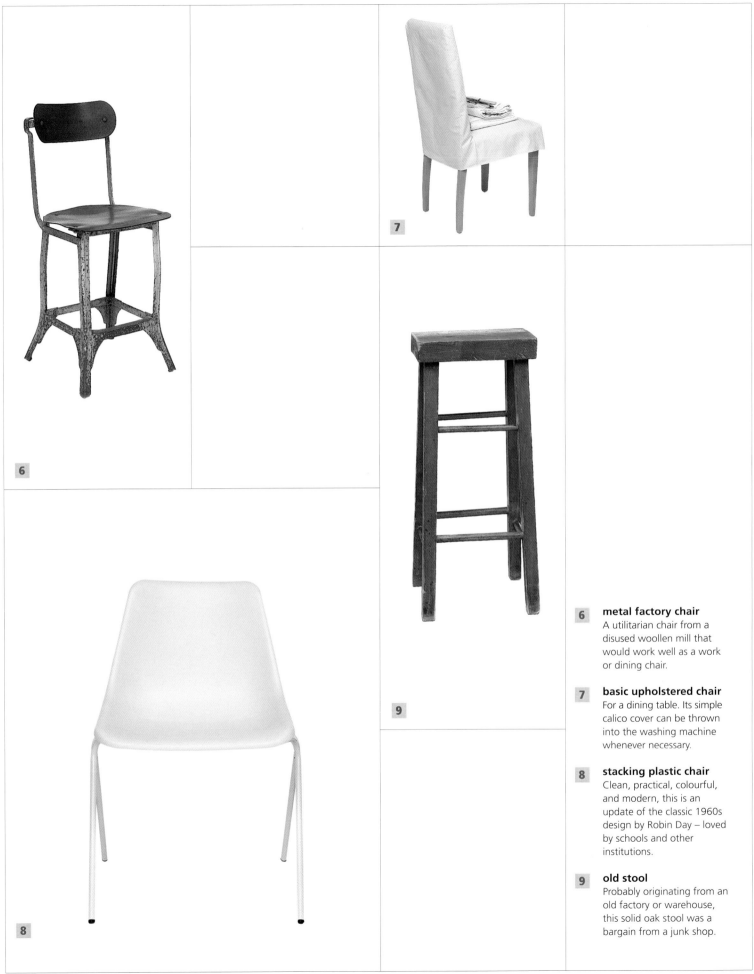

6 **metal factory chair**
A utilitarian chair from a disused woollen mill that would work well as a work or dining chair.

7 **basic upholstered chair**
For a dining table. Its simple calico cover can be thrown into the washing machine whenever necessary.

8 **stacking plastic chair**
Clean, practical, colourful, and modern, this is an update of the classic 1960s design by Robin Day – loved by schools and other institutions.

9 **old stool**
Probably originating from an old factory or warehouse, this solid oak stool was a bargain from a junk shop.

Garden

garden tools

organic produce

pure style flowers

container ideas

Garden data

Gardens are our own little eco-systems, where we can grow nutritious produce and maintain a balance with nature by using organic gardening methods. Making compost from vegetable peelings, eggshells, and even old teabags is an ecological and resourceful way to make the most of household rubbish. It is tempting to use chemical fertilizers that promise rapid rates of growth, but in the long term they can damage the soil structure and their residues are passed into the human body. Equally, chemical pest control can be so effective that it wipes out all bugs in the garden, including useful ones.

Compost

The main source of soil fertility in the organic garden should be recycled organic materials, such as compost and well-rotted manure. Buy **organic compost** and growbags or, better still, make your own **compost heap** using organic household waste. Buy or construct **a compost bin** – ideally made of wire, or plank fencing with ventilation holes; choose or make the largest you can fit into a corner of your garden and place it on earth not concrete. **Keep a bucket** for all organic kitchen waste – fruit and vegetable peelings, tomato skins, eggshells, bread, cereals, tea bags, coffee grounds, and non-animal leftovers; although cooked meat and fish flesh decomposes nicely, it is best avoided as it attracts rats, foxes, and hungry dogs; **dampen** cardboard and newspaper to speed up decomposition before adding to the heap; **use organic material** from outside the garden, for example leaf mould from the park or woods; seaweed from a trip to the beach; leaf sweepings from the street (organic gardeners soon develop an eye for possible compost material); **add different textures** to the heap – woody, grassy, leafy – in alternating layers; **turn the heap** two or three times to add air and generate aerobic activity (that is, activate the oxygen-loving microbes to break down the organic matter); **add nitrogen** in the form of fishmeal to encourage the rotting process further: the compost needs to be very hot for continued decomposition and while young green growth contains enough nitrogen to achieve this heat, dry matter, such as straw, does not; the heat kills most seeds, which is why you don't see tomato plants, apple tree saplings, or even weeds growing out of compost heaps. Once built, cover the heap with a layer of earth and a lid to retain the heat and speed up the rotting process. **Fresh compost can be applied** directly to the soil or dug in according to the garden's needs and the time of year. **Depending on the season** and the weather, a heap 1.5 m high will take between 3 and 6 months to rot down. The complete cycle from food to decomposition and back to food can take as little as two years.

Fertilizers

Overdressing with nitrates and other **artificial fertilizers** leads to soil debility with the result that plants lose their strength. Where supplies of compost are insufficient or there are major deficiencies in the soil, use one or more of the following **organic fertilizers**: bonemeal, which is a slow-release form of organic phosphate that promotes strong root growth; fish, blood, and bone, which contains slow-release nitrogen and phosphate for steady growth and a strong root system; gypsum, a conditioner for heavy clay soils; potash for healthy tomatoes and fruit. Also, **rotate vegetable crops** (that is, don't grow the same crop on the same ground for two years running) to stop the soil becoming depleted of nourishment, which may necessitate the use of chemical fertilizers. **Synthetic pesticides** can do long-term damage as they upset the natural balance of pests and predators; this negative aspect is often overlooked because of the temporary benefits the chemicals produce; in addition, they are toxic to other insects, plants, and humans. **Natural pesticides** include insecticidal soap, which is a liquid soap that kills aphids by dissolving the wax layer on their skins so they dry up and die, and derris with tropical plant derivatives, which kills caterpillars, aphids, trips, and sawfly (don't forget that these insecticides may also kill beneficial insects so use as sparingly as possible).

Pest control

Many plants have chemical defences against pests and disease; by growing them in strategic places or by mixing them with other crops, plant damage can be minimized. For example, **onions** have a fungicidal effect and can be usefully grown between strawberry plants to discourage disease and planted next to carrots to deter carrot fly; **French marigolds** repel a variety of vegetable pests, and interplanted with cabbages and tomatoes **encourage** pollinators and predators; wild flowers attract pollinating bees, which improve fruit yields. **Variety** is the key to attracting wildlife and keeping down pests so don't grow too many plants of the same type close together. **Barriers, traps, and repellents** are all means of keeping pests at bay that don't harm other insects, animals, and humans; for example, bird-scaring tape that hums in the breeze; a good old-fashioned scarecrow; slug and snail tape that repels intruders with a small electric charge; reusable mesh sheet that prevents larger insects from reaching the plants. **Biological pest control** uses one living organism to control another, with no danger to humans, pets, and beneficial insects, such as the mite that feeds on the red spider mite, and a tiny parasitic wasp that lays its eggs in young whitefly.

garden tools

I use an assortment of modern and well-seasoned old implements in the garden

1

2

3

1 **old hoe and fork**
Ideal tools for weeding, digging, and preparing the ground for planting.

2 **besom broom**
For sweeping leaves from grass and stone surfaces.

3 **fine sieve**
For removing stones from soil and rinsing earth off freshly picked cucumbers and other garden produce.

4 **enamelled watering can**
A small can is easy to carry and practical for container plants. Use a hose for general garden watering.

5 **cast aluminium tools**
Easy to clean, compact shapes that can be stored neatly with other garden kit (from left: weeder, fork, trowel, bulb planter).

4

5

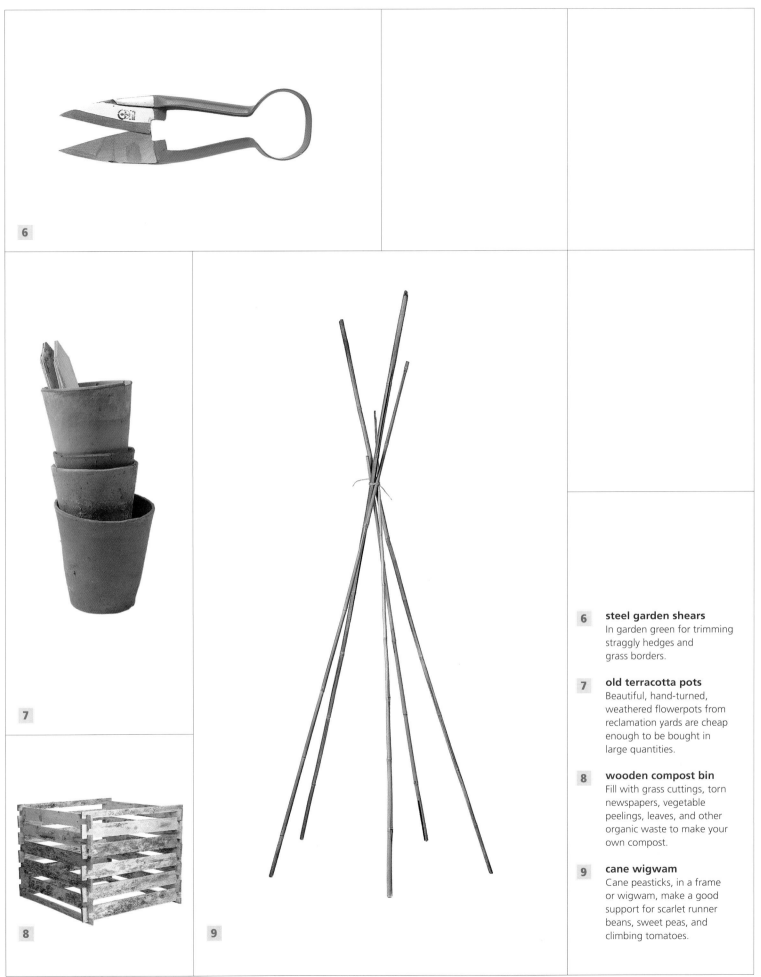

6 **steel garden shears**
In garden green for trimming
straggly hedges and
grass borders.

7 **old terracotta pots**
Beautiful, hand-turned,
weathered flowerpots from
reclamation yards are cheap
enough to be bought in
large quantities.

8 **wooden compost bin**
Fill with grass cuttings, torn
newspapers, vegetable
peelings, leaves, and other
organic waste to make your
own compost.

9 **cane wigwam**
Cane peasticks, in a frame
or wigwam, make a good
support for scarlet runner
beans, sweet peas, and
climbing tomatoes.

organic produce

fruit, vegetables, and herbs from the garden, vegetable plot, and window box

1 **bunch of mint, bay, thyme, and rosemary**
These are favourites for adding flavour to food; grow them in pots on the window-sill or in the garden.

2 **courgettes**
Easy to grow, summer vegetables that come in green and yellow varieties; the flowers can be eaten, too, fried in a light batter.

3 **bramley apples**
Picked from the back garden, cooking apples make perfect autumn fruit crumbles.

4 **gooseberries**
Summer berries for making into jam, wine, and creamy fools.

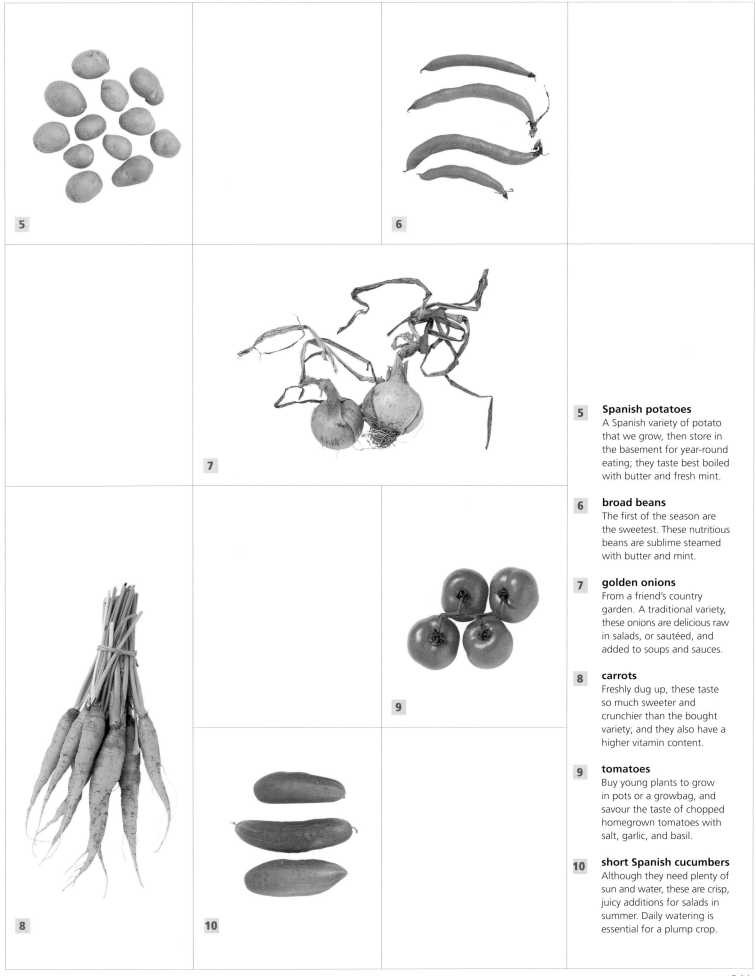

5 Spanish potatoes
A Spanish variety of potato that we grow, then store in the basement for year-round eating; they taste best boiled with butter and fresh mint.

6 broad beans
The first of the season are the sweetest. These nutritious beans are sublime steamed with butter and mint.

7 golden onions
From a friend's country garden. A traditional variety, these onions are delicious raw in salads, or sautéed, and added to soups and sauces.

8 carrots
Freshly dug up, these taste so much sweeter and crunchier than the bought variety; and they also have a higher vitamin content.

9 tomatoes
Buy young plants to grow in pots or a growbag, and savour the taste of chopped homegrown tomatoes with salt, garlic, and basil.

10 short Spanish cucumbers
Although they need plenty of sun and water, these are crisp, juicy additions for salads in summer. Daily watering is essential for a plump crop.

pure style
flowers

grow your own flowers or
visit a flower stall for buds
and blooms to give colour,
scent, and life to the home

1 **allium**
Pink, fluffy balls on tall stems
that look good in metal
buckets. From the onion
family, they also come in
purple, blue, and white.

2 **narcissus**
Buy in bunches for subtle
colour and a heady, fragrant
scent, or grow from bulbs in
the garden or inside in pots.

3 **peony**
To bring back childhood
memories of pink peony
blooms soaked in summer
rain, I buy or pick a few
blowsy heads for the table.

4 **amaryllis**
This is fast growing, especially
if placed in a warm room. I
buy the white variety of this
voluptuous flower, which I
plant in old terracotta pots.

5 **sunflower**
Easy to grow, sunflowers
make dramatic borders,
especially the giant variety
with plate-like heads. In
Spain, we dry the seeds and
nibble them as tapas.

6 **hyacinth**
I grow this heavenly scented
flower indoors from forced
bulbs and outside in warmer
weather in pots on the
patios in Spain. Hyacinths
come in pink, white, and a
deep, purply-blue – probably
my favourite.

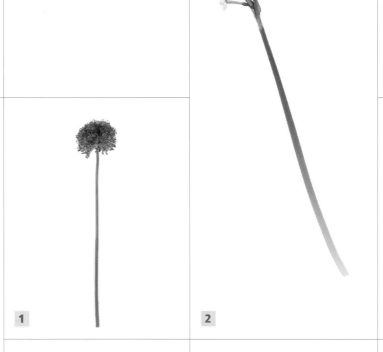

1

3

2

6

4

5

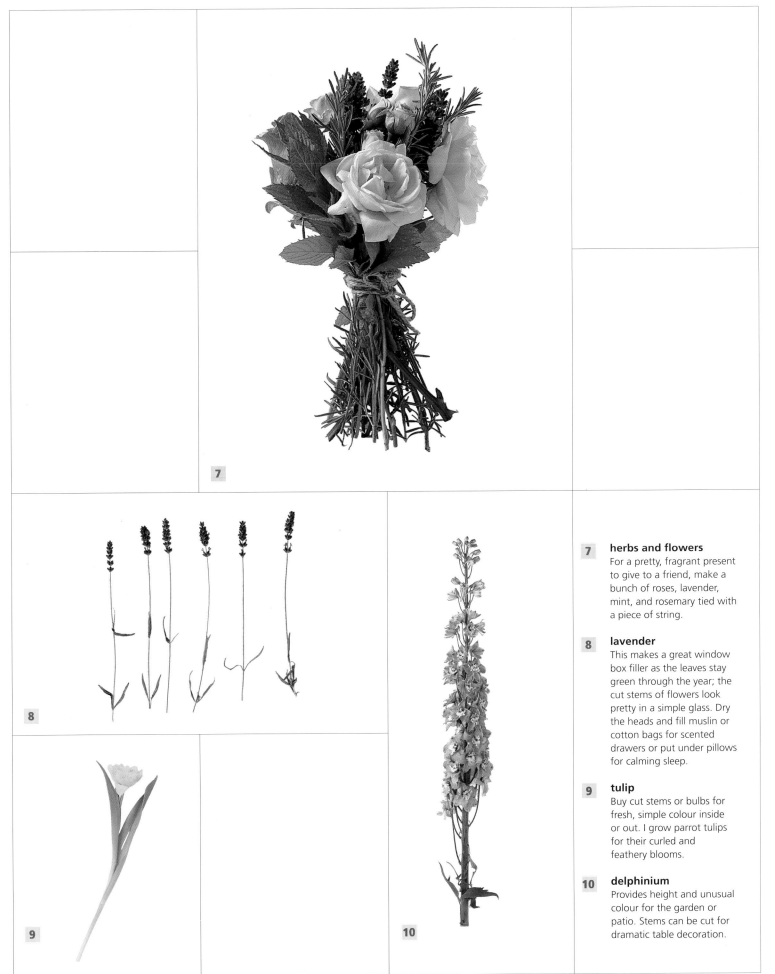

7

8

9

10

7 herbs and flowers
For a pretty, fragrant present to give to a friend, make a bunch of roses, lavender, mint, and rosemary tied with a piece of string.

8 lavender
This makes a great window box filler as the leaves stay green through the year; the cut stems of flowers look pretty in a simple glass. Dry the heads and fill muslin or cotton bags for scented drawers or put under pillows for calming sleep.

9 tulip
Buy cut stems or bulbs for fresh, simple colour inside or out. I grow parrot tulips for their curled and feathery blooms.

10 delphinium
Provides height and unusual colour for the garden or patio. Stems can be cut for dramatic table decoration.

container ideas

flowerpots, boxes, and buckets for patios, yards, and balconies

1

2

3

1 | **wooden window box**
Painted in greeny-blue and planted with lavender, this will bring crisp colour to an urban yard or balcony.

2 | **old terracotta flowerpot**
A small pot is good for nurturing a single bulb. Add a handful of springy moss for a green and earthy effect.

3 | **galvanized steel bucket**
A sturdy, utilitarian container for a miniature olive tree, and other plants suitable for topiary, such as lavender, rosemary, and box.

4 | **galvanized steel window box**
Fill a metal box with daisies for a fresh, modern look.

5 | **modern terracotta pot**
Plant foxgloves in small flowerpots and place in a row along a wall to bring instant, long-lasting colour to your garden.

4

5

6

7

8

6   **old tin can**
Recycle tins to make pots for flowers and herbs; puncture the bottoms with holes for drainage before filling with soil and planting.

7   **natural window box**
A cedarwood container that will weather and look more beautiful and textured with age; plant with rosemary (as here) or lavender for an earthy, organic look.

8   **painted flowerpots**
Paint small pots in different shades of green and plant with lemon verbena, thyme, and other scented herbs.

Rest

seating

fireside accessories

electric lighting

scent

natural lighting

Rest data

For many of us, too much time is taken up with work, either responding to the demands of e-mails, faxes, and phone calls, worrying about office politics, or simply wondering how to make ends meet. It's no wonder that stress-related illnesses are on the increase. We need to remember that taking time off to relax is vital for our mental and physical wellbeing.

Our homes should be refuges from the hurly-burly outside, and we owe it to ourselves to make them as welcoming and as calming as we can. Make time to read a book, to lie back and think about nothing in particular, or stretch out on the sofa to snooze. Rooms to rest in should be peaceful (except for the occasional cathartic burst of opera or loud rock music), with soft comfortable textures. I made sure that one end of our open-plan living space in our London flat should feel snug and homely with comfy chairs and a sofa large enough for us all to flop onto and watch a Saturday night film.

Seating

Choose the biggest sofa you can afford. **A good sofa** should have a solid hardwood frame, with a sprung base and back – the springs are padded with layers of cotton wadding, wool felt, and hair; cheap sofas are foam-filled, and not as durable. **Measure up** before you buy, and not just the space you have available for the sofa – measure the height and width of the front door, and look at narrow corridors, tight corners, and stairs to make sure your sofa can reach its destination. **Cushions** come in different fillings: **feathers** – deliciously soft and cosy, they mould to your shape as you sink in; they need plumping up every day to maintain their shape; **feathers and fibre** – less giving than pure feathers but also less expensive; plump up as for feather-only cushions; **quallofil-foam** – soft and springy, and cheaper, but don't mould to your shape and, therefore, less comfortable. Don't expose sofas directly to **heat sources** – radiators or strong sunlight can cause warping. Sitting on **sofa arms** weakens the structure so avoid at all costs. **Rotate seat and back cushions** weekly to even out wear and fading. To **plump up a cushion**, hold it up in the air, punch from all sides, and finally drop it on the floor to let air filter slowly back into it.

Summer ideas

In the heat of the summer, **airy rooms** should be shuttered during the day to keep out the sun and opened only when the heat has died down later. The **scent of flowers** intensifies in the evening – I have jugs of tuberose and jasmine in Spain. **Make foam-filled cushions** with tough canvas slip-on covers to flop onto for the grass, terrace, or by a swimming pool; when damp, remove covers and dry out. **Wear cool, loose clothing** – linen is best, followed by cotton. **Drink lots of water** – the body quickly dehydrates in the heat, which leads to headaches and irritability. **Put up a makeshift awning** for cool, shady picnics on the beach or at the park (see pp.170–171); choose a dark canvas and secure with rope and old-fashioned tent pegs; it is especially important for babies and small children to be kept out of the sun and they will need hats and high-protection sun cream as well. At the end of the day, **hang strings of lanterns** outside or scatter tealights across a mantelpiece for glowing, flickering light.

Winter ideas

To create warmth and homeliness in the bleaker months, **use natural textures**, such as a woven grass log basket, rough natural matting, wool rugs, and layer sofas in warm, woolly throws and blankets; **warm rooms** with underfloor heating, which is less drying and stuffy than central heating; **keep draughts out** with lined curtains. If you have central heating, **aluminium panels** tucked down behind radiators help to radiate more heat. **Keep yourself warm** with layers of light clothing – wear cotton or silk next to the skin, followed by wool, or polar fleece; keep your feet warm with thick woolly socks. **Build a blazing fire** – it appeals to our primal instincts for warmth and security; **toast marshmallows** and **roast chestnuts** for comforting winter fuel. For **winter scents**, I burn orange-scented candles to mimic the aromatic peel of oranges and tangerines, and fill bowls with dried lavender and rose petal pot-pourri for floral notes. **Make soft glowing pools of light** from low-level lamps – avoid horrors like central overhead lights or naked light bulbs; dark walls absorb more light than pale ones so choose wattage accordingly, and whenever possible use low-energy bulbs – they can give the same intensity of light, last longer, and use less energy than ordinary bulbs.

seating

seats of all sizes in my
favourite neutral shades
with comfort, practicality,
and durability being the
key considerations

1   **junk armchair**
Cover in a plain, white
cotton loose cover to
disguise its origins.

2   **boxy modern sofa**
This creamy yellow sofa
would provide smart seating
in a city loft-style apartment.

3   **1930s second-hand sofa**
A squashy, three-seater
covered in white cotton
loose covers to collapse into
for long afternoon naps.

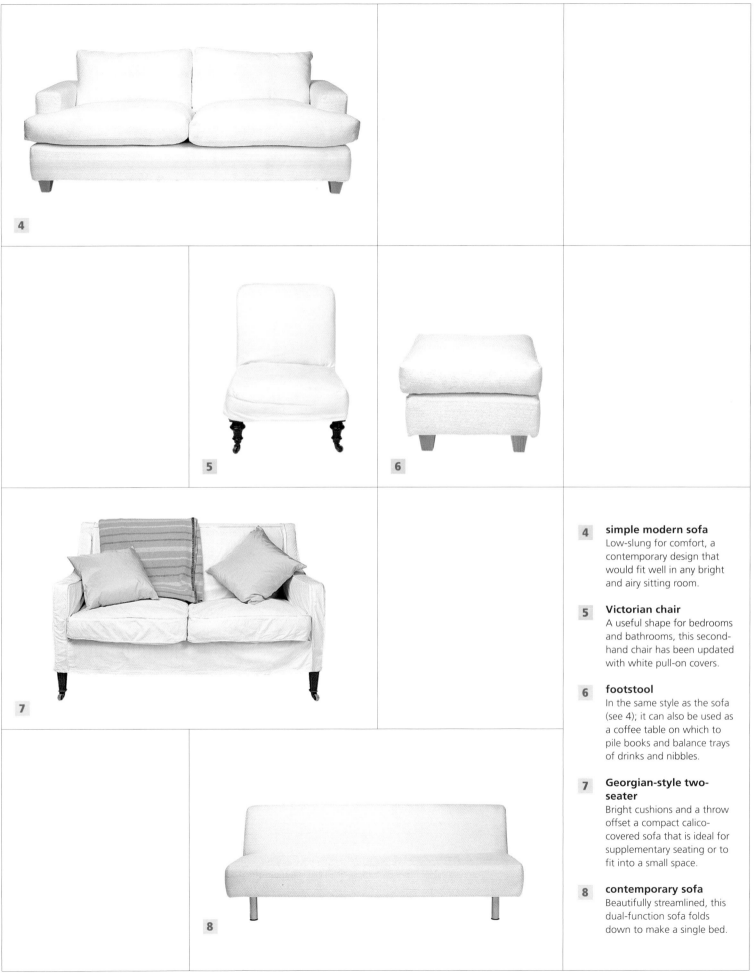

4

simple modern sofa
Low-slung for comfort, a contemporary design that would fit well in any bright and airy sitting room.

5

Victorian chair
A useful shape for bedrooms and bathrooms, this second-hand chair has been updated with white pull-on covers.

6

footstool
In the same style as the sofa (see 4); it can also be used as a coffee table on which to pile books and balance trays of drinks and nibbles.

7

Georgian-style two-seater
Bright cushions and a throw offset a compact calico-covered sofa that is ideal for supplementary seating or to fit into a small space.

8

contemporary sofa
Beautifully streamlined, this dual-function sofa folds down to make a single bed.

fireside accessories

essential equipment for building a blazing fire and other fireside activities

1

2

3

1 **stainless steel pither stove**
Designed to burn smokeless fuel, this is an ecological and stylish choice of home heating for urbanites.

2 **natural toasting fork**
A forked twig from in the garden has been stripped of its bark to use for toasting bread and marshmallows.

3 **poker, tongs, and shovel**
Essential implements for assembling and stoking the fire, and for clearing away the ashes the next day.

4 **metal bucket**
For carrying wood or coal from store to fire, and taking ashes away for disposal.

5 **pile of stacked logs**
Keep logs in a dry place to ensure a good blazing fire, and store in an orderly way to maximize storage space.

4

5

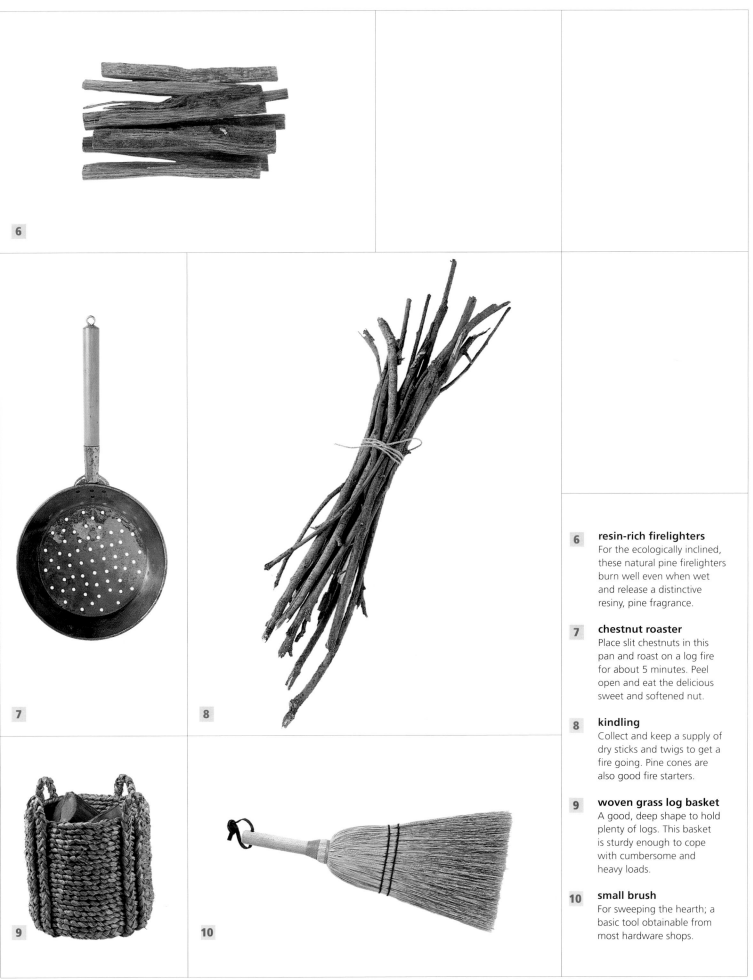

6 **resin-rich firelighters**
For the ecologically inclined, these natural pine firelighters burn well even when wet and release a distinctive resiny, pine fragrance.

7 **chestnut roaster**
Place slit chestnuts in this pan and roast on a log fire for about 5 minutes. Peel open and eat the delicious sweet and softened nut.

8 **kindling**
Collect and keep a supply of dry sticks and twigs to get a fire going. Pine cones are also good fire starters.

9 **woven grass log basket**
A good, deep shape to hold plenty of logs. This basket is sturdy enough to cope with cumbersome and heavy loads.

10 **small brush**
For sweeping the hearth; a basic tool obtainable from most hardware shops.

electric lighting

desk lamps, table lamps, and pendant lights for work, rest, and play

2

1

4

1 **aluminium factory-style pendant light**
A basic shape that is equally at home in the kitchen as in the hallway or workroom.

2 **Philippe Starck's "Miss Sissy"**
Neatly proportioned in translucent plastic, this lamp by the French designer is perfect for a hall or sitting-room table.

3 **reconditioned l930s flexible anglepoise lamp**
Useful for close tasks such as homework, writing, reading, and sewing.

4 **aluminium lampstand with plastic shade**
A modern take on the old-fashioned standard lamp that forms a compromise between overhead and low-level lighting.

3

scent

for a restful and relaxing atmosphere, scent your home with fragrant and natural aromatics

1

2

3

1 **lavender-scented water**
Imparts a delicious scent when sprinkled over freshly ironed bedlinen.

2 **scented candle**
Especially uplifting on a dark winter's evening – my favourite smell is tuberose.

3 **dried rose buds**
Impregnated with a rose-scented oil, these smell almost fresh and look beautiful heaped in simple white bowls.

4 **cedarwood block**
The lovely woody fragrance permeates storage areas and has the benefit of being a natural moth repellent.

5 **incense stick**
Select the perfume of your choice to uplift your spirits or as an antidote to cooking smells in the kitchen.

4

5

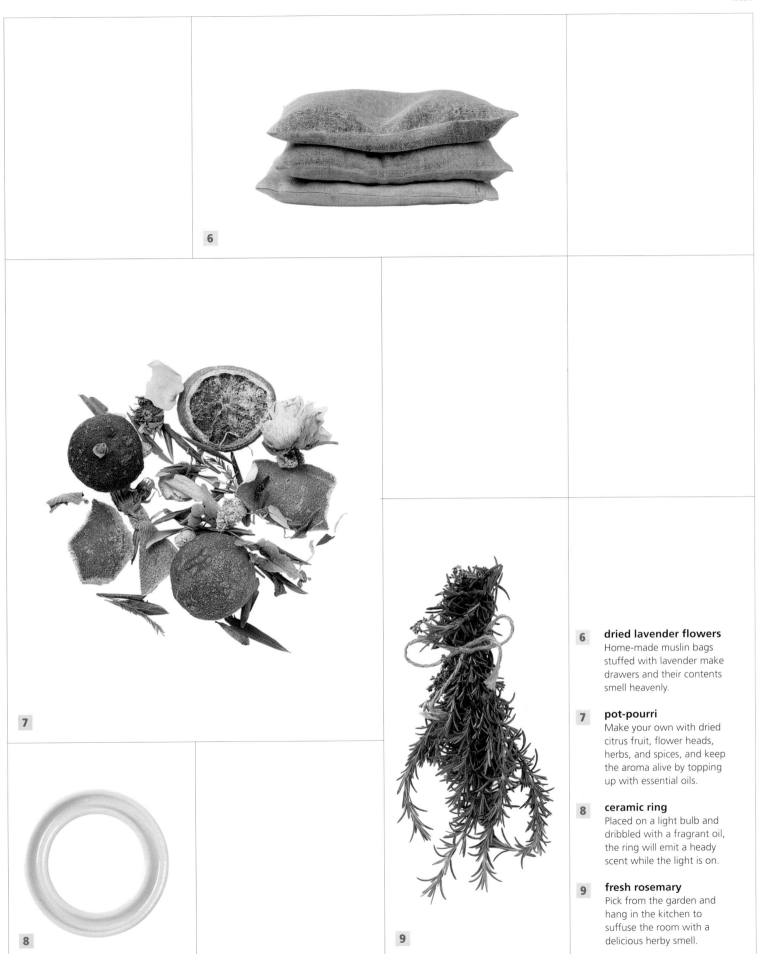

6 **dried lavender flowers**
Home-made muslin bags stuffed with lavender make drawers and their contents smell heavenly.

7 **pot-pourri**
Make your own with dried citrus fruit, flower heads, herbs, and spices, and keep the aroma alive by topping up with essential oils.

8 **ceramic ring**
Placed on a light bulb and dribbled with a fragrant oil, the ring will emit a heady scent while the light is on.

9 **fresh rosemary**
Pick from the garden and hang in the kitchen to suffuse the room with a delicious herby smell.

natural lighting

for moody evenings turn off the electric lights and burn flickering tealights and cream church candles

1

2

3

4

1 **string of aluminium tins**
Filled with tealights, this idea makes the perfect outside lighting for a summer party.

2 **glass storm lantern**
An invaluable asset when you want to sit or eat outside on a windy evening.

3 **traditional metal lantern**
A few strung on wire hung between two trees or put on an outside shelf or wall give ample lighting for a warming winter bonfire party.

4 **tealight in glass jar**
Scatter on a table or line up along a mantelpiece for a magical party atmosphere.

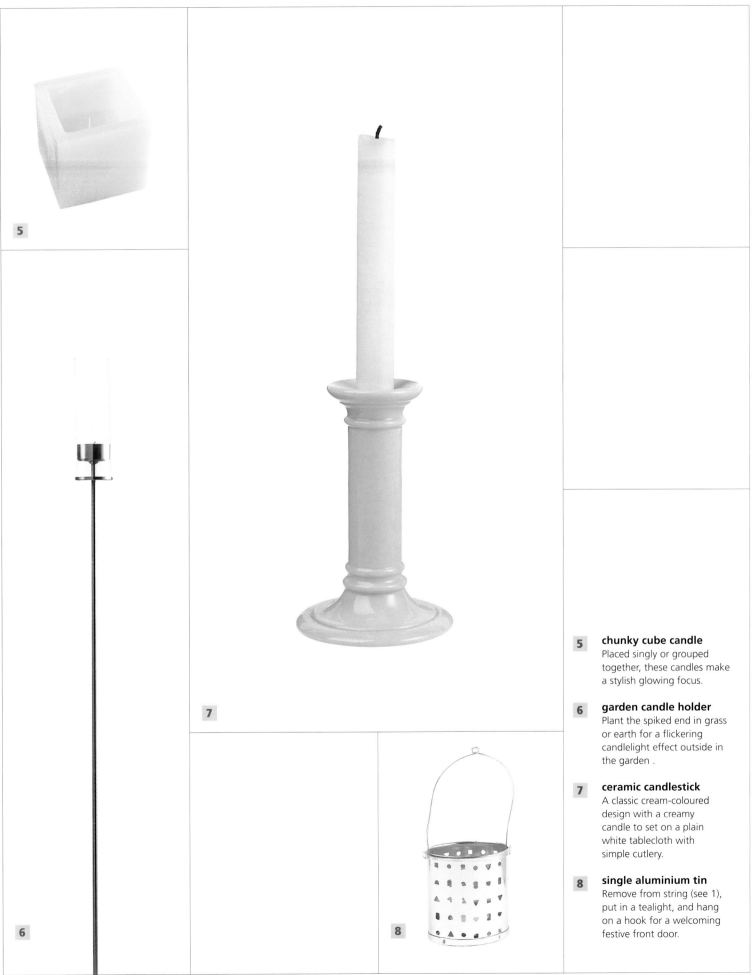

5 **chunky cube candle**
Placed singly or grouped
together, these candles make
a stylish glowing focus.

6 **garden candle holder**
Plant the spiked end in grass
or earth for a flickering
candlelight effect outside in
the garden .

7 **ceramic candlestick**
A classic cream-coloured
design with a creamy
candle to set on a plain
white tablecloth with
simple cutlery.

8 **single aluminium tin**
Remove from string (see 1),
put in a tealight, and hang
on a hook for a welcoming
festive front door.

Play

materials

playtime

Play data

There are plenty of things to do at home that will stimulate and inspire children without incurring extra expense. Empty boxes and cartons can make improvised stables, farms, or garages; dens can be made out of blankets and kitchen chairs; old clothes can be recycled for dressing up; sheets of paper and crayons can be used for drawing: all these activities are more likely to develop creativity than manufactured toys that are complete in every detail. If, like me, you were brought up with that marvellous children's television programme that showed you how to turn a humble washing-up liquid bottle into hundreds of ingenious applications, I am sure you will agree with these old-fashioned sentiments.

Everyday ideas

I keep a supply of paper, felt-tip pens, wax crayons, brushes, poster paints, plain pencils, scissors, and glue for **painting**, **drawing**, **cutting**, and **sticking**. At Christmas, we make potato-cut stamps in star or tree shapes, and coat with paint to print our own wrapping paper and Christmas cards. We also make collages using coloured paper, fabric, and felt, and cut out chains of dancing dolls or Christmas trees from newspapers (see p.202). At Easter, it's time to get out the poster paints and decorate brown eggs with flowers, stripes, and other spring-like patterns (see pp.206–207). When there are about a dozen we pile them into a basket with straw chicks. I encourage the children to **read** anything – from comics to well-known contemporary and classic children's authors. Join the local library to borrow books, audio cassettes, and videos. Also, go to second-hand book stalls and junk shops for cheap paperbacks. For **dressing up**, we keep a big basket of old clothes, including belts, big trousers, grandma's old shirts, and my cast-offs; I have made simple capes from muslin and net for princess games, black capes and tights for superhero fun, and outfits out of white sheets for Halloween ghosts. Living for part of the year in Andalucia means that my daughters embrace the tradition of wearing frilly flamenco dresses at fiestas, and these also become important additions to the dressing-up repertoire. As far as **cooking** is concerned, it's good to start them young but always be around to supervise; my children love to make simple biscuits, using flour, butter, and sugar, or cup cakes or cookies from packets of cake mix; they then decorate them with icing and silver balls – a perfect way to spend a rainy afternoon. Tom, my 12-year-old son, can now rustle up excellent brownies, pancakes, tortillas, and chocolate cake. Try to encourage children to be catholic in their musical taste and expose them to a variety of different types of **music** – opera, classical, reggae, pop, jazz, country, and folk (my children have learnt to appreciate my 1970s heroes, such as Bob Dylan, Neil Young, and Al Green). In addition, if there's an opportunity for your children to learn a musical instrument, make the most of it; start with a basic percussion instrument such as a tambourine, or a recorder.

Parties

The secrets of **successful children's parties** are fizzy drinks, cocktail sausages, crisps, chocolate cake, Madonna blaring in the background, and really good games. The list of party games is infinite, but here are a few of my favourites. **Pass the parcel**: wrap a small prize in layers of newspaper, with a sweet or chocolate secreted in every layer (one for every child); sit children in a circle and pass the parcel round. When the music stops, the child holding the parcel removes one layer and takes the sweet; this continues until one child opens the final layer and claims the prize. **Pin the tail on the donkey**: draw a donkey on a large piece of paper and cut out a separate tail. Blindfold each child – the aim is to pin the tail in the correct position, so the winner is the child who comes nearest to the correct place. **Musical statues**: the children dance until the music stops and everyone has to freeze; those who move are out. Continue until only one contestant remains – the winner (this is good exercise to wear out over-excited children). **Wrap the mummy**: divide children into two teams, each of which is given a loo roll; each team wraps a player in the tissue, and the one who uses up the roll first is the winner (a good Halloween game). **Grandmother's footsteps**: one player stands with his or her face to the wall ("grandmother"); the contestants line up and see who can reach the "grandmother" first; when she turns round the children must freeze and if she catches anyone moving they go back to the starting line. **Apple bobbing**: a traditional Halloween game that can be played all year round. Put eight or nine apples in a large bowl of water; children take turns to see who can grab the most apples with their teeth in a designated time. Although wet and not very hygienic, this game is great fun for participants and onlookers alike. **Potato and spoon race**: each contestant cradles a small potato in a spoon; line up the children and on the order to go, see who can reach the finish without the potato falling off the spoon. **Sack race**: each child stands in a sack or bin bag; the winner is the first to jump to the finishing line.

Holidays

With the right holiday venue, most children will make their own entertainment, but if a new environment isn't enough (or if the weather is foul), here are some ideas. **Keep a diary** – stick in shells, seaweed, tickets, and postcards; **record a whole day** on a roll of film and write captions to the prints; **make a flicker book**; go to the park, **take a picnic**, and play cricket, football, or rounders; have a bonfire or light a disposable barbecue in the back garden and cook sausages and other tasty outside grub; **at the beach**, make sandcastles and decorate with shells and seaweed; have sand-drawing competitions; skim stones across the water; run relay races over the sand; fly a kite; learn to body surf (check the currents, don't let your children go out of their depth, and constantly supervise); collect shells to take home and stick on card to make pictures.

materials

let your children show their creativity with crayons, paints, ribbons, and bright tissue paper

1

2

1 **stick-on stars**
Great for making Christmas cards, decorating labels, and for sticking on incentive charts for good behaviour and other character forming-habits.

2 **ribbons and braids**
Can be cut up and pasted on cards to decorate them. Velvet ribbon makes a classy trim for napkins, bags, cardigans, and skirts.

3 **felt-tip colouring pens**
Store in old jam jars and keep in the kitchen for the children to use when they please. The washable varieties are definitely best.

4 **brown parcel paper**
Makes cheap yet stylish packages when tied with a brightly coloured ribbon.

3

4

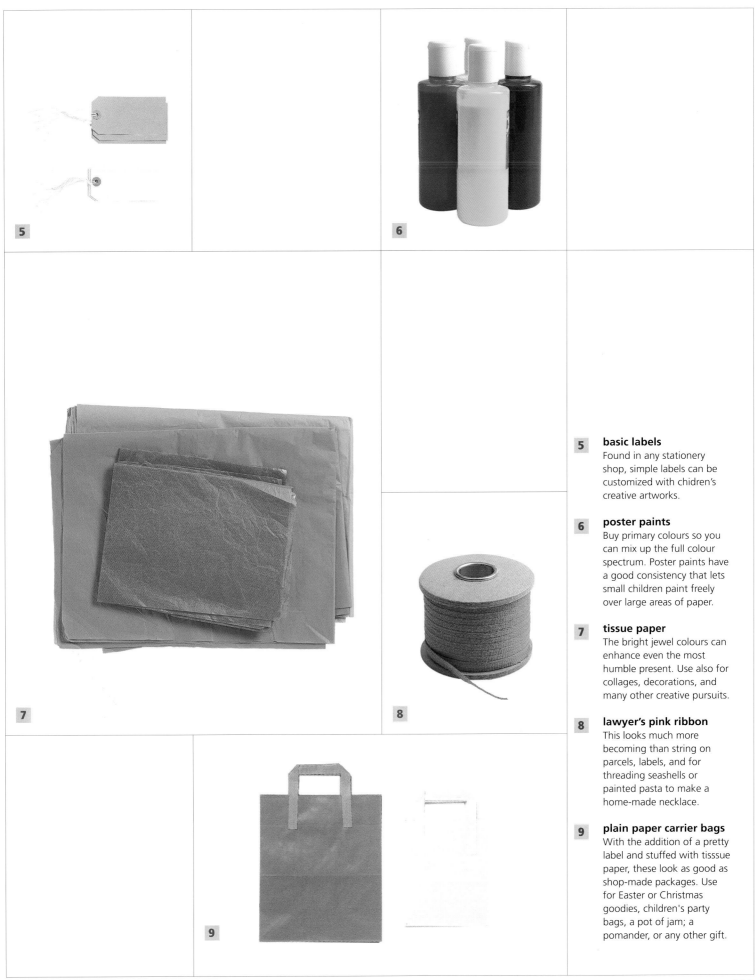

5 **basic labels**
Found in any stationery shop, simple labels can be customized with chidren's creative artworks.

6 **poster paints**
Buy primary colours so you can mix up the full colour spectrum. Poster paints have a good consistency that lets small children paint freely over large areas of paper.

7 **tissue paper**
The bright jewel colours can enhance even the most humble present. Use also for collages, decorations, and many other creative pursuits.

8 **lawyer's pink ribbon**
This looks much more becoming than string on parcels, labels, and for threading seashells or painted pasta to make a home-made necklace.

9 **plain paper carrier bags**
With the addition of a pretty label and stuffed with tisssue paper, these look as good as shop-made packages. Use for Easter or Christmas goodies, children's party bags, a pot of jam; a pomander, or any other gift.

playtime

a selection of ideas to fuel busy young minds and hands and to spark off further imaginative projects

1

2

3

4

5

1 **gummed paper squares**
Cut into shapes and stick on paper to make colourful pictures and collages. Hours of fun can be had by anyone old enough to use a pair of blunt children's scissors.

2 **pretty lantern**
Make an original lantern by sticking a hand-decorated label on an old jam jar, and place a nightlight inside. Add a string handle.

3 **salt dough**
An easy-to-make modelling material that can be cut into all kinds of shapes. Leave to set, and then paint and decorate.

4 **bucket and spade**
Making sandcastles at the beach or in a sandpit gives endless pleasure to children and grown-ups alike.

5 **pair of castanets**
Try some music. Castanets can be played alone or along with other instruments.

6

7

8

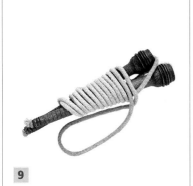

9

10

6 **painted pillowcase**
Children can customize bed-linen or a T-shirt with acrylic felt-tip fabric pens. Iron the design to make it indelible.

7 **rag doll**
Although simple to sew from remnants of fabric and wool, children may need help with the basic pattern for the body and clothes.

8 **tennis ball**
Learning to throw and catch a small ball helps a child to develop and strengthen their co-ordination.

9 **skipping rope**
One of the oldest childhood pursuits, skipping is still a top playground choice and is perfect aerobic exercise.

10 **solid poster paints**
A palette of six colours to inspire artistic creativity. Solid paints are most suitable for older age-group children.

Wash

bathroom fittings

bathroom accessories

bathroom kit

bathroom linen

Wash data

White ceramic surfaces, natural wood and cotton textures, lashings of hot water, and warm, dry, cotton towels are my key bathroom requirements. Kitting out the bathroom and organizing plumbing arrangements can be extremely costly if you go down the route of hi-tech showers, made-to-measure baths, and the latest designer accessories. But if you are prepared to hunt around for basic bath kit in high street showrooms, reclamation specialists, and builders' merchants you can still create a sensual and comfortable bathroom space.

Baths

Although demanding of water, enamelled cast-iron, roll-top baths are durable, heat insulating, and resistant to scratches, cracks, and stains; freestanding on ball-and-claw feet, their deep, curvy proportions provide a luxurious way to take a long hot soak. These baths need sturdy floors to support their own weight, plus the bather, and a bath full of water. **Enamelled** steel baths, coated with vitreous enamel and fired to give a hard finish, are strong and hard wearing, relatively cheap, and available from basic builders' merchants; **acrylic** baths are lightweight, easier to install than cast-iron baths, warm to the touch, less slippery than metal, and stain resistant, but they will scratch easily. Both acrylic and enamelled steel shapes need a supportive frame, which can be boxed in with tiles or wood; **choose a long bath**, as it's much more comfortable for stretching out; **showers in baths** can be contained within a shower curtain – a clear, plastic one is plain and simple; wash and scrub regularly to keep damp and mould at bay. **Dripping taps** waste water and create **limescale stains**; replace the washers as soon as possible. To remove **tidemarks** from an enamel bath, fill with hot water and add several cupfuls of washing soda; swill the solution around the bath and leave overnight. Next morning, work over the whole bath with a stiff cleaning brush. **To remove limescale**, apply a mixture of equal parts of hot vinegar and salt with a toothbrush, and leave until it can be scrubbed off. **Rust marks** can be bleached out with a paste made from salt and lemon juice. Spread the paste over the stain and moisten with more lemon juice for a day or two, then wipe away.

Showers

Showers can range from a simple hand set fitted to the bath taps to a state-of-the-art walk-in room with a drained, sloping floor that serves as a large shower tray. If you are planning such a room, bear in mind that waterproofing a floor needs expert advice. A decent shower depends on an **adequate flow of water** (water pressure varies between areas) and an even water temperature. There are **low- and high-pressure shower** fittings; low-pressure systems rely on the tank in the loft, but they don't deliver a strong flow; high-pressure systems, which give a better shower performance, are used with a combination boiler or unvented or pumped systems. In the UK, it's probably necessary to install a pump in order to ensure a good strong flow of water. **If installing a power shower**, you will probably need to notify the water company (depending on your system). Conservationists encourage us to take showers instead of baths in order to save water, but water usage can be as great with a power shower as with a bath. Depending on the type of shower and for how long it is used, a quick shower can save the 25 litres needed for a bath, but an 8-minute power shower, delivering a therapeutic deluge, uses more water than a bath. To overcome this wastage, some manufacturers make **showers with eco-options** that reduce consumption. Check with the supplier that all shower components – valves, pumps, and the actual shower fittings – are compatible with each other. Showers are either surface-mounted or concealed; for a concealed system, you need to insert the plumbing before the wall surfaces are put in place. To **conceal shower pipes**, the walls need to be at least 7.5 cm thick. Modern thermostatic showers can be encased in period-style bodies, which is ideal if you like old-fashioned, large, rose shower heads.

Flooring

Whatever is used – stone, wood, cork, rubber – it must be sealed or fitted with efficient drainage. Avoid carpet and natural coverings, such as sisal, as they are prone to rot. Use cotton bath mats to soak up water as marble and stone can be slippery; hardwoods, such as teak, are good for shower floors and bath mats. Ceramic tiles with a matt finish in sea blues and green colours are practical together with plain terracotta slabs (provided that the floor has adequate support). Consider installing underfloor heating for warm bathroom floors.

Reclamation

Salvage yards sell a variety of utilitarian and functional 19th- and early 20th-century baths, taps, and other bathroom fittings; reclamation yards are also a good hunting ground for baths, showers, and fittings removed from schools, hotels, and other institutions that are being demolished or updated.

Ventilation

Open windows to let out steam and prevent condensation, which will produce black mould that can cause walls, window frames, and floors to rot. If the bathroom is windowless, install an extractor fan.

bathroom fittings

plain, functional baths and basins, gleaming ceramic surfaces, and gushing hot water are requisites for my bathroom

1

2

1 **early 20th-century cast-iron roll-top bath**
A reclaimed bath brought right up to date with a re-enamelled lining.

2 **modern white ceramic shower tray**
A basic and inexpensive solution for the shower.

3 **1920s French ceramic pedestal basin**
A traditional freestanding white sink for any style of bathroom.

4 **unglazed ceramic mosaic tiles**
In a shower interior or above a bath these need to be protected with a matt sealer.

5 **early 20th-century nickel shower fitting**
Probably rescued from a grand old hotel, this fitting delivers a good flow of water.

3

4

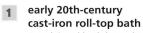

5

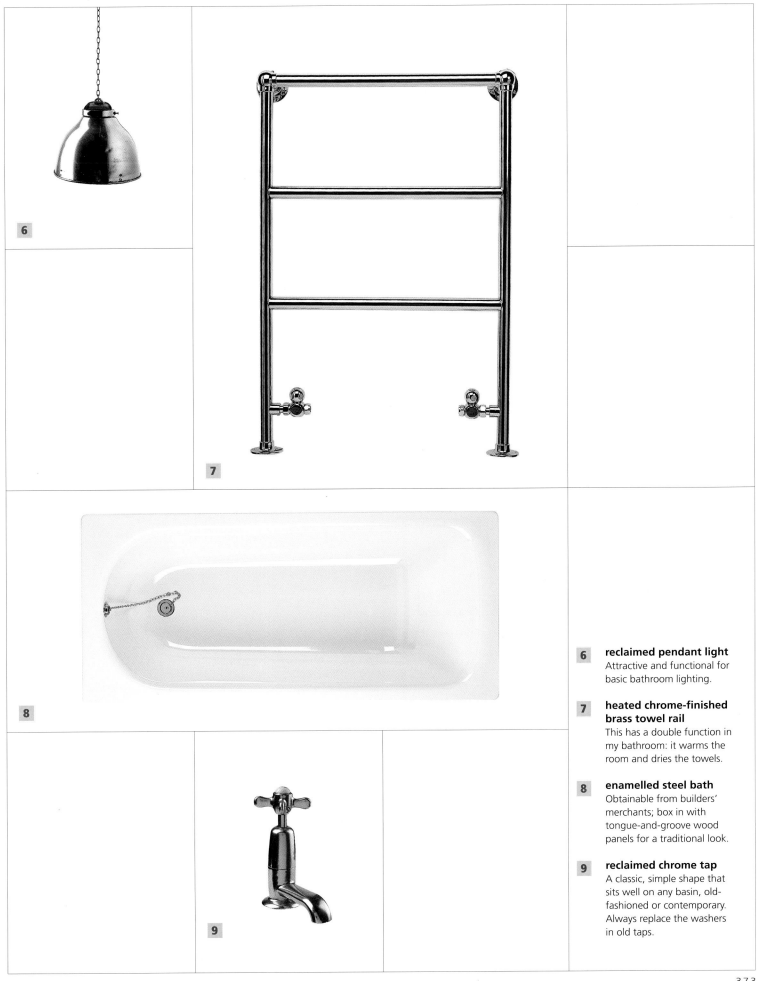

6

7

8

9

6 **reclaimed pendant light**
Attractive and functional for
basic bathroom lighting.

7 **heated chrome-finished
brass towel rail**
This has a double function in
my bathroom: it warms the
room and dries the towels.

8 **enamelled steel bath**
Obtainable from builders'
merchants; box in with
tongue-and-groove wood
panels for a traditional look.

9 **reclaimed chrome tap**
A classic, simple shape that
sits well on any basin, old-
fashioned or contemporary.
Always replace the washers
in old taps.

bathroom accessories

tactile surfaces for bathrooms in wood, metal, and natural fibres

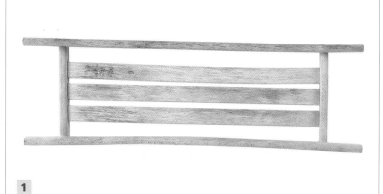

1

2

3

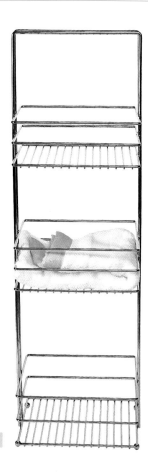

4

5

1 wooden bath rack
Ideal for housing soaps and flannels. Scrub down regularly to prevent mould forming on the damp wood.

2 simple kitchen glass
This makes a good tooth-brush holder and looks better than the typical plastic type.

3 white ceramic soap dish
A plain but functional and essential bathroom ingredient.

4 vertical wire rack
Provides stylish storage for smaller items, such as soaps, lotions, towels, and flannels.

5 drawstring canvas bag
Quick to make, and perfect for storing dirty laundry until wash day (see pp.226–227).

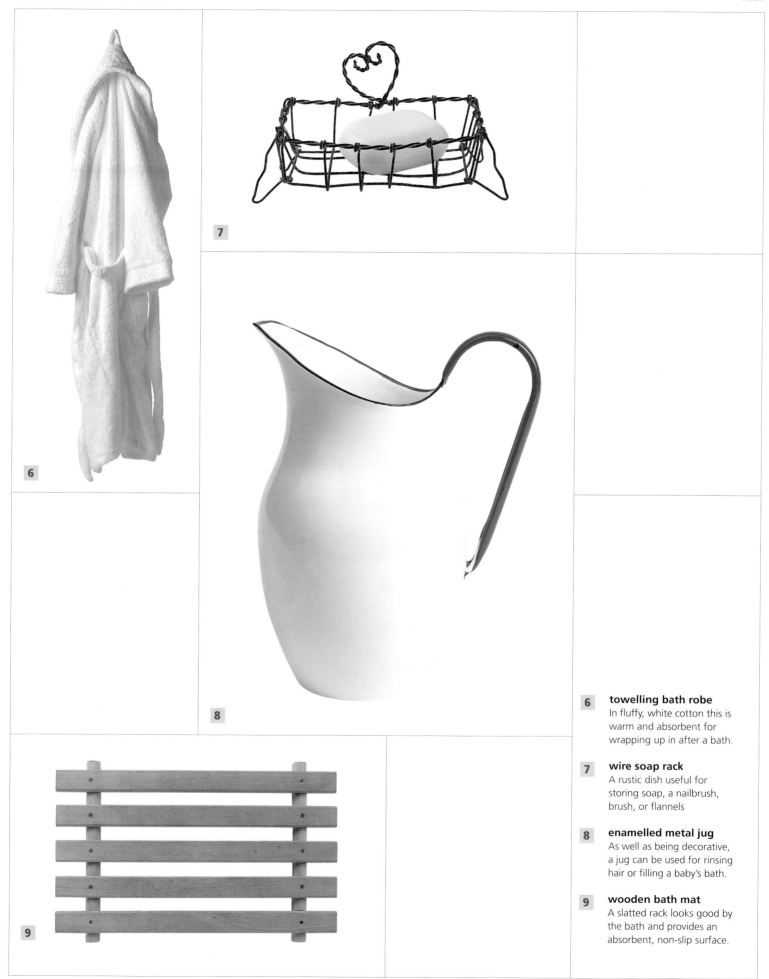

6   **towelling bath robe**
In fluffy, white cotton this is
warm and absorbent for
wrapping up in after a bath.

7   **wire soap rack**
A rustic dish useful for
storing soap, a nailbrush,
brush, or flannels

8   **enamelled metal jug**
As well as being decorative,
a jug can be used for rinsing
hair or filling a baby's bath.

9   **wooden bath mat**
A slatted rack looks good by
the bath and provides an
absorbent, non-slip surface.

bathroom kit

soaps, lotions, and pampering tools for bathtime

1

1 **pure vegetable soaps**
Choose natural plant extracts and rich, earthy colours for bathroom soaps.

2 **pretty bottles**
Filled with a favourite cologne or bath oil. Mine is a delicious, spicy, orange scent from Spain that I decant into old liqueur bottles.

3 **soft face brush**
Made from Japanese hinoki wood (with antibacterial properties). Use for exfoliating and removing the day's accumulated dirt.

4 **natural sponge**
For a soft and lathery skin wash. Always rinse thoroughly after using to prolong the sponge's life.

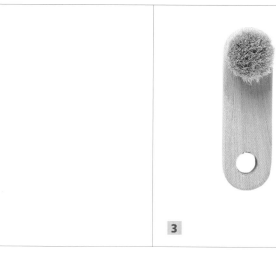

2

3

4

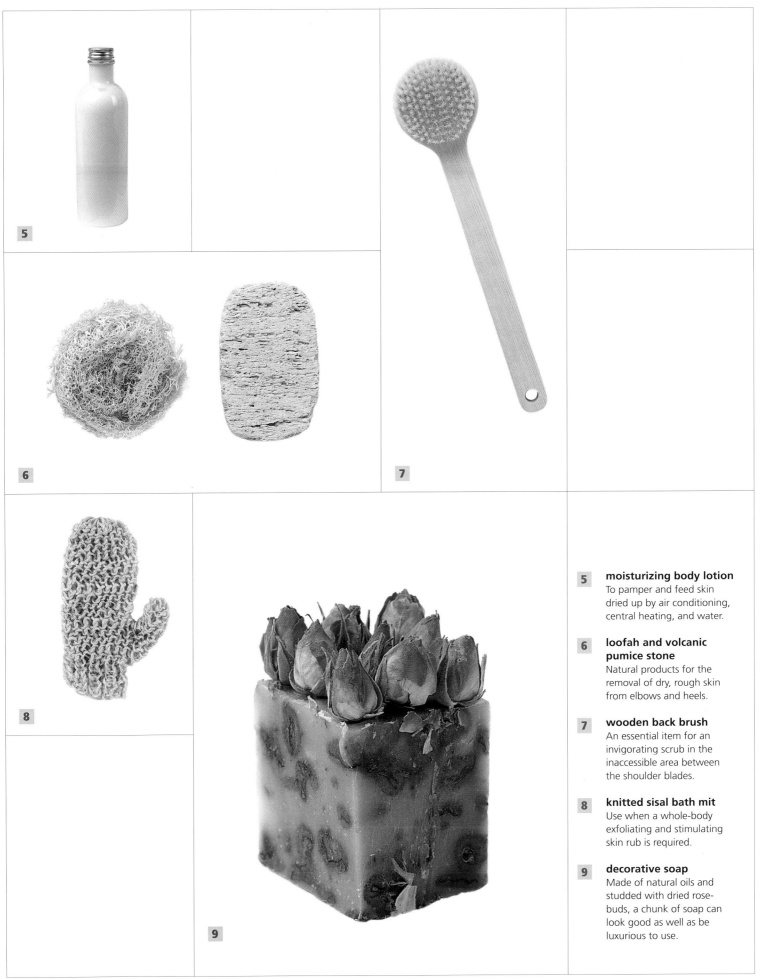

5   **moisturizing body lotion**
To pamper and feed skin
dried up by air conditioning,
central heating, and water.

6   **loofah and volcanic
pumice stone**
Natural products for the
removal of dry, rough skin
from elbows and heels.

7   **wooden back brush**
An essential item for an
invigorating scrub in the
inaccessible area between
the shoulder blades.

8   **knitted sisal bath mit**
Use when a whole-body
exfoliating and stimulating
skin rub is required.

9   **decorative soap**
Made of natural oils and
studded with dried rose-
buds, a chunk of soap can
look good as well as be
luxurious to use.

bathroom linen

piles of fluffy, white cotton
towels for daily bathtime,
and crisp linen hand towels
to pamper friends who
come to stay

1 **edged cotton bath mat**
A warm and absorbent mat
for feet just out of the bath.

2 **textured cotton mat**
Use by the bath or basin,
and keep pristine with a hot
machine wash every two or
three days.

3 **finely woven Indian
cotton towel**
Very light and easily dried,
this towel doubles up as a
sarong, beach throw, or
picnic cloth when travelling.

4 **white cotton towels**
A border of natural linen
adds a touch of colour and
texture to plain towels.

5 **white cotton bath towel**
An essential item for any
stylish bathroom; stock up
at sale time.

6 **knobbly cotton mat**
The heavy texture of this mat
will stimulate the soles of
your feet after a bath.

7 **rough linen hand towel**
Although expensive, linen is
a very hardwearing fabric,
ideal for the bathroom.

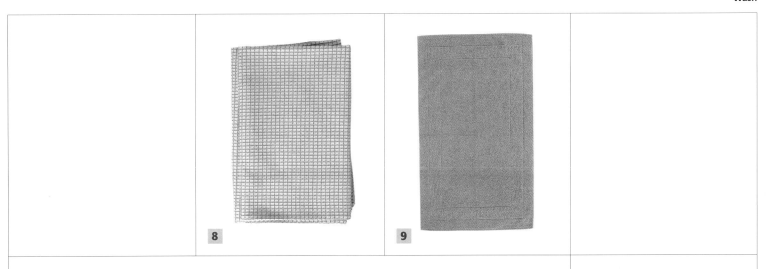

8

9

10

8 **blue-check waffle cotton towel**
Lends a cool, rough texture that is best for summer use.

9 **blue cotton bath mat**
A sea-blue mat to go with the blue-check towel in a holiday bathroom.

10 **linen hand towel**
The ultimate pure style luxury, white linen is perfect for drying hands.

Sleep

beds

bedding basics

bedlinen

bedroom accessories

Sleep data

We are born in bed and die in bed. In between, beds are our havens and retreats from everyday life; a comfort zone layered with soft blankets and crisp cotton sheets. It is here that we stretch out, relax, sleep, make love, work, and play.

The earliest beds were improvised affairs: mediaeval people slept on DIY mattresses of straw ropes and sticks. A woman in labour was known as the "lady in the straws" – a reference to the disposable straw beds on which women delivered their babies. Sailors slept on sacks of waxed linen stuffed with feathers, which could even float if the ship went down. Contemporary bedding needs are no different, demanding practicality, durability, and comfort.

Throughout history beds have been dressed in as many different ways as sartorial fashions have varied, from elaborate four-posters draped in sumptuous brocade hangings favoured by the rich in the 17th and 18th centuries to plain, plaid-covered painted wooden beds in 19th-century Sweden.

Beds

The most basic bed is a **divan** – a mattress placed on a sprung box base. Simple, painted **wooden or metal bed frames** with slats on which to rest a mattress are also comfortable. For small spaces, consider a **futon** mattress, which can be rolled up and stowed in a cupboard during the day. When friends stay, a **folding metal-framed bed** is useful, and a makeshift bed of blankets and sofa cushions on the floor can be warm and cosy. Think big – larger beds are more comfortable. A **single bed** should be at least 10–15 cm longer than the sleeper and at least 90 cm wide. A 135-cm standard **double bed** – not much bigger than a child's bed – accommodates two adults 168 cm tall, which is acceptable if you like being close to your sleeping partner, but not if he or she is restless and snores. Since the main purpose of a bedroom is for sleeping it might be worth sacrificing floor space for the comforts of a large bed to curl up in at night. For good **feng shui**, the Chinese recommend a shared large mattress rather than two twin mattresses lying side by side, and a bed with rounded corners is thought to take the edges off a rocky marriage. The Chinese also believe that during pregnancy you shouldn't dust under a bed or move it if you want to avoid a miscarriage; also, a bed facing east means family life will be happy, rewarding, and peaceful.

Mattresses

Buy for **support and comfort** – not just firmness – for your weight and build. We spend over 29,000 hours on a mattress during its l0-year lifespan so it's important to choose the best you can afford to keep back problems at bay. Most modern mattresses have a **spring interior**; as a rough guide, the more springs the better the support. Spring interiors come in different types: **open springs** – rows of coiled springs joined by a helical wire, which are used mainly in budget beds; although also found in more expensive mattresses, when the spring count is usually higher; **continuous springs** – a variation on open springs that uses one length of wire to knit the spring unit together; usually found at the better-quality end of the market in mattresses with a higher spring count; **pocket springs** – small springs separately housed in fabric pockets so they operate independently for more individual support; these vary in quality and number of springs. **Foam mattresses** have a reputation for being cheap and nasty but have been improved in recent years; performance and price can vary depending on design and quality. **Latex mattresses** are resilient, and don't need to be turned regularly. Old-fashioned, hard-wearing striped ticking makes the best covering for most types of mattress.

Sleep

Make the bed with **natural fibres**, such as cotton and linen, which do not retain moisture and have a cooling effect; synthetics, such as nylon, don't breathe and release static. Cotton cellular blankets are good for regulating the temperature in children's and babies' rooms; wool blankets are cosy in cold weather. Invest in a good duvet and pillows – goose-down is the lightest and warmest filling; anti-allergenic fillings offer an alternative for asthmatics. The **ideal room temperature** is l6–l8°C; a hot, stuffy bedroom is uncomfortable and it's better to wrap up in a cool, ventilated one. **Ear-plugs** cut out disturbances – dogs barking, traffic, or noisy neighbours. **Take exercise** to tire you, but not too close to bedtime to avoid overstimulation; **don't drink or eat** late at night: alcohol sends you to sleep initially but interrupts sleep later, and digesting food is very disruptive. If you are **stressed**, take your mind off your problems and make lists of things to do the next day; **relax and have a bath**; read a good novel; keep the lighting low; listen to soothing music or a story on the radio – all good for relaxing body and mind to induce restful sleep.

beds

the best shapes with crisp bedlinen for comfort and peaceful slumber

1

2

1 hospital-style, metal double bed
A utilitarian shape with simple contemporary detailing which would look good in an urban flat.

2 painted pine double bed
Painted in a stone colour with a mat finish. This is a great shape for both modern and period bedrooms

3 pine, low-level double bed
Dress-up a basic frame with a luxurious wool blanket or throw.

3

4

**painted Swedish-style
single box bed**
A good spare or child's
bed that looks at its best
with crisp cotton sheets
and blankets.

5

single futon
A versatile sleeping solution
for small spaces; roll up
and stow away during
the day.

bedding basics

my vital ingredients for
a good night's sleep are a
firm, unyielding mattress,
soft, malleable pillows, and
a light, goose-down duvet

1

2

3

1 **duck-feather and down all-season duvet**
The ultimate in versatility, this comprises two duvets that can be used singly in warm or cool temperatures and buttoned together when it's very cold.

2 **hand-tufted, open-spring, firm mattress**
Stuffed with cotton and wool felt and covered with classic cotton ticking, this sprung mattress gives good back support.

3 **pillow fillings**
A range of pillow stuffings is available to suit most needs (from top: anti-allergenic synthetic filling; goose-down and feather mix; luxurious goose-down).

4 **feather and down bolsters**
Longer, thinner, and bulkier alternatives to pillows. Use during pregnancy as a good tummy support (lie sideways with the bolster wedged between your legs).

4

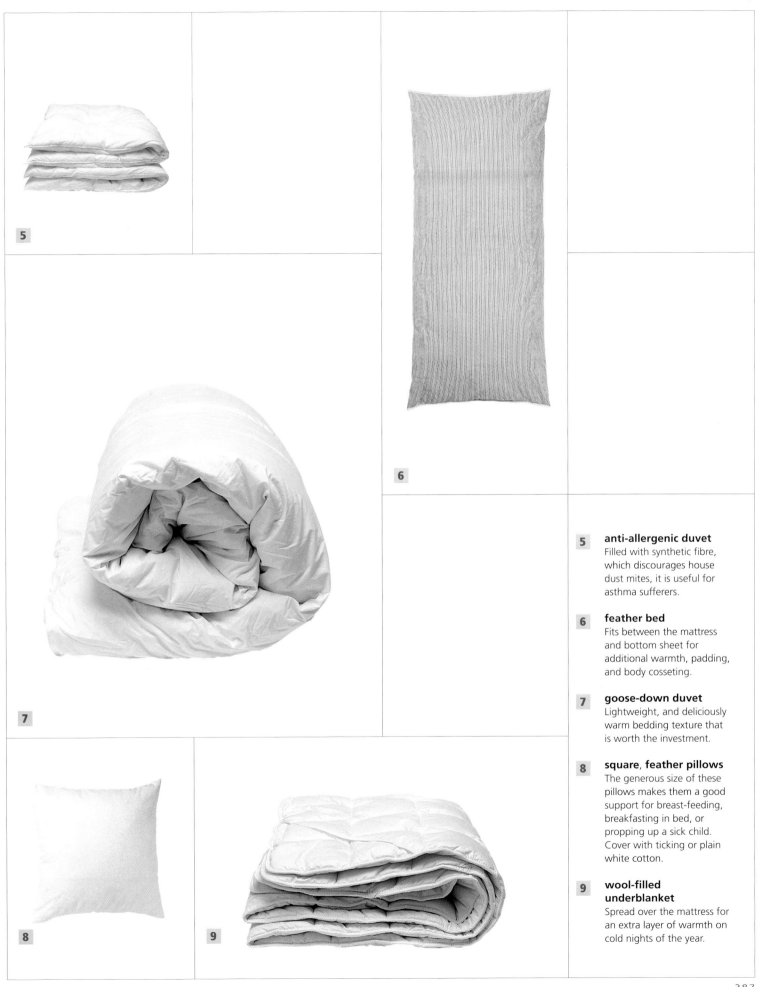

5 **anti-allergenic duvet**
Filled with synthetic fibre,
which discourages house
dust mites, it is useful for
asthma sufferers.

6 **feather bed**
Fits between the mattress
and bottom sheet for
additional warmth, padding,
and body cosseting.

7 **goose-down duvet**
Lightweight, and deliciously
warm bedding texture that
is worth the investment.

8 **square, feather pillows**
The generous size of these
pillows makes them a good
support for breast-feeding,
breakfasting in bed, or
propping up a sick child.
Cover with ticking or plain
white cotton.

9 **wool-filled
underblanket**
Spread over the mattress for
an extra layer of warmth on
cold nights of the year.

bedlinen

scrumptious bedding
textures in linen, cotton,
and wool are essential for
bedroom comfort

1

2

3

1 **worn and washed linen**
This feels extra-soft next to
the skin, and can be picked
up cheaply in markets,
second-hand stores, and
junk shops.

2 **cotton jersey bedlinen**
Soft, warm and cosy
when the nights are cold and
very long.

3 **tactile wool and linen**
Covers in neutral colours
come in a variety of weights
to suit all temperatures.

4 **set of linen sheets**
Costs a king's ransom, but
luxurious and tough. If
looked after the sheets
will last a lifetime.

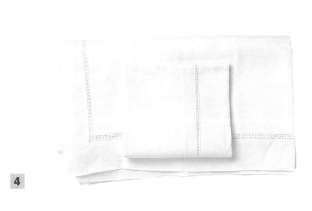

4

5 wool blankets and throws
These look good layered on the bed and can be removed or added to depending on individual needs.

6 crisp, white cotton bedlinen
Whether it is the height of summer or the depths of winter, cotton feels good next to the skin.

7 checked and striped blankets
Key ingredients for adding colour, simple pattern, and texture.

8 cotton flannel sheets
Inexpensive, warm, and comforting, flannel sheets are a favourite with children.

9 knitted bed textures
To give a snug, homely feel to any bedroom (from top: lambswool cushion cover; chocolate-coloured blanket; linen throw; alpaca throw).

bedroom accessories

pretty, practical additions to the bedroom to make it a comfort zone

1

2

3

4

5

1 **white bathrobe**
Wrap up in a soft cotton waffle robe before bedtime. I also have one in a fluffy towelling texture.

2 **cherry stone hottie**
An alternative to the traditional hot-water bottle, this linen bag contains cherry stones and can be heated up in the oven or microwave.

3 **bedside alarm clock**
A necessary device for rousing sound sleepers in the morning.

4 **linen lavender pillow**
Put under a pillow to encourage peaceful sleep.

5 **canvas boxes**
You can never have too many stackable storage boxes for clothes, shoes other bedroom kit. Stow away under the bed if space is limited.

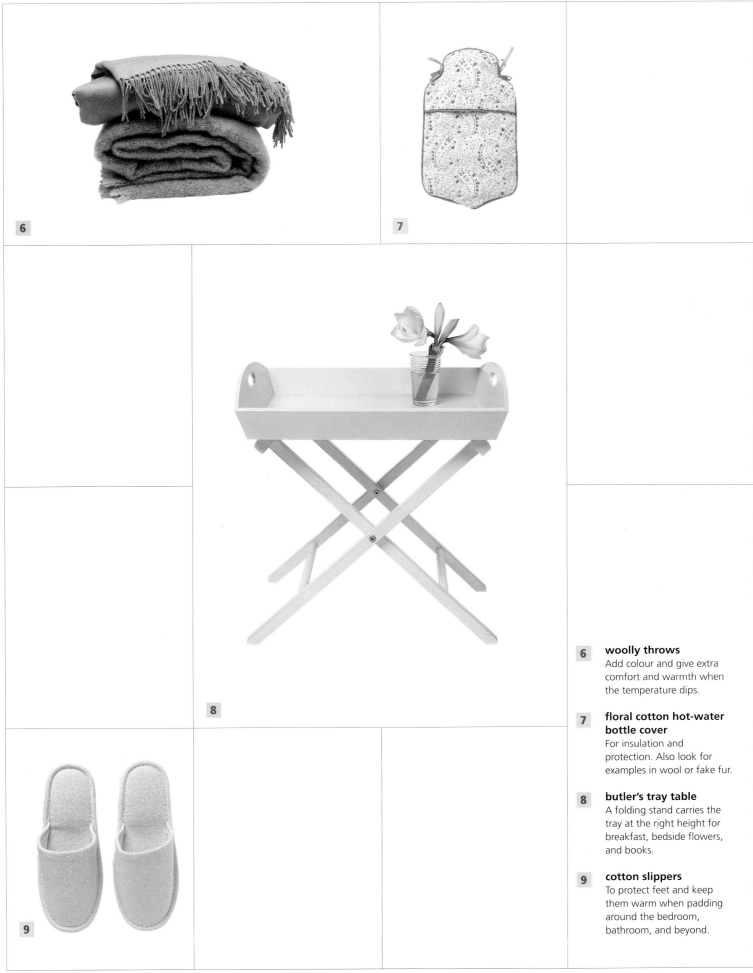

6 **woolly throws**
Add colour and give extra comfort and warmth when the temperature dips.

7 **floral cotton hot-water bottle cover**
For insulation and protection. Also look for examples in wool or fake fur.

8 **butler's tray table**
A folding stand carries the tray at the right height for breakfast, bedside flowers, and books.

9 **cotton slippers**
To protect feet and keep them warm when padding around the bedroom, bathroom, and beyond.

Recipes
Cook up feasts in the kitchen with simple-to-prepare ideas and good ingredients.

Chestnut soup
(p.97) serves 4
A soup with a smooth texture and a rich flavour that is tasty at any time of year.
1 onion, chopped; 2 sticks of celery, chopped; 1 potato, chopped; 2 tbsp olive oil; 500g chestnut purée; 1 litre chicken stock; single cream and parsley to garnish.

Fry the onion, celery, and potato in the oil until soft. Add the chestnut purée and stir in the stock. Bring to the boil and simmer for 1 hour, then blend with a hand-held blender. Season and add single cream and parsley to garnish. A recipe given to me by Arrabella Douglas-Menzies.

Roast chicken with a lemon and herb butter
(p.118) serves 4
Instead of a turkey at Christmas time, chicken is just as delicious – especially with lemon and herb butter between the skin and flesh to give it extra juiciness.
3 tbsp thyme or rosemary, chopped; 2 tbsp parsley, chopped; grated zest and juice of 1/2 organic lemon; 75–125g unsalted butter, softened; 1 free-range chicken, approximately 1.5kg

Preheat oven to Gas 4, 180 C, 350 F. Mix the herbs, lemon zest and juice with the softened butter; season with salt and a little freshly ground black pepper.

Lift the skin around the breast of the chicken and ease the herb butter over both breasts, smoothing it out so it covers all the meat. Press the skin down with the flat of your hands.

Roast in the oven for about 1 hour, depending on weight; allow approximately 20 minutes per 500g. Baste several times to keep the bird moist.

Garnish with sprigs of fresh herbs, and serve warm with vegetables and a wonderful gravy.
Recipe ©Clare Gordon Smith

Chicken stock
(p.118) serves 4
This can be stored in plastic containers in the freezer.
1 chicken carcass; 1 bay leaf; 1 onion, chopped; 1 carrot, chopped

Place all ingredients in a saucepan or casserole dish. Cover with water and season. Bring to the boil and simmer for 1 1/2 hours. Sieve, and use the remaining liquid in soups and risottos.

Brussel sprouts with pinenuts and shallots
(p.118) serves 4
Add extra flavour and texture to sprouts with some sautéed bacon and shallots.

500g brussel sprouts, peeled and marked with a cross at the base; 2 tbsp butter or olive oil; 6 rashers streaky bacon cut into bite-size pieces; 8 shallots, peeled and halved; 75g pinenuts
Steam brussel sprouts over a pan of salted simmering water for about 7–10 minutes.

Heat olive oil or butter in a large frying pan, add the bacon and shallots and gently sauté until the bacon is soft and shallots golden – about 7–10 minutes.

Stir in the pinenuts and drained sprouts and cook for a further 5–10 minutes until the sprouts are just tender and soft and have taken the flavour of the bacon and shallots.

Season with sea salt and freshly ground black pepper.
Recipe ©Clare Gordon Smith

Sautéed leeks
(p.119) serves 4
500g leeks, trimmed; 50g butter; juice and grated zest of 1 lemon; 2 tbsp chopped chives, 4 tbsp single cream or crème fraîche (optional)

Thinly slice leeks on a diagonal; heat the butter in a large frying pan.

Add the leeks and gently sauté until soft and tender, about 7minutes. Remove from heat and stir in the remaining ingredients.

Season with sea salt and freshly ground black pepper. Serve hot.
Recipe ©Clare Gordon Smith

Sautéed carrots
(p.118) serves 4
The combination of carrots with orange is particularly tangy and tasty.
50g butter; 500g carrots, peeled and sliced; grated zest and juice of 1 orange; parsley to garnish

Melt the butter in a saucepan. Sauté the carrots in the butter until soft and tender. Stir in the orange zest and juice, and garnish with chopped parsley. Serve immediately.
Recipe ©Clare Gordon Smith

Roast parsnips and potatoes
(p 118) serves 4
Roast parsnips and potatoes are always good with roast chicken or turkey. Make sure that the oil is hot to ensure crisp vegetables.
500g potatoes, peeled; 500g parsnips, peeled; 4 tbsp olive oil

Preheat oven to Gas 4, 180C, 350 F. Cut the potatoes and parsnips into equal size pieces and parboil in a pan of salted boiling water for about 7–10 minutes.

While they are cooking, heat the oil in a roasting pan; when hot add the drained, parboiled potatoes and parsnips and toss in the hot oil until coated.

Roast in the oven for 40–60 minutes; baste every 10 minutes or so. Alternatively, if there is space, place the vegetables around the roast chicken and cook.
Recipe ©Clare Gordon Smith

Heart-shaped biscuits
(p.217) makes 12–15
Prepare a simple shortbread recipe. Use cutters to cut out hearts and stars for Christmas tree decorations.
125g butter; 150g plain flour; 50g caster sugar; little drop of vanilla extract
To decorate: 125g icing sugar, 1–2 tbsp warm water; silver balls; ribbon

Preheat oven to Gas 4, 180 C, 350 F. Rub butter into flour to resemble breadcrumbs; stir in sugar and vanilla extract.

Pull together to form a smooth dough. Roll out on floured surface to about 5mm deep. Cut out different shapes with cutters and place on greased baking sheet. Use a skewer to make a hole at the top to thread a ribbon through. Bake in preheated oven for 10–15 minutes, until just golden brown.

Cool on a wire rack. Decorate with glacé icing and silver balls.
Recipe ©Clare Gordon Smith

Mince pies
(p.119) makes 12-18
Decorate these mince pies with a simple star. If using ready-made mincemeat, stir in a little brandy or sherry for extra flavour.
200g shortcrust pastry; 200g mincemeat; 1–2 tbsp brandy or sherry; milk; caster or icing sugar

Preheat oven to Gas 4, 180 C, 350 F. Roll out pastry on a floured surface; cut with an 8cm pastry cutter and line mince pie baking tray.

Stir brandy or sherry into mincemeat; add about 2 teaspoons of mincemeat to each pastry case. With a small star cutter, cut out star shapes and place on top of mincemeat. Brush with a little milk and bake for 15–20 minutes, until golden.

Cool on a wire rack and dust with caster or sifted icing sugar.

Chocolate truffles
(p.119) makes 24
The base of the mixture is a soft and gooey chocolate ganache. Keep it firm by chilling in the fridge and use a teaspoon to help shape the truffles. Use good-quality chocolate with a minimum of 70% cocoa solids.
375g plain chocolate, broken into small pieces; 2 tbsp brandy; 250ml double cream; 3–4 tbsp cocoa, sieved

Put chocolate and brandy into a bowl over a saucepan of just simmering water, heat gently, stirring until the chocolate has melted and the mixture is

quite smooth. Transfer to a bowl, add the cream and beat with an electric mixer until cool and thick.

Chill for a few hours to thicken. Use a teaspoon to shape the mixture into balls. Roll in the sieved cocoa. Place on a baking sheet and chill in the fridge until ready to serve.
Recipe ©Clare Gordon Smith

Orange and almond cake
(p.107) serves 6
This moist and orangey-flavoured cake has Moorish origins and is a good choice for puddings.
4 eggs, separated; 125g caster sugar; zest of 2 oranges; 100g ground almonds
For the syrup: juice of 4 oranges; 125g caster sugar; 1 tbsp brandy

Preheat oven to Gas 4, 180 C, 350 F. Beat egg yolks, sugar, orange zest and ground almonds together. In a separate bowl, beat egg whites until stiff, then fold in the yolk mixture. Pour into a greased and floured 20cm loose-bottomed cake tin. Bake for 45 minutes and allow to cool in the tin.
To make the syrup: bring the orange juice, sugar and brandy to the boil and simmer for 5 minutes.

Pierce the cake all over with a skewer; pour the syrup over and leave to soak in.
Based on a recipe from 'Mediterranean cookery' by Claudia Roden; BBC Books

Sterilizing jam jars
(p.92–93)
Make sure that the jars you are using have no cracks, chips, or other flaws.

Wash well in hot soapy water, rinse, and put into a hot oven at 140C/275F/gas mark 1 for 30 minutes. Fill the jars whilst they are warm to prevent cracking.

Grapefruit, orange, and lemon marmalade
(p.92–93) makes 6 jars
Wash and dry the fruit first.
2 grapefruit, quartered and peeled; 2 oranges, quartered and peeled; 4 lemons, quartered and peeled; 3.4 litres wate; 2.7kg sugar

Finely shred all citrus fruit zest, saving the pips, pith, and flesh. Put the pips and pith in a piece of muslin and tie with string (which can be tied to the pan handle). Coarsely chop the flesh of the fruits.

Place the flesh, zest, muslin bag, and water in a large saucepan. Bring to the boil and simmer for 1 1/2 hours.

Remove the muslin bag. Add the sugar to the remaining liquid and stir until it dissolves.

Increase the heat; boil rapidly for 15–20 minutes, or until it wrinkles. Remove from the heat and let stand for 10 minutes. Stir, then ladle the marmalade into sterilized jars and cover.

Addresses

PAINT

Auro Organic Paint Supplies Ltd
Unit 2 Panphillions Farm
Debden
Saffron Walden
Essex CB11 3JT
tel 01799 543077
for stockist or delivery details
fax 01799 542187
website www.auroorganic.co.uk
email sales@auroorganic.co.uk
Natural emulsion, eggshell, and chalk paints in a range of muted colours.

J.W. Bollom & Co. Ltd
Head Office
Croydon Road
Beckenham
Kent BR3 4BL
tel 020 8658 2299 for nationwide stockists
fax 020 8658 8672
Good strong colours available in all the usual finishes; a range of child-safe and flame-retardant paints. Plus chalkboard paint in black and green.

Crown Decorative Products Ltd.
PO Box 37
Crown House
Hollins Road
Darwen
Lancashire BB3 0BG
tel 01254 704951 for stockists
fax 01254 774414
Wide colour range. Available in most large DIY stores.

Designer's Guild
267–271 & 275–277 King's Road
London SW3 5EN
tel 020 7351 5775 for the store
fax 020 7243 7710
tel 020 7243 7300
for general enquires
Bright, light contemporary colours in matt emulsion, environmentally friendly water-based eggshell and emulsion sample pots. A smaller selection from the range is available in branches of Home Base.

ICI Dulux Paints
Wexham Rd
Slough
Berks SL2 5DS
tel 01753 550555 for advice and product information
Vast range of colours and finishes, plus a matching service.

Farrow & Ball
33 Uddens Trading Estate
Wimbourne
Dorset BH21 7NL
tel 01202 876141 for stockists
fax 01202 873 793
email farrow-ball@farrow-ball.co.uk
tel 0171 351 1273 for London showroom
Excellent selection of off-whites, also good range of old-fashioned matt colours, originally created for the National Trust.

Fired Earth
Head Office
Twyford Mill
Oxford Road
Adderbury
Oxfordshire OX17 3HP
tel 01295 814300 for stockists and brochures
fax 01295 810832
website www.firedearth.com
email enquiries@firedearth.com
A range of paints in authentic 18th and 19th-century colours, plus traditional finishes, Dead Flat Oil, Distemper, Emulsion, Oil Eggshell and Sleepy Gloss. There is also a range of water-based and odourless contemporary colours.

Floor Style Vinyl Flair floor paint
Stocked in major DIY stores
tel 01962 717001 for stockists
website www.plascon.co.uk
Paint that can be used to revitalize a vinyl floor; comes in six colours. Also paint for wooden floors, in eight colours, which is touch-dry in one hour and doesn't need varnishing.

Francesca's Lime Wash
24a Battersea Business Centre
99–109 Lavender Hill
London SW11 5GL
tel 020 7228 7694
fax 020 7228 8067
Traditional lime wash for both interior and exterior walls available in 40 colours, but can also be mixed up to customer's specifications.

Homebase Ltd.
Beddington House
Wallington
Surrey SM6 0HB
tel 020 8784 7200 for nearest branch
website www.homebase.co.uk
Their own range of paints has a good selection of colours, in all the usual finishes, and is very good value for money.

Johnstone's Paints
Kalon Decorative Products
Huddersfield Road
Birstall
Batley
West Yorkshire WF17 9XA
tel 01924 354000
fax 01924 354001
website www.kalon.com
Customer services tel
01924 354100 for stockists
fax 01924 354101
Wide colour range. Paint mixing service available that will match your existing paint work, wall coverings, fabrics, and tiles.

Leyland Paint Company
Kalon Decorative Products
Huddersfield Road
Birstall
Bateley
West Yorkshire WF17 9XA
tel 01924 477201 for colour advisory

service and stockists
fax 01924 422210
6000 shades plus a colour matching service.

Nutshell Natural Paints
PO Box 72 South Brent
Devon TQ10 9YR
tel 01364 73801 for orders & advice
fax 01364 73068
website www.nutshellpaints.com
Environmentally friendly paint that has a pleasant fresh smell. A limited but good colour range.

Sanderson
Sanderson House
Oxford Road
Denham
Buckinghamshire UB9 4DX
tel 01895 830000 for stockists
fax 01895 830055
There are hundreds of colours in the spectrum range, available in all of the standard finishes.

FABRIC

Bennison Fabrics Ltd.
16 Holbein Place
Lonndon SW1W 8NL
tel 020 7730 8076
fax 020 7823 4997
The diffusion range of fabrics has pretty floral cottons in fresh colours.

The Blue Door
74 Church Road
Barnes
London SW13 0DQ
tel 020 8748 9785
fax 020 8563 1043
Checks, stripes, and plains in cotton and linen.

J.W. Bollom & Co. Ltd
See Paint for details
Large colour range of flameproof felts (bright pink, green, blue, white are just a few) and muslins.

Cath Kidston
8 Clarendon Cross
London W11
tel 020 7221 4000
tel 020 7229 8000 for mail order
fax 0207 221 4388
email mailorder@cathkidston.co.uk
Bright and fresh 1950s-inspired florals. Fabrics are available by the metre and as pretty coathangers, pyjamas, bags, sheets, and other accessories.

The Cloth Shop
290 Portobello Road
London W10 5TE
tel 020 8968 6001
fax 020 8960 2719
website www.clothshop.co.uk
Everything from winter wools to summery stripes; plenty of natural fibres such as jute, wool, and silk, all well priced. It also stocks sari silks and antique linen.

The Conran Shop
Michelin House
81 Fulham road
London SW3 6RD
tel 020 7589 7401
fax 020 7823 7015
Plains, stripes, and checks in cotton and linen, and a great colour range.

Designer's Guild
See Paint for details
Fresh checks, stripes, and florals. Light sheer organzas, cottons, and linens as well as felt and wool.

GP & J Baker and Monkwell
London Showroom:
Decorative Fabrics Gallery,
322 King's Road
London SW3 5UH
tel 020 7589 4778
fax 020 7823 3329
Modern as well as traditional good quality upholstery fabrics. Plain coloured fabrics in different weaves and textures, from wool and cashmere to light cotton voiles.

Ian Mankin
109 Regents Park Road
London NW1 8UR
tel 020 7722 0997
and
271 Wandsworth Bridge Road,
London SW6 2TX
tel 020 7371 8825
Mankin by Mail tel 020 7722 0997
Excellent stock of utility fabrics; tickings, checks, and stripes, from fine cotton ginghams to heavy linen butchers stripes, plain coloured cottons and linens. All fabrics are reasonably priced.

Ikea
Brent Park
2 Drury Way
North Circular Road
London NW10 0TH
tel 020 8208 5600 for enquiries and branches
website www.ikea.co.uk
Bargain fabrics in simple, modern checks, stripes, and plain colours plus ready-made curtains, cushions, and blinds.

International Textile Company Ltd.
Firth Mill, Skipton
North Yorkshire BD23 2RL
tel 01756 793941
email Heritage@itc-ltduk.com
Good selection of linen, velvet, and cotton in a range of plain colours.

John Lewis
278–306 Oxford street
London W1 1EX
tel 020 7629 7711 for branches
Department stores with great fabric departments selling plastic coated cotton (ideal for outdoors), sheeting, linings, muslin, canvas, ticking, and other utility textiles. Good selection of roller and roman blinds.

K A International
68 Sloane Avenue
London SW3 3DD
tel 020 75847352
website www.ka-international.com
A huge range of fabrics including checks, stripes, and prints as well as woven and textured fabrics. Good value for money.

Kvadrat
62 Princedale Road
London W11 4NL
tel 020 7229 9969 for stockists
fax 020 7229 1543
email kvadrat@kvadrat.co.uk
Very good quality upholstery fabrics. Plain fabrics in excellent colour ranges with various textures from felt to boucle.

Laura Ashley
27 Bagleys Lane
Fulham
London SW6 2QA
tel 0800 868 100 for mailorder
tel 0870 5622 116 for stockists
Florals, stripes, and checks in a good choice of colours.

Liberty plc
Regent Street
London W1R 6AH
tel 020 7734 1234
fax 020 7573 9876
website www.liberty.co.uk
Look amongst the dress fabrics for classic, pretty, lightweight, floral, tana lawn prints and use to make floaty curtains, pilllow slips, and bags.

Malabar
31–33 The South Bank Business Centre
Ponton Road
London SW8 5BL
tel 020 7501 4200 for stockists
website www.malabar.co.uk
email info@malabar.co.uk
Upholstery fabrics at excellent prices. Good range of natural fibres. Plain fabrics in a variety of colours and textures as well as checks and stripes.

Meredith Design
Boynett
2 Aston Road
Cambridge Road
Bedford MK42 0JN
tel 01234 217788 for worldwide stockists.
fax 01234 217469
Good value suede fabric for upholstery that looks and feels just like the real thing.

Olicana Textiles Ltd
Brook Mills
Crimble
Slaithwaite
Huddersfield
West Yorkshire HD7 5BQ
tel 01484 847666
fax 01484 847735
email sales@olicana.co.uk
Quality furnishing fabrics woven from

natural yarns in great *plain colours, stripes, checks, and neutrals; very reasonably priced.*

Pongees
28–30 Hoxton Square
London N1 6NN
tel 020 7739 9130
fax 020 7739 9132
Silk specialists; a wide variety of weights, plus coloured parachute silks.

Romo
Lowmoor Road
Kirkby-in-Ashfield
Nottinghamshire NG17 1DE
tel 01623 750005 for worldwide stockists
Excellent range of plain colours in a variety of textures; I particularly like the range of cotton velvets.

Russell & Chapple
68 Drury Lane
Covent Garden
London WC2B 5SP
tel 020 7836 7521
fax 020 7497 0554
Canvas, cotton, muslin, and linens, both dyed and natural, plus a wonderful green waterproof canvas *for outdoors.*

Sanderson
See Paint for details
Good stripes, checked cottons, *and cotton velvets.*

Texture
84 Stoke Newington Church Street
London N16 0AI
tel 020 7241 0990
fax 020 7241 1991
website
www.texturesfromnature.com
Fabric shop selling organic and eco-friendly fabrics including organically grown cotton, hemp, jute, *and recycled fabrics.*

Wolfin Textiles
64 Great Titchfield Street
London W1P 7AE
tel 020 7636 4949
Cotton, ticking, calico, muslin, and other utility fabrics as well as cotton and linen sheeting *at low prices.*

Z.Butt Texiles
284 Brick Lane
London E1 6RF
tel 020 7247 7776
Denim, silk, calico, white cotton drill, muslin, *all cheaper per metre if you buy at least ten metres.*

FLOORING

Albion Stone Quarries
Wray Coppice
Oaks Road
Reigate
Surrey RH2 0LE
tel 01737 771772
fax 01737 771776
website

www.albionstonequarries.com
British limestone floor tiles.

The Alternative Flooring Company
Unit 3B Stephenson Close
East Portway
Andover
Hampshire SP10 2RU
tel 01264 335111 for stockists
fax 01264 336445
website
www.alternative-flooring.co.uk
email
sales@alternative-flooring.co.uk
Sisal, Coir, Seagrass, Jute, and 100% wool, in various different weaves, which can be fitted wall to wall or made into rugs. All floorings are made from renewable resources.

Carpet Design Studio
No.13, 3rd floor-Centre Atrium
Chelsea Harbour Design Centre
London SW10 0XF
tel/fax 020 7349 8835
A good choice of quality natural carpets *at reasonable prices.*

The Conran Shop
See Fabric for details
Good selection of rugs, *including hand tufted wool and woven sisal examples.*

Crucial Trading
79 Westbourne Park Road
London W2 5QH
tel 01562 825200 for stockists
fax 01562 825117
Natural floor coverings in jute, sisal, and coir.

Dalsouple
PO Box 140
Bridgwater
Somerset TA5 1HT
tel 01984 667233 for stockists
fax 01984 667366
website www.dalsouple.com
email info@dalsouple.com
Textured and smooth rubber floor tiles in a wide range of colours.

Drysdale Timber Mouldings Ltd.
Manufacturers and Timber Importers
36–38 River Road
Barking
Essex IG11 0DM
tel 020 8594 6004
fax 020 8594 6008
Flooring in oak, maple, cherry, and black walnut. They will also make up flooring in any wood specified by the customer, if available.

European Heritage
48-52 Dawes Road
London SW6 7EN
tel 020 7381 6063
fax 020 381 9534
website
www.europeanheritage.co.uk
email sales@europeanheritage.ltd.uk
Reclaimed and quarried stone, sourced from all over Europe, plus marble and granite with a natural unpolished finish.

The Extra Special Tile Co.
38 Albert Road North
Reigate
Surrey RH2 9EG
tel 01737 223030
website www.extrespecialtile.co.uk
Natural stone flooring in slate, terracotta, and limestone.

Fired Earth
See Paint for details
Terracotta floor tiles, both aged and new. Also slate and soft coverings such as sisal, which can be fitted or made into rugs with a choice of edge bindings.

First Floor
174 Wandsworth Bridge Road
London SW6 2UQ
tel 020 7736 1123
fax 020 7371 9812
A really good selection of rubber and vinyl floorings *in various colours and textures, also natural floor coverings such as jute and sisal.*

Graham & Green
4 Elgin Crescent
London W11 2JA
tel 020 7727 4594
fax 020 7229 9717
website
www.grahamandgreen.co.uk
Brightly coloured, woven plastic mats *and rush mats from Africa.*

Granite Marble & Stone Ltd
Office & Warehouse
Spelmonden Estate
Spelmonden Road
Goudhurst
Kent TN17 1HE
tel 01580 212204
fax 01580 211841
A large range of natural floor covering, including slate, limestone, and marble.

Habitat
196 Tottenham Ccourt Road
London W1P 9LD
tel 0645 334433 for nearest store
Lots of cheaper rugs and mats *in contemporary colours, textures and materials as well as more expensive large wool rugs in contemporary designs.*

Ikea
See Fabric for details
Good selection of rugs and laminate flooring *at low prices.*

Jaymart Rubber & Plastic
Woodlands Trading Estate
Eden Vale Road
Westbury
Wilts BA13 3QS
tel 01373 864926 for stockists
fax 01373 858454
email jaymart@compuserve.com
Contract and industrial floorings including rubber which looks equally good in the home and is very hard-wearing.

John Lewis
See Fabric for details

Inexpensive seagrass mats, plain carpets, and vinyl flooring.

Junkers Limited
Wheaton Road Commercial Centre
Wheaton Road
Witham
Essex CM8 3UJ
tel 01376 517512
fax 01376 514401
tel 01376 534710 for information and samples.
website www.junkers.co.uk
email sales/tech@junkers.co.uk
Solid hardwood flooring available in beech, oak, ash, merbau, and sycamore. All wood is sourced from managed forests.

Kersaint Cobb & Company Limited
Gorsey Lane
Coleshill
Birmingham B46 1JU
tel 01675 430430
tel 0800 028 5371 for stockists
fax 01675 430222
email kersaint.cobb@headlam.com
Natural floor coverings; coir, sisal, jute, seagrass, linen, *and* pure wool.

Lassco Flooring
41 Maltby Street
London SE1 3PA
tel 020 7237 4488
fax 020 7237 2564
Both reclaimed floor boards and new wooden flooring.

Limestone Gallery
Arch 47 South Lambeth Road
London SW8 1SS
tel 020 7735 8555
fax 020 7793 8880
Over 150 different types of limestone *as well as* terracotta.

Natural Flooring Direct
46 Webbs Road
Battersea
London SW11 6SF
tel 0800 454 721 for information and brochures
A range of natural floorings including seagrass, sisal, jute, coir, *and wooden laminates.*

Roger Oates
1 Munro Terrace
Cheyne Walk
London SW10 0DL
tel 020 7351 2288
fax 020 7351 6841
tel 01531 631611 for stockists
fax 01531 631361
website www.rogeroates.com
email london@rogeroates.com
Beautiful mats, rugs, and wool stair runners *in wonderful colours and simple stripes.*

Saraband Designs
Rooksmoor Mills
Bath Road
Stroud
Gloucestershire GL5 5ND
tel 01453 872579 for stockists
fax 01453 872420
website saraband-designs.co.uk

email sales@saraband-designs.co.uk
Large, varied range of natural flooring such as sisal, jute, and wool, *which can be fitted wall to wall or made into bordered rugs.*

Siesta Cork Tile Co.
Unit 21
Tait Road
Croydon
Surrey CR0 2DP
tel 020 8683 4055
fax 020 8683 4480
website www.siestacorktiles.co.uk
Cork for flooring or walls, which comes in a choice of different finishes, as tiles or on a roll.

Stone Age
19 Filmer Road
London SW6 7BU
tel 020 7385 7954/5 for branches
fax 020 7385 7956
website www.estone.co.uk
email info@stone-age.co.uk
A large range of natural sandstone and limestone, *and slate for flooring or work surfaces.*

Terracotta Direct
Pinford End Farm
Pinford End
Bury St Edmonds
Suffolk IP29 5NU
tel 01284 388002
fax 01284 388003
website www.terracottadirect.co.uk
Handmade terracotta *tiles from Spain.*

Treework Services Ltd.
Cheston Combe
Church Town
Backwell
Bristol BS19 3JQ
tel 01275 464466
fax 01275 463078
website
www.treeworkflooring.co.uk
Solid wood flooring in Oak, Ash, Elm, and other sustainable timbers.

Walcot Reclamation
108 Walcot Street
Bath
North East Somerset
BA1 5BG
tel 01225 335532
fax 01225 448163
website www.walcot.com
email rick@walcot.com
Hardwood planking, strip, block, and parquet flooring as well as York stone flags.

Wicanders
Amorim (UK) Limited,
Amorim House
Star Road
Partridge Green
Horshem
West Sussex
RH13 8RA
tel 01403 710001 for stockists
fax 01403 710856
website www.wicanders-amorim.co.uk
Cork and wooden flooring.

FOOD

Abbey Parks Asparagus
Parks Farm
East Heckington, Boston
Lincolnshire PE20 3QG
tel 01205 820722
email
lowethAabbeyparks.freeserve.co.uk
Fresh asparagus available by mail order or from the farm shop.

A.Gold
42 Brushfield Street
London E1 6AG
tel 020 7247 2487
Traditional English summer puddings, lemon tarts, jam, pork pies, good cheese, and bread.

Cirencester Farmers' Market
Held at Cirencester's Cattle Market
Old Tetbury Road
(next to the Leisure Centre)
tel 01453 834777 for further information
Local producers gather monthly with stalls selling beef, chicken, pork, lamb, fresh fruit and vegetables, jams preserves, eggs, honey, cheeses, home baked cakes.

Damhead Organic Foods
32a Damhead
Old Pentland Road
Lothianburn
Edinburgh
West Lothian EH10 7EA
tel 0131 445 5591 for mail order
fax 0131 445 5848
website www.damhead.co.uk
Organic supermarket selling meat, vegetables, and a whole range of organic groceries.

Dell Farm
Painswick
Near Stroud
Gloucestershire GL6 6SQ
tel 01452 813382
fax 01452 814363
email harh@hsd.co.uk
Naturally reared whole or half lambs for the deep freeze.

Denhay Farms
Broadoak
Bridport
Dorset DT6 5NP
tel 01308 458963
fax 01308 424846
Farm shop and mail order service selling cheddar cheese, butter, air-dried ham, dried-cure bacon, cured meat sausage, and other locally made produce.

Eastbrook Farm Organic Meats
Bishopstone
Near Swindon
Wiltshire SN6 8PW
tel 01793 790 460 for mail order
fax 01793 791239
email eastbrookfarm@compuserve.com
Sells its own beef, veal, lamb, and pork, cut to your requirements; other products include bacon, gammon, and sausages.

The Fresh Olive Company of Provence
Unit 1
Hanover West Industrial Estate
Acton Lane
London NW10 7NB
tel 020 8453 1918 for enquiries and mail order
fax 020 8838 1913
Olives, oils, antipasti, and vegetables sourced from small family producers in France, Italy, and Spain.

Jones Dairy
23 Ezra Street
London E2 7RH
tel 020 7739 5372
Old-fashioned shop selling wonderful English cheeses, homemade cheese cake, fresh coffee, bunches of fresh herbs. Open 3 days a week.

Ken Watmough
29 Thistle Street
Aberdeen
Aberdeenshire AB10 1UY
Scotland
tel 01224 640 321
A good source of seasonal fish; haddock, turbot, hake, bass, snapper, tuna, wild sea trout, and herring which is bought in fresh every day.

Limited Resources
53 Old Bailey Street
Hulme
Manchester M15 5RF
tel 0161 226 4777
fax 0161 226 3777
website www.limitedresources.co.uk
email office@limitedresources.co.uk
Fruit and vegetables, mostly home grown, and a wide range of other items including cereals, pulses, and dairy products available via home delivery.

Loch Fyne Oysters
Clachan
Cairndow
Argyll PA26 8Bl
Scotland
tel 01499 600 264 for mail order
website www.loch-fyne.com
email info@loch-fyne.com
Pacific oysters, excellent smoked salmon, mussels, scallops, and kippers. They also have a chain of restaurants nationwide where produce can be bought.

London Farmers' Markets
tel 020 7704 9659
website
www.londonfarmersmarkets.com
Fruit, vegetables, bread, and homemade cakes direct from the producers.

Marchents
PO Box 100
Fareham
Hampshire PO14 2SX
tel 0870 900 2900
website www.marchents.com
Meat, vegetables, cheese, cakes, preserves, hand baked biscuits and fresh herbs from a group of small and medium-sized producers brought to you via the website.

Meat Matters
2 Blandy's Farm Cottages,
Letcombe Regis,
Wantage
Oxfordshire OX12 9LJ
freephone 0808 0067426 for mail order
website www.meatmatters.uk.com
Any joint cut to your specifications, ham, sausages, and a few organic vegetables and groceries.

Neal's Yard Dairy
17 Shorts Gardens
London WC2H 9AT
tel 020 7240 5700
tel 020 7645 3550 for branches and overseas stockists
Knowledgeable staff who will give you tastes of the excellent British and Irish cheeses, inluding Applebys Cheshire, Gorwydd Caerphilly, Beenliegh Blue.

Organics Direct
Units A62-A64
New Covent Garden, Nine Elms
London SW8 5EE
tel 020 7622 3003
fax 020 7622 4447
website www.organicsdirect.com
Produce sourced from farms in Hertfordshire, boxed and sold nationwide. A typical box contains aubergines, onions, carrots, beetroot, leeks, mushrooms, and green peppers; the selection changes seasonally.

Out of This World
Gosforth Shopping Centre
High Street Gosforth
Newcastle-upon Tyne NE3 1JZ
Tyne & Wear
tel 0191 213 0421
tel 0191 213 5377 for branches
website www.ootw.co.uk
Organic supermarkets stocking products that contribute to healthy eating, fair trade, environmental sustainability, animal welfare, and community development.

Pata Negra – mail order
for Brindisa foods
28 Parson's Green
London SW6 4UH
tel 020 7736 1959
Jamon from free-range, acorn-fed Black Foot pigs; Spanish cheeses, olive oil, and bottled tomatoes.

Planet Organic
42 Westbourne Grove
London W2 5FH
tel 020 7221 7171
fax 020 7221 1923
A wide range of organic produce; fresh fruit and vegetables, wine, pulses, peeled chestnuts , cereals, and pasta; also has an in-store juice bar.

Sainsburys
PO Box 202
Stamford House
Stamford Street
London SE1 9LL
tel 020 7695 6000 for nationwide branches.

Seville oranges in season; frozen raspberries; Green & Black's organic chocolate; organic chestnuts, fresh in season, puréed and vacuum packed.

Selfridges
400 Oxford Street
London W1A 1AB
tel 020 7629 1234 for branches
fax 020 7495 8321
website www.selfridges.com
Fresh wild mushrooms, white duck eggs, and quinces in season. Spanish Manzanilla sherry.

Spitalfields Market Office
65 Brushfield Street
London E1 6AA
tel 020 7247 8556
Organic market held on Sunday mornings selling fresh vegetables, fruit, dried fruits, and wholesome breads. Wayside Organics sell good tomatoes, spinach, apples, salad leaves, and potatoes, in season, from their smallholding in Sussex.

Sierra Rica
C. La Julianita 7-9
Poligono Cantalgallo
Aracena 21200, Huelva
Spain
tel 00 34 959 127327
website www.sierrarica.com for details of stockists
Organic foods from Andalucia, Spain, including peeled and cooked chestnuts, membrillo soups, and cooking sauces.

Steve Hatt
88–90 Essex Road
London N1 8LU
tel 020 7226 3963
Family-run fishmongers selling oysters, prawns, wild salmon, fresh tuna.

The Tuit Centre
Lewdown
Okehampton EX20 4BS
tel 01566 783327
Properly farmed meat from local north Devon sources, including succulent ribs of beef and joints of pork.

KITCHEN

Builders Iron & Zincwork
Millmarsh Lane
Brimsdown
Enfield
Middlesex EN3 7QA
tel 020 8443 3300
Suppliers of zinc and stainless steel sheets. They will cut pieces to size, and make up made-to-measure worktops.

The Conran Shop
See fabric for details
Good selection of accessories, linen tea towels, and cookware.

David Mellor
See Tableware for details
Good kitchen knives, biscuit cutters, chunky wooden chopping boards.

Divertimenti
See Tableware for details
Big range of practical and stylish kitchen accessories; Sabatier knives, Le Creuset pans, blue & white tea towels, shallow aluminium baking trays.

GEC Anderson Ltd
Oakengrove
Shire Lane
Hastoe
Hertfordshire HP23 6LY
tel 01442 826999 for stockists
fax 01442 825999
website www.gecanderson.co.uk
email email@gecanderson.co.uk
Industrial looking kitchen furniture in stainless steel.

Habitat
See Flooring for details
Contemporary kitchen basics: inexpensive serving bowls. pots, pans and storage jars.

Hansen's Kitchen & Bakery Equipment
Showroom
306 Fulham Road
London SW10 9ER
tel 020 7351 6933
fax 020 7351 5319
email sales@hansens.co.uk
website www.hansens.co.uk
A specialist for the catering trade crammed with everything from industrial kitchen fittings to cutlery, chefs aprons and ice cube trays.

Heal's
See Tableware for details
Stylish kitchen accessories; espresso makers, Kilner® jars, stainless steel tools.

Homebase Cookshop
See Paint for details
Good value kitchen accessories; colanders, sieves, ladles, cotton tea towels, pots, and pans.

Ikea
See fabric for details
Simple style at excellent prices: folding wooden drainers, wooden spoons, pots and pans.

ICTC
The Intercontinental Cooking & Tableware Co Ltd
3 Caley Close, Sweet Briar Road
Norwich
Norfolk NR3 2BU
tel 01603 488019 for stockists
fax 01603 48802
website www.ictc.co.uk
email admin.ictc@dial.pipex.com
Stainless steel Cuisinox pans, baking tins in all shapes and sizes and hand turned wooden bowls.

Jerry's Homestore
See Tableware for details
Good value kitchen tools, checked tea towels.

John Lewis
See Fabric for details
Has just about everything for an efficient kitchen, including brooms, chopping boards, food processors, knives, vegetable racks, and linen tea towels.

Junkers Ltd
See Flooring for details
Solid wooden worktops in maple, beech, or oak.

Kitchen Bygones
c/o Alfie's Antiques Market
13–25 Church Street
London NW8 8DT
tel 0207 253 3405
Retro cream and green enamelware, kettles, graters, and jelly moulds.

Lakeland Ltd
Alexandra Buildings
Windermere
Cumbria LA23 1BQ
tel 015394 88100 for branches and mail order
fax 015394 88300
website www.lakelandlimited
All kinds of kitchen tools and gadgets, including cheap plastic storage boxes, wooden spoons, and food nets.

McCord
London Road
Preston
Lancashire PR11 1RP
tel 0870 908 7005
fax 0870 908 7050
website www.mccord.uk.com
Chunky Dualit toasters for thick slices of toast, stainless steel tools, traditional weighing scales, and stainless steel roasting dishes.

Mills
Witheys Yard
High Street
Stroud
Gloucestershire GL5 1AS
tel 01453 759880
Brilliant kitchen shop selling absolutely everything: cake tins, sieves, food processors, knives, oyster knives, scales, and scissors.

Nisbets
Nisbets Freepost (BS4675)
Bristol BS32 4FA
tel 01454 855555
fax 01454 855565
website www.nisbets.co.uk
email sales@nisbets.co.uk
Fabulous 'Bourgeat' and heavy-based 'Le Creuset' pans, Sabatier knives, cotton tea towels, stainless steel tools, pyrex bowls, maplewood chopping boards and biscuit cutters in all shapes.

Ocean Home Shopping
689 Mitcham Road
Croydon
Surrey CR0 3AF
tel 0870 8484840
fax 0870 8484849
Modern, kitchen kit: Dualit toasters, steel trivets and aluminium colanders.

Pages
121 Shaftsbury Avenue
London WC2H 8AD
tel 020 7565 5934 for the shop
tel 020 7565 5959 for sales
email sales@pagescatering.co.uk
Catering equipment including ovens, trolleys, pots and pans.

Summerhill & Bishop
100 Portland Road
London W11 4LN
tel 020 7221 4566
fax 020 7727 1322
Good source of smart kitchen tools.

TABLEWARE

After Noah
121 Upper Street
London N1 1QP
tel 020 7359 4281
and
261 Kings Road
London SW3 5EL
tel 020 7351 2610
email
mailorder@afternoah.demon.co.uk
Retro kitchenware: glass sugar shakers, schoolroom-style drinking glasses, and chunky white mugs.

The Conran Shop
See Fabric for details
Plain white china, blue and white striped Cornishware, simple wine glasses, and other functional tableware.

David Mellor
4 Sloane Square
London SW1W 8EE
tel 020 7730 4259 for shop and mail order
fax 020 7730 7240
website davidmellordesign.com
Excellent contemporary cutlery, ceramics, and glasses.

The Dining Room Shop
62-64 White Hart Lane
London SW13 0PZ
tel 020 8878 1020
A good range of 19th century cutlery, including bone handled examples.

Divertimenti
See Kitchen for details
Good selection of cutlery, white china, and simple white serving dishes.

Glazebrook & Co.
PO Box 1563
London SW6 3XD
tel 020 7731 7135 for mail order and free sample service
fax 020 7371 5434
website www.glazebrook.com
email sales@glazebrook.com
Classic timeless stainless steel cutlery.

Graham & Green
See Flooring for details
Lots of accessories as well as white china jugs, salt and pepper sets, and place mats.

Habitat
See Flooring for details
Basic white china, simple cutlery, tablecloths and napkins in bright fresh colours.

Heal's
196 Tottenham Court Road
London W1P 9LD
tel 020 7896 7555 for branches
Beautiful white china and simple cutlery

Ikea
See Fabric for details
Unbeatable value tableware; white china, basic tumblers, glasses and cutlery.

Jerry's Home Store
163-167 Fulham Road
London SW3 6SN
tel 020 7581 0909
fax 020 7584 3749
tel 020 7225 2246 for branches
Linen tablecloths and napkins, as well as cutlery and china.

John Lewis
See Fabric for details
All the basics: white china, table cloths, simple cutlery and a range of blue and white striped ceramics.

Liberty
See Fabric for details
Both traditional and contemporary cutlery as well as china and ceramics.

The Master Cutlers
5 Cavendish Place
London W1G 0QA
tel 020 7637 9888
fax 020 7255 1687
website www.cutleryshop.co.uk
Classically designed cutlery in silver, silver plate and stainless steel.

McCord
See Kitchen for details
Galvanised or cream enamel jugs, galvanised vases, simple white ceramics and chunky glasses.

Muji
187 Oxford Street
London W1R 1AJ
tel 020 7437 7503 for branches
Simple, modern white ceramics and stainless steel cutlery.

Old Colonial
56 St John's Road
Tunbridge Wells
Kent TN4 9NY
tel 01892 533993
fax 01892 513281
Classic blue and white enamelware from France.

Robert Welch Designs
Lower High Street
Chipping Campden
Gloucestershire GL55 6DY
tel 01386 840522 for stockists and mail order
fax 01386 841111

Classic simple cutlery in stainless steel, also available to order in silver plate and sterling silver.

Waterford Wedgwood
158 Regent Street
London W1B 5SW
tel 020 7734 7262
website www.wedgewood.com
Simple white bone china dinner plates and tableware.

TABLES AND CHAIRS

The Conran Shop
See Fabric for details
Contemporary tables and chairs plus classic designs from designers like Arne Jacobsen.

Decorative Living
55 New King's Road
London SW6 4SE
tel 020 7736 5623
Second hand weathered and worn tables and chairs.

The Dining Room Shop
See Tableware for details
Lovely old wooden dining tables.

Habitat
See Flooring for details
Simple, modern and affordable tables plus folding slatted white chairs for all around the house.

Heal's
See Tableware for details
Some good simple chairs and tables for inside and outside.

Ikea
See Fabric for details
Good value trestle tables, solid pine kitchen tables, basic chairs and stools.

Jerry's Home Store
See Tableware for details
Contemporary zinc-topped dining tables and plain upholstered dining chairs.

Muji
See Tableware for details
Simple, functional modern chairs and wooden tables.

Purves & Purves
220–224 Tottenham Court Road
London W1T 7QE
tel 020 7580 8223
website www.purves.co.uk
email info@purves.co.uk
Modern tables and chairs.

Sasha Waddell
269 Wandsworth Bridge Road
London SW6 2TX
tel 020 7736 0766
fax 020 7736 0746
website www.sashawaddell.com
email info@sashawaddell.com
Simple swedish style, tables, chairs, and accessories.

ECO

Centre For Alternative Technology
Machynlleth
Powys
Wales SY20 9AZ
tel 01654 702400
website www.cat.org.uk
Working centre on eco-technology which runs courses and a shop; supplies information and a mail order catalogue, Buy Green By Mail.

Community Recycling Network
Trelawny House
Surrey Street
Bristol BS2 8PS
tel 0117 942 0142
fax 0117 908 0225
website www.crn.org.uk
email crnmail@crn org.uk
Advice, support, and information for people interested in community-based recycling.

Computeraid International
Unit 111C Belgravia Workshop
157–163 Marlborough Road
London N19 4NF
tel 020 7281 0091
website www.computer-aid.org
Recycle your old computer (486 and above) by sending it overseas to developing countries.

Construction Resources
16 Great Guildford Street
London SE1 0HS
tel 020 7450 2211
website www.ecoconstruct.com
Building centre with eco-solutions.

Damhead Organic Foods
See Food for details
Eco-cleaning products such as washing-up liquid, detergent, bleach, and kitchen roll.

Energy Efficiency Advice Centre
136 Upper Street
London N1 1QP
tel 0800 512012 for branches
Advice on how to save money and energy in the home.

Energy Efficient Hotline
Energy Saving Trust
21 Dartmouth Street
London SW1H 9BP
tel 0345 277 200
Literature and advice on installers, insulation, and central heating.

Environmental Construction Products
11 Huddersfield Road
Meltham
Holmfirth
West Yorkshire HD9 4NJ
tel 01484 854898
fax 01484 854899
website
www.greenbuildingstore.co.uk
Environmentally friendly loft insulation made from recycled newspapers; a non-toxic, solvent-free paint; varnish stripper; natural paints.

Fair Trade Foundation
Suite 204, 16 Baldwin's Gardens
London EC1N 7RJ
tel 020 7405 5942
fax 020 7405 5943
website www.fairtrade.org.uk
*Certification body for fair trade, with
a list of fair trade suppliers and stockists
on their website.*

Freeplay
Cirencester Business PArk
Love Lane
Cirencester
Gloucestershire
GL7 1XD
tel 0800 731 3052 for stockists
*Manufacturers of the clockwork radio
and solar-powered radio, as well as a
wind-up torch.*

Friends of the Earth
26–28 Underwood Street
London N1 7JQ
tel 020 7490 1555
website www.foe.co.uk
Information on environmental issues.

The Furniture Recycling Network
c/o Community Furniture Service
The Old Drill Hall
17a Vicarage Street North
Wakefield WF1 4JS
tel 0116 233 7007
*Information about furniture
recycling projects.*

Imperial Cancer Research Fund
Unit 14 Bobby Friar Close
Cowley
Oxford
Oxfordshire
OX4 6ZN
tel 01865 716655
website www.imperialcancer.co.uk
*Used printer, fax, or photocopier
toner cartridges can be sold on to be
recycled by ICRF. There is a freepost
service and courier collection in London.*

Lakeland Ltd
See kitchen for details
*Recycled bird feeder, composting bins,
Eco carrier bag bin, can crusher, clothes
airers.*

Natural Collection
Eco House
Monmouth Place
Bath
Bath and North East Somerset
BA1 2DQ
tel 0870 331 3333
fax 01225 469673
website
www.naturalcollection.com
*Eco-friendly products for all areas of
the home by mail order: clockwork
radios, organic sheets, clothes airers.*

Renewable Energy for the Home
NEF Renewables
Natioanl Energy Centre
Davey Avenue
Knowhill
Milton Keynes MK5 8NG
freephone 0800 138 0889

website www.greenenergy.org.uk
*Information for people interested in
using renewable energy in the
home, including technical advice and
supplier lists.*

Twelve
43–44 Durant Street
London E2 7BP
tel 020 7613 4878 for a catalogue
website www.twelvelimited.com
*A small range of stylish interior products
made from recycled materials.*

**UK Steel Can Recycling Information
Bureau**
website www.scrib.org

Wastewatch
Europa House
13–17 Ironmonger Row
London EC1V 3QG
tel 0870 243 0136
website www.wastewatch.org.uk
*Information on where to get just
about anything recycled.*

STORAGE

Action Handling Equipment
The Maltings Industrial Estate
Station Road
Sawbridgeworth
Hertfordshire CM21 9JY
tel 01279 724989 for a catalogue
fax 01279 600224
email ahandling@aol.com
*Industrial lockers and cabinets and
metal mesh clothes lockers which
make great wardrobes.*

Bureau
10 Great Newport Street
London WC2 7JA
tel 020 7379 7898 for mail order
and stockists
*Stylish storage for the office; desktop
drawers, box files, and letter trays.*

Castle Gibson
106a Upper Street
London N11QN
tel 020 7704 0927
*Factory tables, pigeon-hole shelving,
cupboards, and old office and
institutional furniture.*

The Conran Shop
See Fabric for details
Contemporary storage ideas.

The Domestic Paraphernalia Co.
28 Dock Road
Lytham, Lancashire FY8 5AJ
tel 01253 736334
fax 01253 795191
website
www.sheilamaid.com
*Wooden plate racks, plant stands, and
hanging clothes airers.*

Emma Bernhardt
tel 020 8969 4949 for stockists
*Baskets and bags in whacky 1950s-
style brightly coloured plastic.*

Habitat
See Flooring for details
*Boxes, baskets, and shelving in
modern shapes and textures.*

Heal's
See Tableware for details
*Contemporary shelving plus good
ideas when storage space is limited.*

The Holding Company
241–245 Kings Road
London SW3 5EL
tel 0207 352 1600
and
41 Spring Gardens
Manchester M2 2BJ
tel 0161 834 3400
tel 0207 610 9160
for mail order
fax 0207 610 9166
for mail order *Great storage solutions:
baskets, boxes, jars, modular
racking and shelving systems.*

Homebase
See Paint for details
*Various stackable storage boxes in
clear or coloured plastic and untreated
plywood, which looks good as it is or
can be painted.*

Ikea
See Fabric for details
*Inexpensive shelving units, shelving
brackets, plastic and cardboard
stackable containers and white box
files.*

John Lewis
See Fabrics for details
*Cardboard and plastic stackable
boxes, dustbins, and laundry baskets.*

Lakeland Ltd
See Kitchen for details
*Storage ideas for the whole house;
wine racks, plastic containers, under-
bed storage, foldaway crates.*

McCord
See Kitchen for details
*Simple column shelf units, willow
baskets, office storage, hanging
rails, and racking systems.*

Muji
See Tableware for details
*Collapsible canvas boxes, pulp board
shelf units, plastic vegetable racks on
wheels, and lots more affordable
storage ideas.*

Nomad Box Company
Rockingham Road Industrial Estate
Market Harborough
Leicestershire LE16 7QE
tel 01858 464878
fax 01858 410175
*Made-to-measure storage boxes in
aluminium, polypropylene, or resin
fibre board.*

Ocean
See KItchen for details
*Contemporary storage: shelving, sisal
baskets, and laundry baskets.*

Purves & Purves
See Tables for details
*Contemporary storage ideas from
C.D. racks to modular shelving.*

**Slingsby Commercial and Industrial
Equipment**
Preston Street
Bradford
West Yorkshire BD7 1JF
tel 01274 721591 for branches and
information.
*Chrome racking which looks great in
the kitchen and can be built to suit your
storage requirements.*

Voodoo Blue Ltd
Unit 10
Brentford Business Centre
Commerce Road
Brentford
Middlesex TW8 8LG
tel 020 8560 7373
email vb@voodooblue.co.uk
*Rafia baskets in a range of bright
colours, including fuschia pink, available
through mail order.*

OUTSIDE

A1 Laboratory Supplies
2a-4 Avery Hill road
London SE9 2BD
tel 020 8850 0907
fax 020 8859 6026
Glass bell jars to protect seedlings.

Anthony de Grey Trellises
77a North Street
London SW4 0HQ
tel 020 7738 8866
website anthonydegrey.com
email info@anthonydegrey.com
*A good selection of trellises, decking,
and garden furniture.*

Argos
185-197 Old Street
London EC1V 9JS
tel 020 7253 8321
tel 0870 600 3030 for nearest store
Argos Direct
tel 0870 6002020 for orders and
information
website www.argos.co.uk
*Basic self-assembly sheds at low prices,
tools, great picnic and barbecue gear.*

Blacks Camping and Leisure
Brent Cross
Unit 4 Shopping Centre
London NW4 3FP
tel 020 8203 9895 for branches
*Equipment for camping and picnicking;
cool blocks, kettles, cutlery, tin plates.*

Bluebell
28 Kensington Gardens
The North Laines
Brighton
Sussex BN1 4AL
tel 01273 699546 for mail order
website www.bluebellshop.co.uk
*Fold away barbecues, galvanised
watering cans, colourful loungers, cast
aluminium hand tools.*

B & Q DIY and Garden Supercentres
Beckton Triangle Retail Park
Claps Gate
London E6 6LG
tel 020 8591 7666 for branches
*Good variety of plants, bulbs, and
tools.*

Clifton Nurseries
5a Clifton Villas
Little Venice
London W9 2PH
tel 020 7289 6851
*Lots of simple planters, including cedar
wood window boxes; indoor and
outdoor plants and bulbs in season,
including amaryllis, grape hyacinths,
and tête à tête daffodils.*

The Conran Shop
See Fabric for details
*Terracotta, ceramic, and galvanised
planters as well as a small selection
of tools and a range of stylish
outdoor furniture.*

Exterior Timber Designs
7 The Hamlet
London SE5 8AW
tel 020 7733 6269
website www.sexydecks.co.uk
email sales@sexydecks.co.uk
Decking for a roof space or patio.

The Garden Shop
Lydiard Fields
Great Western Way
Swindon
Wiltshire SN5 8UY
tel 01249 656467
website www.thegardenshop.co.uk
*Colourful canvas deck chairs and
hammocks, plaid picnic rugs, and
wooden garden furniture.*

Garden Trading Company
Unit 9 Wychwood Business Centre
Shipton-under-Wychwood
Oxford
Oxfordshire OX7 6XU
tel 01993 832200
fax 01993 832211
website www.gardentrading.com
A wide range of gardening tools.

Habitat
See Flooring for details
*Lots of stylish picnic gear including
bright woven plastic baskets; deck
chairs and planters.*

Heal's
See Tableware for details
*Barbeques, foldaway outdoor furniture,
planters, pots, and hand tools.*

Homebase Ltd
See Paint for details
Garden tools, pots and plants.

Museum of Garden History
Lambeth Palace Road
London SE1 7LB
tel 020 7401 8865
*Worth visiting for traditional garden
ideas.*

The National Society of Allotment and Leisure Gardeners
O'Dell House
Hunters Road
Corby
North Hampshire
NN17 5JE
tel 01536 266 576
website www.nsalg.demon.co.uk
Information about allotments.

Queenswood by Mail
Queenswood Garden Products
FREEPOST HR138
Hereford
Herefordshire HR4 8BR
tel 01432 830015
website www.queenswood.co.uk
Compost containers, wheelbarrows, galvanised watering cans, traditional wooden trugs, fertilizers, and biological pest control products.

Young & D
9F Cadogan Square
London SW1X 0HT
tel 020 7688 0295 for mail order
Traditional Greek barbecues.

ORGANIC GARDEN

Barwinnock Herbs
Barrhill
South Ayrshire KA26 0RB
tel/fax 01465 821338
website www.barwinnock.com
email herbs@barwinnock.com
Organically grown herbs.

The Composting Association
Avon House
Tithe Barn Road
Wellingborough
North Hamptonshire NN8 1DH
tel 019033 227777
fax 01933 441040
website www.compost.org.uk
email info@compost.org.uk
The U.K.'s national composting organisation.

Henry Doubleday
Research Association
National Centre for Organic Gardening
Ryton-on-Dunsmore
Coventry
Warwickshire CV8 3LG
tel 024 76303 517
Advice on composting and gardening organically.

The Organic Gardening Catalogue
The River Dene Estate
Molesey Road
Hersham
Surrey KT12 4RG
tel 01932 253666
fax 01932 252707
website wwwOrganicCatalog.com
email chaseorg@aol.com
Organic fertilisers, pest control solutions, composting bins, large choice of seeds including nasturtiums, sunflowers, foxgloves, broad beans.

Yalding Gardens
Benover Road
Yalding
Maidstone
Kent ME18 6EX
tel 01622 814650
Organic gardens to visit and herbs to buy.

Yorkshire Garden World
Main Road
West Haddlesey
North Yorkshire YO8 8QA
tel 01757 228279
Organic herbs: marjoram, rosemary, basil, coriander, and parsley.

PLANTS & BULBS

Architectural Plants
Cookes Farm
Nuthurst
Near Horsham
West Sussex RH13 6LH
tel 01403 891772
fax 01403 891056
website www.architecturalplants.com
email horsham@architecturalplants.com
Good selection of citrus trees, arbutus, and much more.

Naturescape British Wild Flowers
Lapwing Meadows
Coach Gap Lane
Langar
Nottinghamshire NG13 9HP
tel 01949 851045 (office hours)
tel 01949 860592 (visitor centre)
fax 01949 850431
website www.naturescape.demon.co.uk
email enquiries@naturescape.co.uk
Hedgerow seeds and plants like foxgloves and cow parsley.

Clare Austin Hardy Plants
Bowling Green Lane
Albrighton
Wolverhampton
West Midlands WV7 3HB
tel 01902 376333
Good for peonies and irises.

Columbia Road Flower Market
London E2
Held every Sunday morning; a great source of cheap bulbs, cut flowers, and plants in season.

crocus.co.uk Limited
Nursery Court
London Road
Windlesham
Surrey GU20 6LQ
tel 01344 629 629
fax 01344 629 600
website www.crocus.co.uk
Varieties of sunflowers, hyacinths, convolvulous, agapanthus, alliums, and amaryllis.

David Austin Roses
Bowling Green Lane
Albrighton

Wolverhampton WV7 3HB
tel 01902 376300
fax 01902 372142
website www.davidaustinroses.com
email retail@davidaustinroses.com
Hundreds of varieties; rambling, wild, old fashioned, bush and standard roses. Visit their large rose garden for inspiration.

Dig-it
PO Box 239
Bromley
London BR2 9ZT
tel 0870 120 1630 for a catalogue
fax 020 7576 6427
website www.dig-it.co.uk
Galvanised planters and vases, cast aluminium tools, Victorian style glass bell jars, blue hyacinth bulbs, and Christmas roses.

E W King & Co Ltd
Monks Farm
Kelvedon
Colchester
Essex CO5 9PG
tel 01376 570000
fax 01376 571189
Flowers and vegetables, including 100 sweet pea and 40 lettuce varieties.

Geffrye Museum Herb Garden
Kingsland Road
London E2 8EA
tel 020 7739 9893
Visit this traditional herb garden in the summer for inspiration.

Grooms
Pecks Drove Nurseries
Clay Lake
Spalding
Lincolnshire PE12 6BJ
tel 01775 722421
fax 01775 712252
website www.grooms-flowers.co.uk
Good selection of bulbs for autumn and winter planting, including tulips and narcissi.

Hardy's Cottage Garden Plants
Freefolk Proirs
Freefolk
Whitchurch
Hampshire RG28 7NJ
tel 01256 896533
fax 01256 896572
Specialist in herbaceous perennials: geraniums, irises, delphiniums, and foxgloves.

Hexham Herbs
Chesters Walled Garden
Chollerford
Hexham
Northumberland NE46 4BQ
tel 01434 681483
Herb specialists.

Jekka's Herb Farm
Rose Cottage
Shellards Lane
Alverston
Bristol BS12 2S
tel 01454 418878
fax 01454 411988

website www.jekkasherbfarm.com
email farm@jekkasherbfarm.com
A large variety of herbs; culinary, medicinal, and aromatic; rosemary, peppermint, and lavender.

Merriments
Hawkhurst Road
Hurst Green
East Sussex TN19 7RA
tel 01580 860666
fax 01580 860324
website www.merriments.co.uk
email info@merriments.co.uk
Well-stocked nursery plus summer bulbs: dahlias, lily-of-the-valley, and cannas.

New Covent Garden Market
Nine Elms Lane
London SW8 5NX
tel 020 7720 2211
An early morning market, great for boxes and trays of wholesale cut flowers, bedding plants and flowering bulbs in season. Cash only.

Parkers Dutch Bulbs
452 Chester road
Old Trafford
Manchester M16 9HL
tel 0161 877 4247
fax 0161 877 8350
website www.jparkers.co.uk
Specialise in tulips – try the beautiful feathery parrot tulip varieties.

The Plant Room
47 Barnsbury Street
London N1 1TP
tel 020 7700 6766
Fig trees and olive trees. Expert advice and gardener's accessories.

PW Plants
Sunny Side
Heath Road
Kenninghall
Norfolk NR16 2DS
tel 01953 888212
email pw.plants@paston.co.uk
Many different types of grasses.

The Romantic Garden Nursery
The Street
Swannington
Norwich
Norfolk NR9 5NW
tel 01603 261488
Evergreens and topiary.

SEEDS

Raising flowers and vegetables from seed is a satisfying business as you watch them sprout and grow. Sunflowers, nasturtiums, and herbs such as basil, rocket, and coriander are all easy to grow from seed.

Chase Organics
River Dean Business Park
Molesey Road
Hersham
Surrey KT12 4RG
tel 01932 253 666

fax 01932 252 707
Organic seeds.

Chiltern Seeds
Bortree Stile
Ulverston
Cumbria LA12 7PB
tel 01229 581 137
for mail order
fax 01229 584 549
Good range of flowers and herbs.

Mr Fothergill's Seeds Ltd
Gazeley Road
Kentford
New Market
Suffolk CB8 7QB
tel 01638 751 161 for stockists and mail order
fax 01638 751 624
Traditional favourites including runner beans and tomatoes.

Sarah Raven's Cutting Garden
Perch Hill Farm
Brightling
East Sussex TN32 5HP
tel 01424 838 181
Colourful flowers from raven's impressive repertoire.

Suttons
Woodview Road
Paignton
Devon TQ 7NG
tel 01803 696 321 for stockists and mail order
Everything for basic gardening: carrots, lettuces, beans, and tomatoes.

Terre de Semences
Ripple Farm
Crundale
Canterbury
Kent CT4 7EB
tel 0966 448379 / 01227 731815
fax 01227 730790
website www.terredesemences.com
email commenta@terredesemances.com
Huge selection of organic seeds; varieties of tomatoes, peppers, pupmkins, sunflowers, lavender, and allium.

Thompson & Morgan
Poplar Lane
Ipswich
Suffolk IP8 3BU
tel 01473 688 821
fax 01473 680 199
A mouth-watering range of flowers, vegetables, and herbs.

Unwins Seeds
Head Quarters
Impington Lane
Histon
Cambridge
Cambridgeshire
CB4 4LE
tel 01945 588 522 for mail order
Buy wild flower mixes – they are perfect for giving to a child for their own flower patch.

FLORISTS

Below are some of the best florists in London for seasonal buds and blooms – roses, narcissi, delphiniums, tulips, rannuculus, and so on – and simple bunches and bouquets.

Paula Pryke
20 Penton Street
London N1 9PS
tel 020 7837 7336

Jane Packer
56 James Street
London W1M 5HS
tel 020 7935 2673
website www.janepacker.com

McQueen's
126 St John St
London EC1V 4JS
tel 020 7251 5505
for branches

Wild at Heart
49a Ledbury Road
London W11 2AA
tel 020 7727 3095
for branches

POTS & PLANTERS

Barbary Pots
45 Fernshaw Road
London SW10 0TN
tel 020 7352 1053
Hand-thrown terracotta pots from Morocco.

Clifton Little Venice
3 Warwick Place
London,
W9 2PX
tel 020 7289 7894
Old and worn terracotta and stone pots and planters.

Ikea
See Fabric for details
Wooden, galvanised, and terracotta pots and window boxes.

Judy Green's Garden Store
11 Flask Walk
London
NW3 1HJ
tel 020 7435 3832
Good selection of plants, pots, and window boxes.

Ocean
See Storage for details
Simple planters both white ceramic and galvanised steel.

Pots and Pithoi
The Barns
East Street
Turners Hill
West Sussex
RH10 4QQ
tel 01342 714793
Handmade terracotta urns, both old and new.

UPHOLSTERY

Aero
347-349 Kings Road
London SW3 5ES
tel 0207 351 0511 for stockists
Contemporary sofas and chairs by B&B Italia and Hitch Mylius.

The Conran Shop
See Fabric for details
Modern shapes and big sofas for sinking into.

The Cube
14 Holland Street
London W8 4LT
tel 020 7938 2244
fax 020 7938 1920
website www.thecube.co.uk
email info@thecube.co.uk
Simple cube-shaped chairs and sofas.

David Seyfried
1/5 Chelsea Harbour Design Centre
Lots Road
London SW1 0XE
tel 020 7823 3848
Well constructed traditional sofas and chairs, and good compact shapes for smaller rooms.

Designer's Guild
See Fabric for details
Modern seating, upholstered in contemporary fabric and colours.

The Furniture Union
Bankside Lofts
65a Hopton Street
London SE1 9LJ
tel 020 7928 5155
fax 020 7928 5253
website
www.thefurnitureunion.com
Contemporary sofas including some modular systems.

George Sherlock Antiques Ltd
588 King's Road
London SW6 2DX
tel 020 7736 3955
fax 020 7371 5179
Big squashy sofas.

George Smith
587-589 King's Road
London SW6 2EH
tel 020 7384 1004
fax 020 7731 4451
website www.georgesmith.com
Traditional sofas and chairs.

Habitat
See Flooring for details
Made-to-order modern sofas as well as cheaper off-the-peg examples.

Heal's
See Tableware for details
Simple designs that can be upholstered in fabric or leather.

Highly Sprung
310 Battersea Park Road
London SW11 3BU
tel 020 7924 1124
fax 020 7924 1150
website www.highlysprung.com
Modern sofas at reasonable prices.

Hitch Mylius Limited
Alma house
301 Alma road
Enfield
Middlesex EN3 7BB
tel 020 8443 2616
fax 020 8443 2617
website www.hitchmylius.co.uk
Sofas and chairs made mainly for contract use, so should be long lasting.

Ikea
See Fabric for details
Very affordable upholstery in modern styles; also sell sofa beds.

Nordic Style
109 Lots Road
London SW10 0RN
tel 020 7351 1755
fax 020 7351 4966
website www.nordicstyle.com
Traditional Scandanavian-style chairs and day beds.

Pentonville Rubber
104 Pentonville Road
London N1 9JB
tel 020 7837 4582
Foam and rubber for upholstery, bean bag filling, cubes, and poufs.

Peter Guild
84–92 College Street
Kempston
Bedford
Bedfordshire MK42 8LU
tel 01234 273372 for stockists
fax 01234 270838
website www.peterguild.co.uk
Traditionally made sofas in both classic and more simple modern styles.

Purves & Purves
See Tables for details
Modern upholstery and design classics.

Recline & Sprawl
604 King's Road
London SW6 2DX
tel 020 7371 8982
fax 020 7371 8984
Good range of reasonably priced sofas.

SCP
135-139 Curtain Road
London EC2A 3BX
tel 020 7739 1869 for stockists
fax 020 7729 4224
website www.scp.co.uk
Contemporary designs from Jasper Morrison and Matthew Hilton and others.

Sofa Workshop
Lords Wood Barn
Lodsworth
Petworth
West Sussex GU28 9BS
tel 01798 343400 for branches
fax 01798 345321
website www.sofaworkshop.com
Sofas and chairs in both traditional and modern shapes. Choose from a range of cushion fillings.

Viaduct
1-10 Summers Street
London EC1R 5BD
tel 020 7278 8456
website www.viaduct.co.uk
Contemporary sofas from top Italian companies such as Cappellini.

FIRESIDE

Albrissi
1 Sloane Square
London SW1W 8EE
tel 020 7730 6119
fax 020 7259 9113
email albrissi@netscapeonline.co.uk
African woven rush log baskets.

The Conran Shop
See Fabric for details
Baskets for logs, plus pokers and tongs.

CVO Fire
Studio 1
Adelphi House
Hunton
Bedale
North Yorkshire DL8 1LY
tel 01677 450111
website www.cvo.co.uk
Contemporary gas fires.

Dovre
Unit 1 Weston Works
Weston Lane
Tyseley
Birmingham
West Midlands B11 3RP
tel 0121 706 7600
website www.dovre.co.uk
Cast iron wood-burning stoves.

House of Steel
400 Caledonian Road
London N1 1DA
tel 020 7607 5889
Fireplaces and accessories such as buckets, pokers, tongs, and grates.

SCAN manufactured by:-
Krog Iversen & Co. A/S
Postbox 60
DK-5492 Vissenbjerg
Denmark
tel/fax +45 64 47 30 98
website www.krog-iversen.dk
Imported into UK by:
LHA – SCAN
28 Darmonds Green
West Kirby CH48 5DU
tel/fax 0151 625 0504
for stockists
email scanstoves@FSBDial.uk
Simple wood-burning stoves with an environmentally friendly combustion system, made to order in Denmark.

Mr W Tierney
7 Berkley Close
Moor Lane
Staines
Middlesex TW19 6ED
tel 01784 457896
fax 01784 457475
Made to order utilitarian pither studio stoves. Really efficient and designed to burn natural anthracite smokeless fuel.

Valantique
9 Fortis Green
East Finchley
London N2 9JR
tel 020 8883 7651
Fireplaces, old fashioned grates, pokers and other fireside accessories.

LIGHTING

After Noah
See Tableware for details
Reconditioned original 1930's angle-poise lamps.

Best & Lloyd
Cambray Works
William Street West
Smethwick
West Midlands B66 2NX
tel 0121 558 1191 for stockists
fax 0121 565 3547
website www.bestandlloyd.co.uk
Classic, anglepoise desk and floor standing lamps.

Central
33-35 Little Clarendon Street
Oxford
Oxfordshire OX1 2HU
tel 01865 311141
fax 01865 511700
website www.central-furniture.co.uk
A good range of modern lighting.

The Conran Shop
See Fabric for details
Modern lighting: spun aluminium pendants, white ceramic pendants, aluminium desk lights.

Davey lighting
Unit 2
Martlesham Creek Industrial Park
Sandy Lane, Martlesham
Suffolk IP12 4SD
tel 01394 386768 for stockists
50's retro style functional white bakelite wall mounted lamps - once used in boats and caravans.

Habitat
See Flooring for details
Anglepoise desk lamps, paper shades, simple lamps and candles.

Heal's
See Tableware for details
Simple turned wooden lamp bases, glass pendant shades, simple candle holders, beeswax candles.

Ikea
See Fabric for details
Large lighting department with fisherman's pendants, paper shades, children's night lights, and a large selection of energy saving bulbs.

Intoview Ltd
239 Deansgate
Manchester M3 4EN
tel 0161 834 1313
Simple, contemporary lighting.

Le Paul Bert
198 Westbourne Grove
London W11 2RH
tel 020 7727 8708
Antique lighting, lots of American 50's table lamps.

McCord
See Kitchen for details
Tin hurricane lanterns.

Ocean
See Tableware for details
White china pendants and simple metal candle holders.

Price's Candles
110 York Road
London SW11 3RU
tel 020 7801 2030
Huge selection including beeswax and scented candles.

Purves & Purves
See Tables for details
Polypropylene shades, plain and Frosted glass pendants and colourful children's lights.

Young & D
see Garden for details
Fisherman's pendant lamps and Greek tapered candles.

MATERIALS

Atlantis Art Materials Ltd.
7-9 Plumbers Row
London E1 1EQ
tel 020 7377 8855
fax 020 7377 8850
Huge range of artists materials, plus poster paints and paper for children, pens and paints for fabrics, china, glass and metal.

Barnett Lawson Trimmings Ltd
16-17 Little Portland Street
London W1W 8NE
tel 020 7636 8591
fax 020 7580 0669
email info@bltrimmings.com
website www.bltrimmings.com
A huge selection of ribbons and braids.

C. Olley & Sons Ltd
Iberia House
Finchley Avenue
Mildenhall
Suffolk IP28 7BJ
tel 01638 712076
fax 01638 717304
Established in 1844, they supply cork in every conceivable form, including straight from the tree.

Creative Beadcraft Limited
20 Beak Street
London W1R 3HA
tel 0207629 9964

website www.creativebeadcraft.co.uk
email beads@creativebeadcraft.com
All sorts of beads.

Early Learning Centre
36 King's Road
London SW3 4HG
tel 01793 443322 for general enquiries and stockists
tel 08705 352 352 for mail order
website www.elc.co.uk
Art materials for creative kids; finger paints, cut and stick packs, packs of paper and card, brushes, block paints and ready mix paints, pens, brushes, crayons and chalks.

Gardners
149 Commercial Street
London E1 6BJ
tel 020 7247 5119
Paperbag wholesaler with packs of white or brown carriers for simple and stylish home wrapping.

Ikea
See Fabric for details
Great for simple toys and art materials; building bricks, musical instruments, paper, crayons and paint, miniature tea sets.

John Lewis
See fabric for details
Ribbon, buttons, felt squares, beads, cotton and zips.

J.W. Bollom & Co. Ltd
See fabric for detail
Large colour range of felts by the metre.

London Yacht Centre Ltd
13 Artillery Lane
London E1 7LP
tel 020 7247 2047
All sorts of rope and twine, great for making drawstring bags, or guy lines for a sun shelter.

Paperchase
213 Tottenham Court Road
London W1P 9TS
tel 020 7467 6200 for branches and mail order
website www.paperchase.co.uk
Huge range of hand made paper and art materials.

Suasion
35 Riding House Street
London
W1P 7PT
tel 020 7580 3763
Fabric dyes and paints, as well as lots of help and advice. They also stock a selection of natural fabrics and ready made items for dyeing.

VV Rouleaux
6 Marylebone High Street
London W1M 3PB
tel 020 7224 5179 for branches
website www.vvrouleaux.com
Beautiful ribbons: cotton velvet in bright greens and pink, esecially stylish; braids and trimmings.

WH Smith Retail Ltd.
Customer Relations
Greenbridge Road
Swindon
Wiltshire SN3 3LD
tel 01793 695195 for stockists
website www.whsmith.co.uk
String, brown paper, packs of card and play paper.

Woolworths
Woolworth House
Royal Barn Road
Castleton
Rochdale & Lancashire OL11 3DU
tel 01706 862789 for stockists
website www.woolworth.co.uk
Children's section has packs of sugar paper and card, stick on stars, gummed squares, paints and pens.

INSPIRE

Many museums and art galleries run art and activity courses during school holidays to help keep children occupied. Look on the internet for details in your area

Even if they might loathe the idea of trailing around a gallery, every child should experience the sheer spatial magnificence of Tate Modern and the terrific views across the Thames to the city of London from the top floor.

Tate Modern
53 Bankside
London SE1 9TG
tel 0207 887 8888 for exhibition detaills.

Bridgewater Pottery Café
735 Fulham Road
LondonSW6 5UL
tel 020 7736 2157
fax 020 7384 2457
and
Lichfield Street
Hanley
Stoke on Trent
ST1 3EJ
tel 01782 269682
fax 01782 201836
website www.bridgewater-pottery.co.uk
Studio run by Emma Bridgewater for learning how to decorate ceramics.

Big and little feet can learn flamenco rhythms and steps at:

El Mundo Flamenco
62 Duke Street
London W1
tel 020 7493 0033
and
Las Estrellas Tango & Flamenco Dance Studio
2-3 Inverness Mews
London W2
tel 7221 8170

Learn sensual latin salsa at:

Salsa-Fusion
tel 020 7837 3752 for information and details of salsa lessons.

and
Salsa Rapido & Salsa UK
tel 020 8444 3723 for Covent Garden, Farringdon and Harrow
tel 020 7794 6021 for Islington, Brixton and Croydon
website www.streetbeat.co.uk

Tooting Bec Lido
Tooting BEc Common
Tooting BEc Road
London SW16 1RT
tel 020 8871 7198
For refreshing and invigorating al fresco swimming in one of the largest outdoor 1930s lidos in the country; packed on hot weekends but normally less crowded on a cloudy day. Ring your local council for details of other lidos (Gospel Oak, Kentish Town and Brockwell Park Lido, Brixton are also great) around the country. Be quick they are fast becoming a rarity.

BATHROOM

Aston Matthews
141-147 Essex Road
London N1 2SN
tel 020 7226 3657
fax 020 7354 5951
website www.astonmatthews.co.uk
Good basic bathroom kit, baths, showers, taps and heated towel rails in simple shapes.

Bathcare
207a Linketty Lane East
Crownhill
Plymouth
Devon PL6 5JX
tel 01752 769567
website www.bathcare-uk.com
email sales@bathcare-uk.com
Restored, re-enamelled original cast-iron roll top baths as well as Victorian and Edwardian sanitary ware.

Bath Doctor
34 London Road
Faversham
Kent ME13 8RX
tel 01795 591711
fax 01795 591860
email sales@thebathdoctor.com
Specialist in restoring worn out old fashioned baths and sanitary ware.

Bisque
15 Kingsmead Square
Bath
Bath & North East Somerset BA1 2AE
tel 01225 469244 for stockists
fax 01225 444708
website www.bisque.co.uk
Modern radiators and towel warmers.

CP Hart
Newham Terrace
Hercules Road
London SE1 7DR
tel 020 7902 1000
fax 020 7902 1001
website www.cphart.co.uk
email centralsales@cphart.co.uk
Vast range of baths, fittings and

accessories, *plus basic range of utilitarian baths, sinks and taps.*

Criterion Tiles
196 Wandsworth Bridge Road
London SW6 2UF
tel 020 7736 9610 for stockists
Swimming pool style tiny blue mosaic tiles and white matt square tiles.

Eurobath International Ltd
Eurobath House
Wedmore Road
Cheddar
Somerset BS27 3EB
tel 01934 744466
fax 01934 744354
website www.eurobath.co.uk
Chrome rose shower heads, traditional style chrome taps, and simple chrome towel rails.

Ideal Standard
The Bathroom Works
National Avenue
Hull
East Yorkshire HU5 4HS
tel 01482 346461 for stockists
fax 01482 445886
website www.ideal-standard.co.uk
Plain and functional fittings, baths, sinks and loos.

Samuel Heath
Leopold Street
Birmingham
West Midlands B12 0UJ
tel 0121 772 2303 for U.K. and overseas stockists
fax 0121 772 3334
website www.samuel-heath.com
email mail@samuel-heath.com
Traditional and modern bathroom fittings and accessories.

Screwfix Direct
Freepost
Yeovil BA22 8BF
freephone 0500 41 41 41
freefax 0800 056 2256
website www.screwfix.com
email online@screwfix.com
Good value modern towel warmer/ radiator and basic white bathroom fittings.

Twyfords
Lawton Road
Alsager
Stoke–on–Trent
Staffordshire ST7 2DF
tel 01270 879777 for stockists
fax 01270 873864
Good range of bathroom kit in clean lines and simple shapes.

Vitra
121 Milton Park
Abingdon
Oxfordshire OX14 4SA
tel 01235 820400 for stockists
fax 01235 820404
Modern chrome fittings and streamlined white bathroom ware.

West One Bathrooms
60 Queenstown Road
London SW8 3RY
tel 020 7720 9333 for branches
fax 020 7498 0661
website www.westonebathrooms.com
Chrome towel warmers, beech cabinets, modern taps and shower roses.

BATHROOM ACCESSORIES

Aero
See Tableware for details
Chrome and beach accessories and cabinets, which are minimal in design.

Graham & Green
See Flooring for details
Soap dishes, toothbrush cups and cotton towels.

Habitat
See Flooring for details
Ceramic accessories, soap dishes, toothbrush cups, beech bath racks, and duck boards.

Heal's
See Tableware for details
Chrome cabinets, fittings, accessories and up to the minute baths and showers.

The Conran Shop
See Fabric for details
Wooden bath racks, duckboards, good soaps, simple fittings, cotton bath robs, linen and cotton towels.

Ikea
See Fabric for details
Great value cotton bath mats, towels in good colours, shower curtains, cabinets and toothbrush holders.

John Lewis
See Fabric for details
The best place for white towels in absorbent cotton textures, also shower curtains in towelling and canvas.

Linea @ House of Fraser
Head Office
1 Horwick Place
London SW1P 1BH
tel 020 7963 2000 for branches
Waffle cotton shower curtains, towelling lined waffle robe, ribbed towels and linen blend towels.

Ocean
See Kitchen for details
Contemporary stainless steel sinks, sleek chrome cabinets, mirrors and fittings.

The White Company
Unit 30 Perivale Industrial Park
Greenford, Middlesex
UB6 7RJ
tel 08701 601610
fax 08701 601611
website www.thewhiteco.uk
email orders@thewhiteco.co.uk
Simple white ceramic accessories; soap dishes, toothbrush cups and stylish cotton towels.

The White House
102 Waterford Road
London SW6 2HA
tel 020 7629 3521
tel 020 7629 8269
website www.the-white-house.com
email sales@the-white-house.co.uk
cotton towels, bath mats and robes.

SMELL

Aveda Ltd
7 Munton Road
London SE17 1PR
tel 020 7410 1600 for stockists
fax 020 7410 1899
website www.aveda.com
Cosmetics, skincare, hair products and scented candles made with natural flower and plant essences. Try the Valencia candle that smells like a Spanish olive grove.

Cologne & Cotton
791 Fulham Road
London SW6 5HD
tel 020 7736 9261 for stockists
Linen lavender pillows, soaps, and lotions.

The Conran Shop
See Fabric for details
Bath oils, scented candles, cedar balls and incense.

Couverture
310 Kings Road
London SW3 5UH
tel 020 7795 1200
website www.couverture.co.uk
email info@couverture.co.uk
Beautiful lavender cushions.

Crabtree & Evelyn
55 South Edwardes Square
London W86HP
tel 020 7603 1611 for stockists
website www.crabtree-evelyn.com
Traditional English fragrances such as rose and lavender in a range of products.

The Flower Room
Columbia Road
London E2 7QD
Wonderful room scents, linen water, burning oils and pot pourri created by Angela Flanders. Open Sunday mornings.

The Holding Company
See Storage for details
Cedar wood blocks, balls, and clothes hangers.

Heal's
See Tableware for details
Good soaps, colognes, candles for burning at bathtime and other scented bathroom goodies.

Immaculate House
57 Brushfield Street
London
E1 6AA
tel 020 7375 1844

and 4–5 Burlington Arcade
London W1J 0PD
tel 020 7493 5852
Lotions and oils in simple bottles.

Linens Select
PO Box 99
Holmfirth
Huddersfield
West Yorkshire
HD3 14ZB
tel 01484 422400
fax 01484 530856
Lavender bags and scented linen water.

L'Occitane
237 Regent Street
London W1B 2EJ
tel 020 7290 1420 for stockists
fax 020 7290 1421 for mail order
Beautiful soaps, lotions, incense, and burning oils.

Lush
40 Carnaby Street
London
W1V 1PD
tel 01202 668 545 for branches and mail order
fax 01202 661 832
website www.lush.co.uk
email sales@lush.co.uk
Handmade cosmetics made with vegetable products; soaps, bath balls, moisturisers, and cleansers.

Muji
See Tableware for details
Basic soaps and lotions simply packaged, and incense sticks and cones.

Savonnerie
57 Brushfields Street
London E1 6AA
tel 020 7375 1844
Handmade vegetable soaps and toiletries.

Space.NK
P.O. Box 18025
London
EC2A 3RJ
tel 0870 169 9999 for mail order
Wonderful scented candles – try Tuberose by Diptique.

BEDS

After Noah
See Tableware for details
Reconditioned original metal beds.

Big Table Furniture Co-Operative Limited
56 Great Western Road
London
W9 3NT
tel 020 7221 5058
fax 020 7229 6032
Handmade wooden beds in simple styles at affordable prices. The wood used is Scandanavian pine which is part of a long established reforestation programme.

Bump
2 Dunston Street
London E8 4EB
tel 020 7249 7000
email email@bumpstuff.com
Simple wooden box beds which are supplied unpainted.

Daniel Spring
158 Columbia Road
London E2 7RG
tel 020 7923 3033
Handmade metal beds, including a hospital style, or to your own design.

The Feather Bed Company
Crosslands House
Ash Thomas
Tiverton
Devon EX16 4NU
tel 01884 821 331
fax 01884 821 328
website www.featherbed.co.uk
email featherbed@eclipse.co.uk
Makers of traditional feather-filled mattresses, pillows, and bolsters.

The Futon Company
138 Notting Hill Gate
London W11 3QG
tel 020 7727 9252 for nearest stockist
fax 020 7792 0159
A range of simple wooden beds and futons and plain coloured tab top curtains.

The Futon Shop
168-170 Devonshire Street
Sheffield S3 7SG
tel 0114 272 1984
fax 0114 278 0369
website www.futonshop.co.uk
email sales@futonshop.co.uk
Beds and futons in a range of hard and soft woods.

Hypnos Limited
Princes Risborough
Buckinghamshire HP27 9DN
tel 01844 348200
fax 01844 346112
website www.hypnos.ltd.uk
email info@hypnos.ltd.uk
Well-made mattresses.

Ikea
See fabric for details
Good value cotton bed linen sets, pillows, duvets and simple modern beds including children's beds and bunks.

Judy Greenwood Antiques
657 Fulham Road
London SW6 5PY
tel 020 7736 6037
fax 020 7736 1941
Large selection of antique beds, old white damask bed covers, and antique patchwork quilts.

Linea Home @ House of Fraser
See Bathroom Accessories for details
Mohair and lambswool throws, silk quilts, suede cushions, linen and cotton bedlinen.

Nordic Style
See Upholstery for details
Swedish-style wooden day beds.

Pentonville Rubber
See Flooring for details
Made to measure foam mattresses, covered in a basic ticking or your own fabric, at very reasonable prices.

Warren Evans
158a Camden Street
London NW1 9PA
tel 0207 284 1132
fax 020 7267 6604
website www.warrenevans.com
Handmade wooden beds in simple styles and finishes.

Yakamoto Futon Centre Ltd.
339b Finchley Road
London NW3 6EP
tel 020 7794 8034
fax 020 7435 4545
website www.futoncentre.co.uk
Futon mattresses with a choice of fillings.

BEDDING

Alma Home
Greatorex Street
London E1
tel 020 7377 0762
Leather and suede cushions and throws in all shapes and sizes.

Anta
Fearn, Tain
Ross-shire IV20 1XW
Scotland
tel 01862 832477
fax 01862 832616
website www.anta.co.uk
email sales@anta.co.uk
Tartan blankets, rugs and china in contemporary colourings.

Cologne & Cotton
See Smell for details
Beautiful cotton, linen and striped flannel bedlinen.

Cath Kidston
See Fabric for details
1950s-inspired floral bedding, pyjamas, night dresses, and robes.

The Cloth Shop
See Fabric for details
Antique bed linen & towels, night dresses and pyjamas.

Colefax & Fowler
110 Fulham Road
London
SW3 6RL
tel 020 7244 7427
fax 020 7373 7916
tel 020 8877 6400 for U.K.stockists
Checked throws.

The Conran Shop
See Fabric for details
Luxurious wool and cotton throws and crisp cotton bed linen.

Debenhams
Head Office
91 Wimpole Street
London W1M 7DA
tel 020 7408 4444 for branches
tel 0845 6099 099 for mail order
Great for bedding basics with a full range of pillows and duvets; hypoallergenic fillings and goose down.

Grimes & Co
James town Business Park
Fingas
Dublin 11
Ireland
tel 00 353-1-806 8918
fax 00 353 1 806 8920
website www.grimesco.ie
email info@grimesco.ie
Pure new wool and lambswool throws and chunky cotton waffle weave bedspreads.

Habitat
See Flooring for details
Bedding basics: duvets, pillows, and cotton bedlinen in stylish colours.

John Lewis
See Fabric for details
Great selection of bedding and bedlinen, including warm cream-coloured wool blankets.

Laura Ashley By Post
See fabrics for details
Floral print bed linen.

The Linen Mill
103 Wandsworth Bridge Road
London SW6 2TE
tel 020 7731 3262
fax 020 7731 3250
website www.thelinenmill.com
email info@the linenmill.com
Pure linen bedding, towels and robes, and wool throws.

Linens Select
See Smell for details
Pure Irish linen and cotton bedding, lambswool and cotton waffle blankets, duvets, and pillows.

McCord
see Kitchen for details
Egyptian cotton and jersey bedlinen, feather-filled and hypoallergenic pillows, all seasons goose down duvets.

Melin Tregwynt
Castle Morris
Haverfordwest
Pembrokeshire SA62 5UX
tel 01348 891225
fax 01348 891694
website www.melintregwynt.co.uk
email info@melintregwynt.co.uk
Wool blankets, throws, and cushions in contemporary checks and stripes and colours.

Ocean
See Storage for details
Pure linen bedlinen, pyjamas, and robes.

The Scotch House
165 Regent Street
London W1B 4PH
tel 020 7734 0203
fax 020 7434 2620
Pure wool, mohair, lambswool, and cashmere blankets.

Shaker
72-73 Marylebone High Street
London W1U 5JW
tel 020 7935 9461
fax 020 7935 0581
website www.shaker.co.uk
email shaker@shaker.co.uk
Earthy-coloured throws in pure wool and alpaca.

Toast
Unit D LAkeside
Llansamlet
Swansea SA7 9FF
Wales
tel 0870 240 5200 for mail order
website www.toastbypost.co.uk
email contact@toastbypost.co.uk
Pure linen, flannel, and jersey bed linen, blankets, pyjamas, and robes.

Tobias and the Angel
68 White Hart Lane
London SW13 0PZ
tel 020 8878 8902
fax 020 8296 0058
Antique bed linen and pretty faded quilts.

Wallace Sewell
Unit 168 Clerkenwell Workshops
27-31 Clerkenwell Close
London EC1R 0AT
tel/fax 020 7251 2143
email studio@wallacesewell.com
Checked and striped woollen cushions and throws.

The White Company
See Bathroom Accessories for details
White bedding in cotton and linen, and pure wool cellular blankets.

The White House
See Bathroom Accessories for details
Cotton and linen bedlinen with classic pinstitch detail.

Earth Tones
36 Trent Avenue
London W54TL
tel 020 7221 9300 for mail order
fax 020 8579 3180
website www.earthtones.co.uk
email info@earthtones.co.uk
A collection of decorative cushions and throws from designers such as Morgan & Oates.

CUSTOM MADE

Steve Toms
Joinery
tel 04104 00271

Jim Howitt
42 Brushfield Street
London E1 6HE

Made to order box beds.

Tessa Brown
33 Rainbow Street
London SE5 7TB
tel 0207 708 1793
Bespoke clothes maker.

The Cotton Tree
High Street
Yoxford
Suffolk IP1Z 3ER
tel 01728 667000
website www.thecottontree.co.uk
Specialists in soft furnishings, loose covers, curtains, and upholstery.

RECLAMATION

Andy Thornton Architectural Antiques
Victoria Mills
Stainland Road
Greetland
Halifax
West Yorkshire HX4 8AD
tel 01422 377 314
fax 01422 310372
website www.aata.co.uk
email antiques@ataa.co.uk
Lighting, wooden panelling, terracotta pots and troughs.

Architectural Antiques
70 Pembroke Street
Bedford
Bedfordshire MK40 3RQ
tel 01234 213 131
Reclaimed tiles, building materials, and period fittings.

Architectural Heritage
Taddington Manor
Taddington
Nr Cutsdean
Cheltenham
Gloucestershire GL54 5RY
tel 01386 584414
fax 01386 584236
website www.architectural-heritage.co.uk
email puddy@architectural-heritage.co.uk
Antique garden ornaments, fireplaces and antique wall panelling.

Architectural Reclaim
Theobalds Park Road
Crews Hill
Enfield
Middlesex EN2 9BG
tel 020 8367 7577
fax 020 8367 6668
Old baths, fireplaces, and radiators.

Au Temps Perdu
5 Stapleton Road
Easton
Bristol BS5 0QR
tel 0117 955 5223
Specialities are fireplaces and old sanitary ware.

Chauncey's
15–16 Feeder Road
Bristol BS2 0SB

tel 01179 713131
fax 01179 712224
website www.chauncey.co.uk
email sales@chauncey.co.uk
Both old and new timber.

Edinburgh Architectural Salvage Yard
Unit 6 Cooper Street
Edinburgh EH6 6HH
tel 0131 554 7077
fax 0131 554 3070
website www.easy-arch-salv.co.uk
Reclaimed baths, sinks and bathroom fittings, doors and fireplaces.

Grate Expectations
Barncoose Terrace
Redruth
Cornwall TR15 3ES
tel 01209 314234
Everything related to fires and fireplaces.

Great Northern Architectural Antiques
New Russia Hall
Chester Road
Gatesheath
Tattenhall
Chester
Cheshire CH3 9AH
tel 01829 770 796
fax 01829 770971
website www.greatnorthern.co.uk
email archantiques@greatnorthern.co.uk
A good range of fittings and fixtures, including doors, taps, and fireplaces.

The House Hospital
68 Battersea High Street
London SW113HX
tel 020 8870 8202
Reclaimed baths, sinks, and cast iron radiators.

Lassco St Michael's
Mark Street
London EC2A 4ER
tel 020 7749 9944
fax 020 7749 9941
website www.lassco.co.uk
Chimney pieces, garden ornaments, and door furniture.

Lassco Radiators, Bathrooms & Kitchens
101 Britannia Walk
London N1 7LU
tel 020 7336 8221
fax 020 7336 8224
website www.lassco.co.uk
Roll top baths, all kinds of sinks, restored taps, and shower fittings.

Lassco Warehouse
101–108 Britannia Walk
London N1 7LU
tel 020 7490 1000
fax 020 7490 0908
website www.lassco.co.uk
A large selection of reclaimed doors.

Northend Reclamation
Northend
Luckington
Chippenham

Wilts SN14 6PN
tel 01666 841040
Mainly heavier reclaimed building materials, but also has sanitary ware.

Pew Corner
Old Portsmouth Road
Guildford
Surrey GU3 1LP
tel 01483 533 337
fax 01483 535554
website www.pewcorner.co.uk
email sales@pewcorner.co.uk
Furniture and fittings from churches including old wooden pews.

Walcott Reclamation
see Flooring for details
Baths and radiators, panelling, doors, and fireplaces.

SECONDHAND

Alfie's Antique Market
13–25 Church Street
London NW8 8DT
tel 020 7253 3405
Everything from old fabrics to 1960s furniture.

Bermondsey Market
London SE1 (London Bridge Tube)
Held early Friday mornings: antiques plus junk furniture and accessories.

Brick Lane
London E1 (Liverpool Street tube)
Market held every Sunday morning: old catering equipment, factory tables and chairs, junk chairs, tables, tablelinen, and kitchenware.

Ginnel Antique Centre
18–22 Lloyd Street
Manchester M2
tel 0161 833 9037
Post-war and retro junk.

Lifestyle
17 Lamb Street
Spitalfields Market
London E1 6EA
tel 020 7247 3503
fax 020 7247 3498
Lots of retro furniture; a good place to find classic chairs.

Overdose on Design
182 Brick Lane
London E1 6SP
tel 020 7613 1266
Classic furniture such as Panton and Bertoia chairs.

Portobello Road Market
London W11 (Notting Hill Gate tube)
Held every Friday & Saturday: an array of stalls selling junk furniture and accessories.

Index

Credits

Page 15 Bulb vase and hyacinth, Clifton Nurseries.
Page 24 - 25 Wool blanket, John Lewis. basket, hand made in Spain
Page 28 - 29 Espresso Maker, Heal's.
Page 34 Changing rooms at Tooting Bec Lido.
Page 35 London flat, Jane Cumberbatch; solid oak flooring, Drysdale Timber Mouldings.
Page 38 Kitchen, Sierra Rica, Aracena, Spain.
Page 44 - 45 Box files, Ikea. Kilner® jars, John Lewis
Page 48 - 49 Ribbons, John Lewis; cork based basket, handmade in Spain. Cotton for skirts, Wolfin Textiles; rick-rack braid, John Lewis.
Page 51 Emulsion-proof green fabric, Russell and Chapple.
Page 54 - 55 Dried rose buds, Clifton Nurseries. Bag made by Kate Storer using tana lawn fabric, Liberty.
Page 56 - 57 From the top: home made cushion covers in cotton by Laura Ashley, Colefax & Fowler, Ikea; checked cloth, Divertimenti; striped bag, market stall.
Page 60 White duck egg, Selfridges.
Page 61 Enamel jug, The Conran Shop.
Page 65 Terracotta pot, Clifton Little Venice.
Page 67 Green chairs, outside a Spanish café.
Page 73 Kitchen lights, Spitalfields house, London.
Page 77 Bertoia chair, Lifestyle; seat pad made by Kate Storer from Davina felt, Kvadrat.
Page 82 - 83 Quinces and wild mushrooms, Selfridges.
Page 84 - 85 Kitchen, London flat, Jane Cumberbatch; cabinets painted in Bollom white eggshell; Kilner® jars, John Lewis; white tiles, Aston Matthews; solid maple worktop, Junkers; checked tea towel, Divertimenti.
Page 87 Folding plate rack, Habitat; white bone china plates, Wedgewood.
Page 88 Kitchen, The Battery, Whitstable, England.
Page 90 Kitchen, London, designed by Alastair Hendy.
Page 91 Kitchen, London flat, Jane Cumberbatch.
Page 92 - 93 Seville oranges, Selfridges; bowl and ladle, Divertimenti; recycled jam jars.
Page 94 - 95 Napkins, The Conran Shop; cutlery and china, Ikea; table cloth and glasses, Habitat.
Page 96 London flat, Jane Cumberbatch; cupboard doors made by Steve Toms; vase and tulips, Paula Pryke; table, Ikea; chairs, secondhand.
Page 97 Bone china soup bowl, Wedgwood.
Page 99 Kitchen, Spanish House, Jane Cumberbatch; custom made table and cupboards from chestnut; folding chairs, Habitat.
Page 100 - 101 Cotton fabric, John Lewis; velvet ribbon, VV Rouleaux; plates,Wedgwood; chair, Habitat.
Page 103 Green cloth homemade using Malabar Quara 13; white chair, Habitat.
Page 104 - 105 Patio, Spanish house, Jane Cumberbatch; chairs, Habitat; sheet used as tablecloth, Peter Reed @ John Lewis.
Page 108 Beach house, Portugal, Nick and Hermione Tudor; chair cover made by Kate Storer, cotton fabric, The Cloth Shop; tablecloth in cotton, Laura Ashley; fisherman's pendant light and tealights, Ikea; basket from a Spanish market.
Page 112 Enamelled tin plate, Blacks; table cloth, Divertimenti.
Page 116 Table, Ikea; cotton tablecloth, Habitat.
Page 122 - 124 Work room, London home, Tessa Brown, bespoke clothes maker.
Page 126 Chairs, Habitat.
Page 127 Work room, Spitalfields house, London.
Page 128 - 129 Raw cork, C. Olley & Sons Ltd.; painted baked bean tin; notice board and shelving constructed by Steve Toms; secondhand filing cabinets painted in white eggshell, J W Bollom.
Page 131 Trestle table and shelving, made by Steve Toms
Page 132 - 133 Blue felt, J W Bollom; ribbon, VV Rouleaux; push pins, Muji.
Page 134 Clothes airer, Domestic Paraphernalia Company; linen tea towel, John Lewis.
Page 136 Utility room, London home, Simon and Liz Brown.
Page 144 - 145 Cotton pyjama top, Cath Kidston
Page 150 - 151 Garden, Marianna Kennedy, Spitalfields, London.
Page 153 Roof terrace, A. Gold, Spitalfields, London.
Page 154 - 155 Secondhand chair; eggshell paint, Farrow & Ball; sandpaper, brush and primer, Homebase.
Page 157 Village house, Spain
Page 160 - 161 Téte à téte daffodil bulbs, Clifton Nurseries.
Page 164 - 165 Allotment, London, John Matheson.
Page 170 - 171 Sun shade made by Kate Storer in cotton fabric, The Conran Shop; rope, London Yacht Centre Ltd; tent pegs,Blacks.
Page 172 - 173 Mattress, made by Kate Storer in cotton fabric, The Conran Shop; foam, Pentonville Rubber; cushions in emulsion-proof green fabric, Russell & Chapple
Page 175 Awning made by Kate Storer from emulsion-proof green waterproof canvas, Russell & Chapple; table cloth, Tobias and the Angel.
Page 176 Cotton curtain, Ikea; homemade cotton cushion covers.
Page 178 - 179 Striped cotton, KA International; interlining, John Lewis.
Page 180 Sofa, George Sherlock; loose cover fabric, Ian Mankin; coffee table, Habitat; director's chair, Heal's.
Page 181 Table, The Dining Room Shop; director's chair, Heal's.
Page 182 - 183 Folding side table, junk shop; lamp, John Lewis; Chesterfield sofa, second hand; throw, Colefax & Fowler; large folding table, Ikea; blinds, John Lewis; small sofa, David Seyfried; large sofa, secondhand.
Page 184 Cushion cover fabric, Designers Guild.
Page 186 - 187 Blind, John Lewis; Bertoia chairs, Lifestyle; table, junk shop.
Page 188 - 189 Chair, secondhand; loose covers made by Kate Storer; floral cotton, Cath Kidston; cotton ticking, Ian Mankin; green cotton, Malabar; white cotton, Designers Guild.
Page 190 - 191 Sofa, George Sherlock.
Page 195 Log baskets, hand made in Spain; shadow box frames, Atlantis.
Page 197 Shadow box frames, Atlantis; specimen jars, LASSCO.
Page 209 Chalk board paint, J W Bollom.
Page 214 - 215 Acrylic paints, Atlantis; card, WH Smith; paper bags, Gardners.
Page 220 - 221 bathroom, London, designed by Alastair Hendy.
Page 224 Bathroom, London flat, Jane Cumberbatch; heated towel rail, Aston Matthews; towel, The Conran Shop.
Page 225 Bathroom, Spanish house, Jane Cumberbatch; bath rack, Habitat.
Page 226 - 227 Canvas, Z. Butt; rope, London Yacht Centre Ltd; striped cotton ticking, Ian Mankin.
Page 228 - 229 Chair and duck board, Habitat; bath rack, The Conran Shop; basket, Spain; sink, taps and bath, Aston Matthews; wood panelling, by Steve Toms; light, The Conran Shop.
Page 231 Bathroom, Spitalfields house.
Page 232 - 233 tea light glasses, The Conran Shop.
Page 234 - 235 Bathroom, Spitalfields house, Jane Cumberbatch.
Page 237 Bathroom, Scotland, Lachlan and Annie Stewart.
Page 242 - 243 Bed, Ikea; orange blanket, Designers Guild; bed linen, Peter Reed @ John Lewis; checked cotton curtain, Ikea.
Page 244 Bed and bedspread, Habitat.
Page 248 Bedroom, The Battery, Whistable; striped flannel bed linen, Cologne and Cotton; blankets, Melin Tregwynt.
Page 250 - 251 Children's bedroom, London flat, Jane Cumberbatch; side table, junk shop; trestle table, by Steve Toms; angle poise lamp, Ikea; blanket, Anta.
Page 252 - 253 Cotton sheeting, Wolfin Textiles; rubber gloves, Homebase; Procion dye & soda ash fixer, Suasion; Velcro®, John Lewis.
Page 255 White cotton bed linen, John Lewis.
Page 256 - 257 Bedroom, London home, Tessa Brown.
Page 258 Bedroom, London, fashion consultant Vanessa de Lisle.
Page 259 Bedroom, Spitalfields house, Jane Cumberbatch.
Page 260 - 261 Calico, Z Butt; trim, VV Rouleaux.
Page 263 Bed, made by Jim Howitt; bed spread, Judy Greenwood.
Page 272 - 273
1. Off-White U/C1 emulsion, Farrow & Ball.
2. Strong White U/C1 emulsion, Farrow & Ball.
3. Lime White U/C1 eggshell, Farrow & Ball.
4. Oyster White Lt. 4-14P eggshell, Sanderson.
5. Blackened U/C1 floor paint, Farrow & Ball.
6. New White U/C1 eggshell, Farrow & Ball.
7. Great White U/C1 eggshell, Farrow & Ball.
8. 70BB 83/013 exterior eggshell, Dulux.
9. 10BB 83/014 emulsion, Dulux.
Table painted in 70BB 83/013, Dulux.
Page 274 - 275
1. 20YY 39/419 eggshell, Dulux.
2. 20YY 65/285 eggshell, Dulux.
3. 20YY 47/344 emulsion, Dulux.
4. 30YY 61/300 eggshell, Dulux.
5. 45YY 66/512 eggshell, Dulux.
6. 25YY 85/108, eggshell Dulux
7. Dorset Cream U/C1, eggshell Farrow & Ball.
8. Olive Yellow 3-16M emulsion, Sanderson
9. Cloudy Amber-w 4-3M eggshell, Sanderson.
Crate painted in 30YY 61/300, Dulux
Page 276 - 277
1. 50YR 23/365 emulsion, Dulux.
2. Mexicana 9-24D eggshell, Sanderson.
3. Porphyry Pink U/C49 eggshell, Farrow & Ball.
4. 90YR 38/239 Weathershield quick drying satin, Dulux.
5. 70YR 25/349, eggshell Dulux.
6. Brick Pink-w 16-22M, eggshell Sanderson.
7. Orange Buff 9-17M exterior eggshell, Sanderson
8. Fowler Pink U/C37 masonry emulsion, Farrow & Ball.
9. Orange Rust 10-11M emulsion, Sanderson.
Table painted in Dulux 90YR 38/239.
Page 278 - 279
1. Mayan Green 41-6D emulsion, Sanderson.
2. Colour World E9-23 emulsion, J.W. Bollom.
3 Chatham Green 41-23M eggshell, Sanderson.
4. 10GY 54/238 eggshell, Dulux.
5. Powder blue U/C22 exterior eggshell, Farrow & Ball.
6. 76GY 73/187 emulsion, Dulux.
7. Springtime 41-3M emulsion, Sanderson.
8. Olive Mist 41-9M emulsion, Sanderson.
9. 30GY 75/105 eggshell, Dulux.
Terracotta Vase painted in Colour World E9-23, J.W.Bollom.
Page 280 - 281
1. 16BB 41/268 eggshell, Dulux.
2. Blue Day Lt 24-14P eggshell, Sanderson.
3 54BB 41/237, eggshell, Dulux.
4. 30BB 47/179 Weathershield quick drying satin, Dulux
5. Regatta 24-17M eggshell, Sanderson
6. Swiss Blue 25-4M emulsion, Sanderson.
7. 10BG 63/166 Weather sheild quick drying satin, Dulux.
8. Phantom Blue 31-15M, exterior eggshell Sanderson.
9. 10BG 63/166 eggshell, Dulux.
Drawers painted in Swiss Blue 24-17M, Sanderson
Page 282 - 283
1. 10RR 25/437 eggshell, Dulux.
2. 86RB 47/274 emulsion, Dulux.
3. 07RB 43/231 emulsion, Dulux.
4. 10BB 47/149 eggshell, Dulux.
5. 64RR 45/245 exterior masonry, Dulux.
6. 41RB 58/162 emulsion, Dulux.
7. Chic Pink 18-16M eggshell Sanderson.
8. 24-3M eggshell, Sanderson.
9. Delicacy Lt. 22-2P emulsion, Sanderson.
Tin can painted in 10RR 25/437, Dulux.
Page 288 - 289 1. Muslin, Russell & Chapple; 2. Medium weight calico, Russell & Chapple; 3.Tandragee White F494/01, Designers Guild; 4. Flax 14oz. , Wolfin textiles; 5. Iona, Monkwell; 6. 10 oz cotton duck, Wolfin Textiles; 7. Silk Muslin, The Cloth Shop; 8. Tonus 2000 100, Kvadrat; 9. Jute, The Cloth Shop; 10. Linen FD170 White, Wolfin Textiles Ltd.; 11. Natural linen, International Textile Company; 12. Bamboo Zinc, Malabar.
Page 290 - 291 1.Tonus 2000 630 blue, Kvadrat; 2. Cotton drill, The Cloth Shop; 3. Dyed muslin, Z. Butt.; 4. Springfield felt, J.W. Bollom; 5. Divina 712, Kvadrat; 6. Dyed muslin, The Cloth Shop; 7. Linara Lavendar RF 2494/36, Romo; 8. Dyed muslin, The Cloth Shop 9. Divina 732 lilac, Kvadrat. 10. Tippo lime, John Lewis; 11. Lamonta Sky Suedette, Meredith Design; 12. Buchan K0307, G.P.& J. Baker.
Page 292 - 293 1. Spanish Green Check, International Textile Company; 2. Beige Square Check, International Textile Company; 3. Linum Nisha, The Blue Door; 4. 100% cotton ticking 6, Ian Mankin; 5. Checkmate 2 Green, PVC, John Lewis; 6. Azores Cuadritos Amarilla, KA International; 7. Azores Gales Azul, KA International; 8. Blue check, Ikea; 9. 100% cotton ticking 1, Ian Mankin; 10. 100% cotton ticking 2, Ian Mankin; 11. Linen/cotton ticking Union 14, Ian Mankin; 12.100% cotton ticking 2, Ian Mankin
Page 294 - 295 1. Rose Sprig, Cath Kidston; 2. Ditsy, Laura Ashley; 3. Rosie Print, Cath Kidston; 4. Rose Paisley, Cath Kidston; 5. Morello, Laura Ashley; 6. Felbrigg, Bennison Fabrics Ltd. Diffusion range; 7. Abbeville, Laura Ashley; 8. Rose Wiggle, Cath Kidston; 9. Hearts, Laura Ashley; 10. Wickmere, Bennison Fabics Ltd. Diffusion range; 11. Tana Lawn, Liberty; 12. Rose gingham, Cath Kidston
Page 300 - 301 1. Antique oak boards, Lassco Flooring; 2. Oregon reclaimed pine boards, LASSCO Flooring; 3. Muhuhu parquet, LASSCO Flooring; 4. unsealed cork tile, Siesta Cork Co.. 5. 'Vert d'eau' rubber tile, Dalsouple @ First Floor; 6. 'Bleu Pastel' rubber tile, Dalsouple @ First Floor; 7. 'Ton Pierre' rubber tile, Dalsouple @ Pentonville Rubber; 8. Antique Pammet terracotta tile, Fired Earth; 9. Pietra Laro, Stone Age; 10. Portland Blue, Stone Age. 11. Vidraco Crème, Stone Age
Page 302 - 303 1. Mat, John Lewis; 2. herringbone coir, Natural Flooring Direct; 3. basketweave seagrass, Natural Flooring Direct; 4. mini boucle sisal, Natural Flooring Company; 5. woven rug, The Conran Shop; 6. African woven plastic rug, Graham & Greene; 7. rag rug, Ikea; 8. checked rug, author's own.
Page 308 - 309 1. Wooden spoon, hardware shop; 2. pudding basin, Divertimenti; 3. Sabatier knife, Divertimenti; 4. balloon whisk, Divertimenti; 5. colander, Woolworths; 6. corkscrew, The Conran Shop; 7. griddle pan, Spanish hardware shop; 8. chopping board, Muji; 9. ladle, Divertimenti; 10. kitchen scissors, Muji; 11. Le Creuset casserole, John Lewis.
Page 312 - 313 1. Fly net, Divertimenti; 2. vegetable trolley, Muji. 3. cutlery tray, junk shop; 4. enamel biscuit tin, market stall; 5. stainless steel container with plastic lid, Muji; 6. enamel bread bin, Brick Lane market; 7. Kilner® jar, John Lewis; 8. plastic clip handled containers, Muji; 9. basket, author's own; 10. plate rack, Habitat; plate, Ikea.
Page 314 - 315 1. Bistro cutlery, The White Company; 2. stainless steel cutlery, Divertimenti; 3. small Duralex glass, Spanish supermarket; 4. espresso maker, Jerry's Home Store; 5. salt shaker, hardware shop; 6.pepper shaker, hardware shop; 7.1930's jelly bowl, junk shop; 8. glass, Habitat; 9. sugar shaker, After Noah; 10. secondhand cutlery, The Dining Room Shop; 11. wine glass, Habtiat; 12. Duralex glass jug, hardware shop.
Page 316 - 317 1. White china mug, Habitat; 2. White china plate, Wedgwood; secondhand cutlery, The Dining Room Shop; 3. Striped linen cloth & napkins, Cath Kidston; 4. Ceramic mug with blue stripe, After Noah; 5. Oilcloth, John Lewis; 6. Checked cloth & napkins, Divertimenti; 7. Ceramic cup & saucer, After Noah; 8. White ceramic serving bowl, The Conran Shop; 9. Traditional ceramic jug, Divertimenti; 10. Cornishware mug, The Conran Shop; 11. White cloth & napkins, Jerry's Home Store; 12. Ceramic egg cup, Divertimenti.
Page 318 - 319 1. Secondhand oak desk, junk shop; 2. Metal folding table, Muji; 3. Slatted folding table, Habitat; 4. Pine table, Ikea; 5. Folding table, Ikea; 6. 'Bra' table top & trestle legs, Ikea; 7. 'Estel' table, Habitat; 8. Beech table with zinc top, Jerry's Home Store.
page 320 -321 1. Sun hat, author's own; 2. Camping kettle, Black's; 3. Basket, Spanish market; 4. Greek barbeque, Young & D; 5. Cool blocks, Black's. 6. Plastic beakers, Habitat; 7. Deck chair, Habitat; 8. Blanket, Melin Tregwynt; 9. Storm kettle, Buy Green by Mail; 10. Cutlery, Ocean.
Page 326 - 327 1. Drying rack, The Domestic Paraphernalia Company; 2. Candles, hardware shop; 3. Cotton duster, hardware shop;

4. Door mat, hardware shop; 5. Wicker basket, Tobias and the Angel; 6. String, hardware shop; 7. Laundry basket, Ikea; 8. Cotton tea towel, Divertimenti; 9. Galvanized dustbin, Aero; 10. Broom, hardware shop

Page 328 - 329 1. Washing up brush & spare heads, Buy Green by Mail; 2. Milk bottle, milk man; 3. Freeplay radio, Buy Green by Mail; 5. Water filter, Natural Collection; 6. Wash balls, Buy Green by Mail; 7. Cushion made by Kate Storer from fabric samples; 8. Newspaper log (logmaker from Buy Green By Mail); 9. Recycled jar; 10. organic cotton bag, Natural Collection

Page 330 - 331 1. Canvas collapsible boxes, Muji; 2. Wire mesh lockers, Action Handling Equipment Limited; 3. Victorian open shelving, Castle Gibson; 4. Square grass baskets with lids, The Holding Company; 5. Rattan lidded baskets, The Holding Company; 6. Pulp board shelving, Muji; 7. 19th-century shelved cupboard, Castle Gibson; 8. Fold-up cardboard drawers, Muji; 19. Plastic basket boxes, The Holding Company.

Page 332 - 333 1. Bertoia chair, Lifestyle; 2. Folding wooden chair, After Noah; 3. Folding slatted chair, Habitat; 4. Wooden stool, Habitat; 5. Old sewing factory chair, author's own; 6. Upholstered dining chair, Jerry's Home Store; loose cover made by Kate Storer, calico, Z.Butt; 7. Robin Day chair, Habitat; 8. Secondhand stool, junk shop.

Page 338 - 339 1. Antique hoe & fork, The Conran Shop; 2. Besom broom, Clifton Nurseries; 3. Ssieve, Clifton Nurseries; 4. Enamel watering can, House of Steel; 5. Cast aluminium tools, Clifton Nurseries; 6. Shears, Clifton Nurseries; 7. Terracotta pots, author's own; 8. Compost container, Queenswood;

9.Cane sticks, Homebase.

Page 344 - 345 1. Painted planter, Ikea; 2. Terracotta pot, Clifton Little Venice; 3. Galvanized bucket, hardware shop; 4. Galvanised window box, Homebase; 5. Terracotta pot, The Conran Shop; 6. Tin can, recycled baked bean can. 7. Cedarwood window box, Clifton Nurseries. 8. painted terracotta pots, author's own.

Page 350 - 351 Secondhand armchair, junk shop; loose cover, The Cotton Tree; cushion, Heals; 2. Hitch Mylius sofa, Aero; 3. Sofa with loose covers, George Smith; 4. 'Man Ray' sofa, The Sofa Workshop; 5. Secondhand chair, junk shop; loose cover, The Cotton Tree; 6. 'Man Ray' footstool, The Sofa Workshop; 7. Sofa, David Seyfried; blanket, Designers Guild @ Heals; cushions, Heals; 8. Sofa-bed, Muji.

Page 352 - 353 Pither stove, Mr W. Tierney; 2. Toasting fork, found stick; 3. Poker, tongs & shovel, Valantique; 4. Stripped bucket, House of Steel; 6. 'Mayasticks', Buy Green by Mail; 7. Chestnut roaster, Spanish hardware shop; 9. African log basket, Albrissi; 10. Hearth brush, market stall.

Page 354 - 355 'Pigsty' pendant, Aero; 2. 'Miss Sissi' lamp by Philippe Starck, Aero; 3. Reconditioned 1930s 'chroom' angle poise lamp, After Noah; 4. 'Constanza' floor lamp, Aero; 5. Metal desk lamp, Habitat; 6. 'Hector' pendant, The Conran Shop; 7. Wooden lamp, Heals.

Page 356 - 357 Linen water, The Flower Room; 2. Acqua di Parma scented candle, The Conran Shop; 3. Rose buds, Laura Ashley; 4. Cedarwood blocks, The Holding Company; 5. Incense sticks & holder, Muji; 6. Lavender pillows, Couverture; 7. Melissa pot pourri,

The Flower Room; 8. Ceramic oil ring, The Flower Room; 9. Rosemary, home grown.

Page 358 - 359 Hanging tea light holders, Habitat; 2. Glass storm lantern, Heals; 3. Tea light lantern, Habitat; 4. Tea light glass, The Conran Shop; 5. Cube candle, Heal's; 6. Ceramic candlestick holder, junk shop; 7. Stick in the ground tea light holder, The Conran Shop; 8. Tea light holder, Habitat.

page 360 Wax crayons, Ikea.

page 364 - 365 1. Stick on stars, WH Smith; 2. Ribbons & braid, John Lewis and VV Rouleaux; 3. Felt tip pens, Woolworths; 4. Brown paper, WH Smith; 5. Luggage tags, WH Smith; 6. Paints, stationery shop; 7. Tissue paper, Paperchase; 8. Legal ribbon, stationery shop; 9. Paper bags, Gardeners.

Page 366 - 367 1. Gummed paper squares; childrens' scissors, both stationery shop; 2. Home made tea light holder, recycled jam jar; 3. Salt dough, home made; 4. Metal bucket, Ikea; plastic spade, market stall; 5. Wooden clacker, Ikea; 6. Cotton pillow case, John Lewis; fabric pens, Suasion; 7. American rag doll, author's own; 8. Tennis ball, sport shop; 9. Skipping rope, junk shop; 10. Block paints, Ikea.

Page 372 - 373 1. Reclaimed roll top bath, LASSCO RBK; 2. Shower tray, Aston Matthews; 3. Reclaimed sink, LASSCO RBK; 4. Mosaic tiles, Criterion Tiles; 5. Reclaimed shower, LASSCO RBK; 6. Refurbished light, LASSCO RBK; 7. Heated towel rail, Aston Matthews; 8. Bath, Aston Matthews; 9. Reclaimed tap, LASSCO RBK.

Page 374 - 375 1. Bath rack, The Conran Shop; 2. Glass, hardware shop; 3. Ceramic soap dish, The Conran Shop; 4. Chrome wire rack, Heal's;

5. Laundry bag, made by Kate Storer; 6. Towelling robe, Heal's; 7. Wire soap dish, author's own; 8. Jug, The Conran Shop; 9. Duck board, The Conran Shop.

Page 376 - 377 1. 100% pure vegetable soaps, The Flower Room; 2. Recycled liqueur bottle filled with Godas De Oro cologne; 3. Face brush, Muji; 4. Natural sponge, The Conran Shop; 5. Body lotion, Immaculate House; 6. Circular loofah, & pumice stone, Muji; 7. Back brush, Muji; 8. Bath mit, The Conran Shop; 9. 'Flower Garden' soap, Savonnerie.

Page 378 - 379 1. Waffle mat, The Conran Shop; 2. Bath mat, Heal's; 3. Towel, The Conran Shop; 4. Linen edged towels, linens select; 5. White towel, John Lewis; 6. Bathmat, Heal's; 7. Linen towel, Ocean; 8. Waffle towels, The Conran Shop; 9. Bath mat, Heal's; 10. Linen guest towel, Linens Select

Page 384 - 385 1. Bed, Daniel Spring; 'Florence' pillow cases, Habitat; percale duvet cover, Cologne & Cotton; 'Seafoam Crepe' blanket, The Conran Shop; secondhand linen sheet, The Cloth Shop; 2. 'Suffolk' bed, Laura Ashley; 'Madeira' bedspread, The White Company; pillow cases, Cologne & Cotton; 3. 'Shaker' bed, Warren Evans; 'Domino' blanket, The Conran Shop; striped flannel pillow cases, cotton duvet cover, both Cologne & Cotton; 4. 'Anna' bed, Nordic Style; antique french monogrammed sheet, The Cloth Shop; waffle blanket, The White Company; 5.Futon mattresses, both Yakamoto Futon Centre; natural linen sheet, Toast; herringbone sheet, The Linen Mill; Waffle blanket, The White Company.

Page 386 - 387 1. All weather duvet, The Iron Bed Company; 2. 'Orthos' mattress,

Hypnos; 3. Anti-allergenic pillow, Debenhams; goose down pillow, The Feather Bed Company; goose down & feather pillow, Debenhams; 4. Bolster & body pillow, The Feather Bed Company; 5. Anti-allergenic duvet, Debenhams; 6. Feather bed, The Feather Bed Company; 7. Goose down duvet, Debenhams; 8. Square pillow, The Feather Bed Company; 9. Underblanket, The Linen Mill.

Page 388 - 389 1.Secondhand linen pillow cases, monogrammed French linen sheet, antique heavy linen sheet, all The Cloth Shop; 2. Jersey duvet cover & pillowcases, Muji; 3. Herringbone duvet cover, The Linen Mill; 'Empress' bedspread, waffle blanket, 'Madeira' bedspread, all The White Company; 4. 'Victoria' duvet covet & pillowcases, Linens Select; 5. Striped 'Etienne' throw, The Conran Shop; cream cellular blanket, The White Company; soft wool blanket, Linens Select; 6. Percale pillow case and duvet cover, Cologne & Cotton; 7. Plaid blanket; fine checked blanket, both Melin Tregwynt; secondhand Welsh blanket, The Cloth Shop; 8. Flannel duvet cover & pillow cases, Cologne & Cotton; 9. Cushion cover, Melin Tregwynt @ Earth Tones; alpaca throw; Shaker; knitted linen throw, Eastern Trading Alliance; alpaca throw, Shaker.

Page 390 - 391 1. Waffle bath robe, Linens Select; 2. Cherry stone hottie, Toast; 3. traditional alarm clock, Aero; 4.Lavender pillow, Cologne & Cotton; 5. Canvas collapsible boxes, Muji; 6. Grey mohair blanket, lilac cashmere throw; both Couverture; 7. Hot water bottle cover, Cath Kidston; 8. Tray table, Nordic Style; 9. Canvas slippers, Muji.

Author's acknowledgments

Putting together *Pure Style Living* has been a team effort and I am grateful to everyone who has helped to make it such a beautiful and informative book.

I am indebted to the commitment, creativity, and enthusiasm of the multi-talented Kate Storer and it has also been a joy to collaborate with such a creative designer and art director as Vanessa Courtier, who has clearly and stylishly interpreted my vision. Many thanks too, to her assistant Gina Hochstein.

Thank you to all the suppliers (see above) who have loaned me products for photography.

I would like to thank the following photographers: Steve Gorton; assistant Andy Komorowski; Pia Tryde. I would also like to extend special thanks to Henry Bourne, Simon Brown, and James Merrell.

Thank you to the following people for allowing me to photograph in their homes:
Ian and Safia Thomas, A.Gold, London; Marilyn Phipps, The Battery, Whitstable; Simon and Liz Brown; Jon White and Tessa Brown; Vanessa De Lisle, Fashion Consultant; Alastair Hendy, food writer and

stylist; Richard Naylor and Sidonie Winter, Jones Dairy, London; Marianna Kennedy and Charles Gledhill; John and Colleen Matheson; Annie and Lachlan Stewart, Anta, Scotland; Nick and Hermione Tudor, Finca el Moro, Spain; Emma and Damon Heath; David and Carolyn Fuest; Pia Tryde.

Thank you to food writer and stylist Claire Gordon-Smith for her styling and recipes to illustrate Christmas food ideas, and to Emma Heath for her marmalade recipe.

A big thank you to Christopher Davis who commissioned me, and to the editorial and design team at Dorling Kindersley, Judith More, Janis Utton, and Neil Lockley.

Thank you to Clare Conville, my agent, who has always been a voice of creative reason and support.

Photographs by: Steve Gorton – all cut out images – and Pia Tryde except for the following:
©Henry Bourne for pages 234-235, 239 far right, 259; ©Simon Brown for pages190-191; Jane Cumberbatch pages 168, 222-223; James Merrell pages 61, 139 far right.